ANCIENT EGYPT
MESOPOTAMIA AND PERSIA

HISTORY OF THE ANCIENT WORLD
ANCIENT EGYPT
MESOPOTAMIA AND PERSIA

A. J. Koutsoukis

Longman Cheshire

Longman Cheshire Pty Limited
Longman House
Kings Gardens
95 Coventry Street
Melbourne 3205 Australia

Offices in Sydney, Brisbane, Adelaide
and Perth. Associated companies, branches
and representatives throughout the world.

Designed by Elizabeth Douglass
Set in 10/13 Palatino
Produced by Longman Cheshire Pty Ltd
Printed in Malaysia
by Percetakan Jiwabaru Sdn Bhd, Bangi, Selangor Darul Ehsan

National Library of Australia
Cataloguing-in-Publication data

Koutsoukis, A. J. (Albert J.), 1933–
    Ancient Egypt.

    Includes index.
    ISBN 0 582 86829 7.

    1. Egypt–History–To 332 B.C.
    I. Title.

932

CONTENTS

INTRODUCTION   vii

1
SUMER AND BABYLONIA   1

2
THE RISE AND FALL OF ASSYRIA   22

3
THE PREDOMINANCE OF PERSIA   43

4
KINGDOMS OF THE NEAR EAST   67

5
EGYPT: THE GIFT OF THE NILE   88

6
THE OLD KINGDOM (c. 2686–2180)   103

7
THE MIDDLE KINGDOM (c. 2040–1786)   122

8
THE NEW KINGDOM PART 1 (c. 1570–1379)   142

9
THE NEW KINGDOM PART 2 (c. 1379–1085)   161

ACKNOWLEDGEMENTS   179
INDEX   181

INTRODUCTION

This book begins with a discussion of the early dominance of Sumer in the Mesopotamian world, and the history of the Assyrian and Persian empires. The discussion then turns to ancient Egypt, and covers each major historical period from the earliest Egyptian civilisation to the end of the Twentieth Dynasty. With constant reference to archaeological evidence, a comprehensive picture of the life, politics, culture and conflicts of ancient Mesopotamia and Egypt emerges.

The book has been written specifically with the needs of senior high school students in mind. Care has been taken to present the material in a simple, readable style that students will find easy to understand, and so enjoy.

Numerous documents have been included to highlight essential points in the history, and to indicate the various points of view held by different ancient historians. Accompanying these documents are thought-provoking questions designed to stimulate students into a greater appreciation of the motives that stirred the men and women of the past.

Also included are special feature articles that highlight points raised in the text that deserve special further consideration. Numerous questions based on the examination of archaeological material, and others based on the enquiry approach to effective learning encourage students to extend beyond the information in the text and form their own interpretations. There is a summary of main events for each chapter, and the many maps, diagrams and photographs make the book a valuable visual resource.

As all events in this history took place before Christ, BC has been omitted from dates throughout the book.

1
SUMER AND BABYLONIA

CIVILISATION IN MESOPOTAMIA

The earliest civilisation of the Near East was the one based in Mesopotamia, a Greek name which means 'between the rivers'. It refers to the land between the Tigris and the Euphrates rivers from the Persian Gulf in the south up to the modern frontier between Iraq and Turkey in the north. To the west of Mesopotamia stretched the vast Arabian desert, while to its east were the Zagros mountains.

The northern part of Mesopotamia was called Assyria. Babylonia was the southern part, comprising the region of Akkad in the north and Sumer in the south. Sumer lay in a rich river delta where the fertile soil was watered by widespread irrigation systems. The people grew fruit, vegetables, dates, barley and a variety of wheat called emmer. They also raised sheep, goats, cattle and camels, and caught fish in the rivers.

WHO WERE THE SUMERIANS?

Despite its early dominance of the Mesopotamian world, all knowledge of Sumer was lost for thousands of years. It was not till 1834 that archaeologists first became interested in its ruined cities. The kingdom was shrouded in mystery, and much painstaking research had to be done before any clear picture began to emerge of the people and their civilisation. Even today, there is some dispute among experts about the origin of the Sumerians. One group believes that the Sumerians only arrived in their land about 3500. Calling themselves the 'black-headed people', they came as migrants from the hill country to the north-east. They displaced an earlier people (the Ubaids) who already knew how to build houses with sun-baked bricks, construct temples, and use the wheel.

A second school of thought agrees that the Ubaids were the original settlers, but denies any later influx of migrants about 3500. It states that the Ubaids continually maintained and built up their civilisation, and that only later were they known as Sumerians. The name Ubaid comes from Al 'Ubaid, a small site near Ur where some distinctive pottery was first found. In time, Ubaid culture spread northwards into Akkad, whose inhabitants were a Semitic-speaking people who had largely migrated from what is now Saudi Arabia. Semites are peoples who are supposed to have descended from Shem, the eldest son of Noah. In ancient times they comprised the people of Babylonia, Assyria, Aramaea, Canaan and Phoenicia. Today, the Semitic

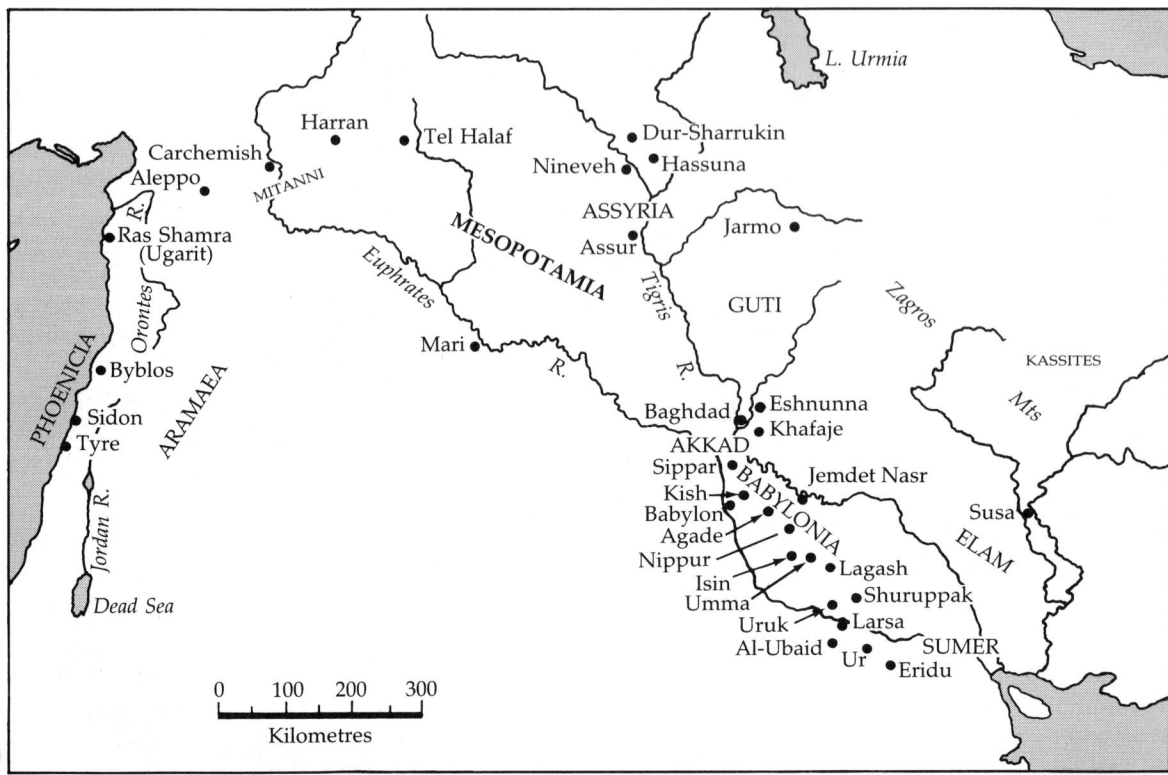

Fig. 1.1 *Mesopotamia—the land between the Euphrates and the Tigris rivers, stretched like a corridor between desert and mountains. It was constantly subject to attack by desert nomads from the west, and mountain tribes from the east. This map shows the position of the Persian Gulf in ancient times.*

people are the Jews, and the Arabs of south-western Asia. There are a number of Semitic languages spoken, mainly in northern Africa and the Near East.

Whatever their origins, the Sumerians are credited with the invention of writing about 3100. This shows that their society was a very complex one which needed to keep a record of its activities. These activities were so involved that human memory alone was no longer sufficient to recall them.

SUMERIAN WRITING

The oldest example of Sumerian writing was discovered at the ancient city of Uruk (called Erech in the Bible) and is known as the Uruk IV script. The writing on it was *pictographic*,

that is, the objects were represented as pictures. A later development occurred when the Sumerians used a small wedge-shaped stylus to write on soft clay tablets which were then baked hard in the sun. As time passed, the pictures underwent a change, reflecting the use of the wedge-shaped stylus. Because the Latin for wedge is *cuneus*, this new style of writing is now called *cuneiform* writing. The drawings in Fig. 1.3 indicate how those changes developed.

What did the Sumerians write about?

Many thousands of clay tablets bearing cuneiform writing have been discovered by archaeologists, not only in Sumer, but in all parts of Mesopotamia. The Uruk tablets mainly con-

Fig. 1.2 *These temples at Eridu show the continuity of culture in Sumer from the Al-Ubaid period to Sumerian times. The foundations of the later shrines enclose the remains of those that were built before them. What difficulties does this create for archaeologists?*

tain lists of livestock and farming equipment, showing that writing was invented as a method of bookkeeping. This emphasis on economic matters continued for centuries, and most of the tablets that have been discovered deal with such business matters as sales of land and loans. However, other subjects *were* treated, but to a lesser degree. They included records of a king's military victories or building projects, personal letters, myths, and mathematical and astronomical texts. Although they came in various sizes, most tablets were rectangular, and could be held easily in one hand.

Despite its cumbersome nature, cuneiform writing was used in the Mesopotamian region for nearly three thousand years. Writing was generally restricted to a small class, however, as most of the people were illiterate.

The invention of writing enabled the Mesopotamians to record all sorts of matters that were important to them. It also enabled later historians to trace a reasonable picture of what Mesopotamian life was like.

THE GROWTH OF CITY STATES

The time from 3500 to 2800 is known as the Proto-Literate Period. This era saw the development of small farming villages into large city states. The process started when farmers, by employing such techniques as ploughing and irrigation, grew more food than they required for their own needs. They were able to use some of their surplus to pay artisans to make tools, and traders to bring goods from

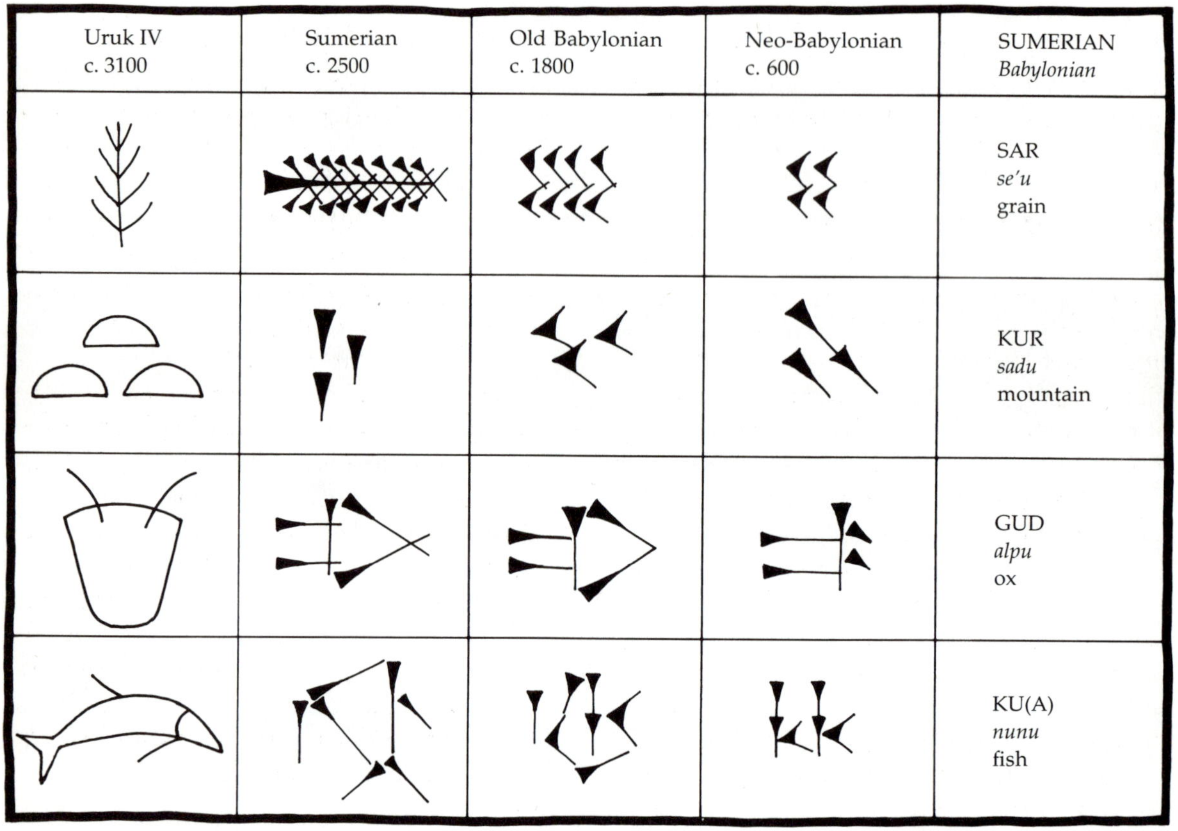

Uruk IV c. 3100	Sumerian c. 2500	Old Babylonian c. 1800	Neo-Babylonian c. 600	SUMERIAN *Babylonian*
				SAR *se'u* grain
				KUR *sadu* mountain
				GUD *alpu* ox
				KU(A) *nunu* fish

Fig. 1.3   *The four stages of Mesopotamian writing.*

other places. Thus started two groups of people who were not directly involved in farming.

The process developed further because the people believed that their welfare depended not only on their own efforts, but on the good-will of the gods. Therefore, they gave their religious leaders a lot of power so that they could intercede with the gods on their behalf. These religious leaders not only organised public worship and built temples, but directed irrigation and agriculture as well. As the communities grew bigger, more priests and government officials were needed and their activities were paid for by the farmers through contributions of food. Gradually the priests and officials became a group apart, a wealthy and noble class with a lot of power. They con-centrated in cities, and used the services of

artisans and traders to attend to their needs. These artisans and traders formed a middle class who dwelt in the cities but who served both the nobility and the farmers.

Each city was regarded as the personal property of its god, and the god's temple was the central feature of the city. Often there were smaller temples nearby that were dedicated to the god's wife and children. Much of the city's surrounding land was owned by the god, and was administered by the priests. They employed labourers to work it, and used the crops both to pay their salaries and to honour the god in various ways.

THE CITY STATES

Some of the earliest city states in Sumer were Uruk, Ur, Eridu, Lagash, Kish and Nippur.

These were all close to the Euphrates, and not the Tigris. The Euphrates flowed much more slowly than the Tigris, and so was an easier source of irrigation water. Because the Euphrates was sluggish, it tended to silt up. As a result, it changed its course from time to time. The present-day course of the Euphrates is quite different from those of ancient times.

The city states named above were all separated by stretches of desert, and this tended to make each one cherish its own independence. Sometimes they fought among themselves for supremacy , but any victory was usually only temporary. Nippur had a special religious significance because it was the home of the god Enlil (see page 9).

Although the city states were probably first governed by a council of elders and an assembly of the citizens, it was not long before kings emerged. Because fighting between the cities was so widespread, good military leaders had to be chosen. In time, these leaders became kings, and their position became secure when their titles were eventually made hereditary, thus introducing dynastic rule. In general, kings worked closely with the priests, and both were seen as servants of the gods. At first the kings took the title of *ensi*, but later this term was reserved for a city governor, who ruled the city on behalf of a great king, or *lugal*. The ensi had enormous power when he was alive, and on his death was given great honour. His tomb was filled with all sorts of treasure for use in the next life, and dozens of slaves were killed to accompany and serve him in the hereafter.

ORGANISATION OF THE CITY STATE

The city state consisted of the city and the surrounding countryside where the farmers grew their crops. The city was surrounded by a high brick wall to keep out enemies. The main building would be the temple, and close to it, the king's palace. Temples, palaces and houses were all built of brick. Although the houses of the nobles might have courtyards, most people lived in cramped houses jammed close together on narrow, winding streets.

Outside the city walls spread the fields, irrigated from the nearest water supply. Here and there were dotted small rural villages. The farmers grew barley, wheat and vegetables and cultivated a few animals. Meat was usually eaten only on festive occasions, and the main source of protein was fish.

Since there were constant quarrels between the various cities over territorial boundaries and water rights, each city state maintained its own army. The soldiers wore protective battle clothing, and fought with bows and arrows, spears, clubs and axes. Although most soldiers fought on foot, some went to war in four- and two-wheeled battle carts drawn by onagers (wild asses). The troops were well trained and disciplined, and usually formed a phalanx in battle.

Two by-products

Apart from unending victories and defeats, this constant warfare had two interesting by-products. The first was the introduction of slavery. People captured in battle were kept to work for the victors, and no doubt they preferred slavery to having their throats cut.

The second by-product was the stimulation of technology. Early experiments in making stronger metals grew out of the demand for weapons, and the use of the war chariot helped in the perfecting of the wheel. First the Sumerians learned that metals could be extracted from ores and hammered or cast into useful shapes. Then they discovered from the Turks and the Persians that a mixture of tin and copper made a strong new alloy: bronze. They imported both metals from these neighbouring countries and perfected the techniques of making the strongest possible bronze implements. Their products were so good that

Fig. 1.4 *Akkadian conquerors such as Sargon the Great frequently erected stelae to commemorate their victories. This fragment of a diorite stele shows an Akkadian soldier escorting naked prisoners after a battle. It was discovered at Susa, where it had been taken following an invasion of Babylonia, probably in the twelfth century* BC. *How did Sargon's reign affect Mesopotamia?*

they created an extremely busy export trade in the region.

THE RISE OF SARGON OF AKKAD

About 2500, King Messalim of Lagash seized control of most of Babylonia, and his dynasty maintained control of the region for about 150 years. Then the rulers of Lagash fought among themselves, and seriously weakened their position. Their plight was seen by the ruler of Umma, Lugal-zagesi, who defeated them in battle and established his own rule. But this was short-lived, due to the rise of Sargon of Akkad (c. 2334–2279).

Sargon came from the city of Agade in northern Babylonia. It was from this city that the surrounding region got its name of Akkad. The site of Agade has never been discovered, but it is probably somewhere near Kish or Babylon. Around 2300 Sargon defeated Lugal-zagesi and soon controlled all of Sumer. In time he extended his empire as far north as Mari on the Euphrates, and effectively ruled the whole of Babylonia. From there he pushed forward into northern Syria and then on up to the mountains of southern Turkey. He also moved east, and conquered many cities in Elam (western Iran). In addition to these conquests, he established trading contacts with India, the coast of Oman, the Persian Gulf, Lebanon, Crete and possibly even Greece. He reigned for fifty-six years, and had thirty-four successful battles. In view of his long and successful reign, he was designated Sargon the Great.

Fortunately, we know a great deal about Sargon and his achievements because his scribes made many tablets describing them in detail. As well, statues and *stelae* (pillar-shaped monuments with writing on them) were erected in the temple of Enlil at Nippur. Although these latter did not survive, the inscriptions on them were copied faithfully by an unknown scribe and are available for research today.

Unlike the Sumerians, Sargon and his people were Semites. These were originally desert nomads from whom both the Arabs and the Hebrews were descended (see page 1). Sargon ruled his empire from Akkad, appointing his own people as governors of the Sumerian cities, and sending military garrisons to keep order.

SARGON'S SUCCESSORS

Sargon lived to a ripe old age, and towards the end of his reign had to deal with many rebellions. One account even claims that he was forced back to Agade and besieged in his own capital. Apparently he recovered from this setback, however, and was able to hand power on to his son Rimush in c. 2278.

Rimush ruled for eight years, and spent most of his time fighting a series of rebellions against Akkadian rule. It appears he was successful, for a fragment of vase was found at Tell Brak in Syria bearing his name and the claim that he held all the land from the Upper

Fig. 1.5 *This triple-horned crown of divinity is similar to the one found on statues depicting Naram-Sin. What was the importance of his claiming to be not the servant of a god, but a god himself?*

to the Lower Sea on behalf of the god Enlil. In c. 2270 he was assassinated, and succeeded by his brother Manishtushu. The new king's reign lasted till c. 2254, when he suffered the fate of his brother in a palace revolt.

Naram-Sin, son of Manishtushu, ruled from c. 2254 to 2218. A worthy successor of his grandfather, he increased the empire to its greatest extent. His long and successful reign is commemorated by many stelae, the most famous of which is the one discovered at Susa. Originally set up at Sippar in Babylonia and obviously carried off to Susa at a later time, it recorded the defeat of the Lullubi, an Elamite border tribe. In Susa itself, many buildings were constructed with bricks bearing the king's name, and the local laws were written in the Akkadian rather than the Elamite language. Naram-Sin claimed to be a living god, and this strengthened his position of authority.

The last of the Akkadian kings was Shar-kali-sharri (c. 2217–2193). For most of his reign he had to contend with rebellions and invasions, and during his time the Akkadian empire fell to pieces.

ACHIEVEMENTS OF THE AKKADIAN EMPIRE

Trade

The Akkadians created the world's first empire. It extended from southern Turkey down to the Persian Gulf and for some distance into Elam. This empire was used to enrich the Akkadians in three ways:

- forced tribute from the conquered territories
- a monopoly of trade for Akkadian merchants
- free access by Akkadians to the resources of their conquered peoples

As a result of its commercial policies, Akkad traded with all parts of the adjacent world, buying and selling as far away as the Indus River in India.

Administration

The administration of the empire was generally in the hands of Akkadian nobles, who acted as governors. Occasionally, a conquered native ruler was allowed to remain in office, but only if he accepted the direction of a resident Akkadian official. The governors acted under the direction of the central government and so were able to put imperial policy into practice.

In an attempt to curry favour with the Sumerians, Sargon established the office of high priestess of the moon-god at Ur, with his own daughter Enheduanna as the first office holder. For the next 500 years, this office was held by a royal princess, and served to unify the Sumerian cities even in times of apparent conflict.

The idea of god-kings

It was the Akkadians who first came up with the idea that the king was also a god. The first to act on this idea was Naram-Sin when he put the sign for 'god' in front of his own name. He got his servants to refer to him as 'the god of Agade' in all official correspondence, and in statues made of him, he invariably wore the triple-horned crown that was normally reserved solely for the gods.

Naram-Sin's claim to divinity was a complete departure from the previous practice, where the king merely claimed to be the god's representative. His example was later followed by other eastern kings when they came to power in their turn.

THE GUTIANS

The downfall of the Akkadians was mainly caused by a people called the Gutians, who came from the mountainous country of the east. The Gutians replaced the Akkadians for about a hundred years as rulers of Babylonia, but in about 2135 they were defeated by the

Fig. 1.6 *These pictures from the famous Standard of Ur show scenes typical of daily life in Sumer. At the top is a banquet scene showing courtiers drinking while musicians play for them. In the centre, servants are leading animals to be killed. At the bottom, servants are carrying heavy loads which may well be the spoils of war. Dating from about 3000 BC, the Standard of Ur is a mosaic, with stones set firmly into a background of bitumen. Why is the Standard of Ur so important in the study of archaeology?*

Sumerian king of Uruk, Uterhegal. Uterhegal was soon replaced by his ensi, Ur-Nammu, who then made Ur the leading city of Sumer. Under the rule of Ur-Nammur, Ur became the centre of a new Sumerian empire. This was known as the Third Dynasty of Ur, and lasted from c. 2112 to 2004.

THE SUMERIAN REVIVAL

Ur-Nammur (who reigned from c. 2112 to 2095) was an outstanding military commander who conquered one Sumerian city after another to create a new Sumerian empire. With the title of 'King of Sumer and Akkad', he eventually extended his empire to include most of the territory formerly ruled by the Akkadians. Proud of his achievements, he built many fine buildings in his capital, including a huge *ziggurat* (see Fig. 1.8 on page 12). He also constructed temples at Eridu, Nippur, Lagash, Adab and Larsa. Interested in legal matters, he erected a stele on which he outlined punishments for various offences. The stele has long since been lost, but copies of the writing have survived as the Codex of Ur-Nammur.

Under Ur-Nammur and his four successors, the empire was tightly organised so that all production and distribution of goods was regulated by the government. Much of the surplus production was used to build temples and to make offerings to the gods. All people were assigned a specific role in life and were expected to work hard for the good of the empire. Records show that men worked in the fields, dug canals, and loaded and towed canal boats. Women cut reeds, drained the fields, helped with the harvesting and worked as weavers. All were paid in the form of beer, bread, oil, onions and fish. A whole host of bureaucrats supervised the process and kept strict records of work done and payments made.

As events were to show, the Third Dynasty of Ur lasted less than a century. During the reign of King Ibbi-Sin, fierce desert tribes known as Amorites raided Babylonia from the north-west, while the people of neighbouring Elam attacked from the east. Under this combined onslaught, the Sumerian empire collapsed, leaving the region in chaos.

SOME ASPECTS OF SUMERIAN CULTURE

Religion

Religion was very important to the Sumerian people. It dominated their lives, and controlled most of their actions. Temples were built in every city, and a numerous class of priests constantly admonished the people to make more offerings to the gods. Having the goodwill of the gods was the most important consideration of every Sumerian citizen, for without that goodwill disaster was inevitable.

The Sumerians believed in a wide variety of gods. All were in human form, but were immortal and had immense powers. Some were more powerful than others, and the more important ones were ranked in a definite order. First in rank was Anu, god of the all-encircling sky, and father and king of all the gods. He had a colourless wife named Antum who was later replaced by Ishtar, goddess of both love and war. Another name for Ishtar was Innana. Although he was particularly associated with the city of Uruk, Anu was a shadowy figure. Since Anu had little contact with humans, it was Enlil, the god of the wind, who received the most attention.

Enlil was Anu's son. Although his chief temple was at Nippur, he was generally considered the national god of Sumer. Together with Anu, Enlil granted power to all kings, and they owed their positions to him. The wind he represented was not just the raging, destructive desert storm, but the moist reviving wind of spring that brought the precious rain.

Third in importance was Ea, or Enki, the water god. He was considered to have brought civilisation to mankind, and taught them wisdom, medicine and writing. Eridu was the city associated with his worship. Some sources say he was the father of Marduk, a god who became all-important in later Babylonian times.

Lesser gods

Of the many goddesses, the chief was Ishtar. She was represented by the planet Venus, and her sacred animal was the lion. Often she was portrayed as a huntress, leading a pack of hunting dogs, and she usually carried a bow and arrows. Although her chief city was Uruk, both Kish and Agade also showed her special reverence. By the second millenium

BC, Ishtar had become the most widely worshipped deity in Babylonia.

One other god who should be mentioned here is Shamash, the sun-god. He was judge of both heaven and earth, and as the god of justice, was specially concerned with the protection of the poor. His image appeared on the famous stele which featured Hammurabi's Code (see Fig. 1.11 on page 16).

In addition to the gods just mentioned, there were many who were important to a particular city. Should that city be successful in war, the god was given the credit and became more revered. Then there were the agricultural gods, whose blessings were needed if the crops were to grow. Some people even had a personal god to whom they prayed when they wanted a blessing, and whom they might forsake if that blessing didn't eventuate.

The priests were in charge of all the rituals that had to be performed. These included

Fig. 1.7 *This impression of an Akkadian cylinder seal shows two of the Sumerian gods. One is Shamash, whose head and shoulders are emerging from between two mountains. On his right is Ea (or Enki), the water god. He can be identified by the streams full of fish flowing from his shoulders. Why were such seals used?*

sacrifices, the making of offerings, the saying of prayers and the organisation of processions.

Some features of Sumerian religion

The main feature of Sumerian religion was the belief that mankind was created purely to serve the gods. In the temples, the gods had to be 'fed' every day, usually behind linen curtains. After the gods had 'eaten', the food was sent to the king and his court to be consumed. Enormous quantities of food were used up in this fashion. One ancient text from Uruk describes a daily offering as: '500 kilograms of bread, forty sheep, two bulls, one bullock, eight lambs, seventy birds and ducks, three ostrich eggs, dates, figs, raisins and fifty-four containers of beer and wine'.

Another main feature of Sumerian religion was the importance of the image of the god itself. The god was considered to reside in the image, which was thus treated with great reverence. In the temples, most images were made of wood, and richly ornamented with clothes and jewels. Most households also had clay replicas of the main images, and these too were treated with the utmost respect.

A considerable number of religious festivals were conducted in Sumer. The most important was the celebration of the New Year. Others celebrated the gathering of harvests and the shearing of sheep.

One final aspect of religion was the practice of divination. This was the process by which learned and holy men were able to detect the will of the gods, and if possible, avert the approach of impending tragedy. One of their methods was to examine the entrails of slaughtered animals. Others were to note carefully the action of oil poured in water, or the behaviour of birds and animals, especially in the temple precincts. Those skilled in the art predicted success or failure in such activities as war, and their advice was heeded most carefully when decisions on such matters were being taken.

Literature

Our knowledge of Sumerian and Babylonian literature comes from two main sources. Firstly there are the royal libraries of Assur and Nineveh, and secondly, the scribal schools of the Old Babylonian period. Very few original Sumerian tablets have been found. Those that have been unearthed are mainly copies of the original texts.

Sumerian literature had strong religious overtones. For example, there were several stories about the creation of the world. These stressed that mankind was created solely to serve the gods. There were other stories about a great flood that wiped out life on earth. The hero of one such story was Utnapishtim who, when Enlil decided to destroy the world by flood, built an ark and saved himself, his wife, and pairs of every living creature. For his action, he was granted immortality. Another similar tale involved a righteous king named Ziusudra. These tales are similar to the Hebrew story of Noah's ark.

A well-known poem was the *Epic of Gilgamesh*. A descendant of Utnapishtim, Gilgamesh was a great hero, a King of Uruk in Sumer's earliest period. The poem tells of Gilgamesh's search for the plant of immortality to bring back to life his friend Enkidu. He has many adventures but eventually returns empty handed. The story confirms the Sumerian belief that man could never achieve immortality, and that there was nothing to look forward to after death.

At one stage of his journeying, Gilgamesh is told by a friend that his search is vain in these words:

Gilgamesh, whither are you wandering?
Life, which you look for, you will never find.
For when the gods created man, they let death be his share, and life withheld in their own hands.
Gilgamesh, fill your belly —

day and night make merry,
let every day be full of joy,
dance and make music day and night.
Put on clean clothes,
And wash your head and bathe.
Gaze at the child that is holding your
    hand, and let your wife delight in your
    embrace.
These things alone are the concern of
    men.

In general, the Sumerians were pessimistic about their relationship with the gods. The gods could do anything they liked to mankind, despite all the efforts of people to honour and appease them. Life was hard and often unjust, and when it was over, all people, both good and bad, went to the same land of the shades.

Architecture

Sun-dried bricks made of mud and clay were the only materials available to Sumerian builders. Since these bricks were not permanent, and fairly easily damaged, no Sumerian building has remained intact to the present day. This situation contrasts with that of the Egyptians, the Greeks and the Romans, who all erected enduring buildings made of stone.

The most distinctive form of architecture in Sumer was the ziggurat, a massive temple something like a step-pyramid. The temple had several storeys, with each level smaller than the one below it, similar to several platforms of various sizes placed one on top of the other. A great staircase led from the base right up to the summit. Ziggurats could take years to build, and many of the walls and columns were richly decorated with copper and mother of pearl. The first known ziggurat was constructed in about 2100 during the reign of Ur-Nammu at Ur. With a base measurement of sixty-one by forty-five metres, it rose to a total height of about twenty-six metres. Its ruins can still be seen today. It is reasonably well preserved because it was carefully renovated by the last kings of Babylon 1500 years after it was first built.

Another distinctive form of Sumerian architecture was the idea of a precinct enclosing a large open space, in which a special building

Fig. 1.8 *The first known ziggurat, constructed at Ur c. 2100 BC.*

Fig. 1.9 *A reconstruction drawing of the ziggurat at Ur. (Adapted from a drawing at the British Museum, London.)*

was constructed. This led to a series of internal courtyards which were very attractive.

The exclusive use of sun-dried mud bricks for constructing buildings has led to problems for modern archaeologists. Because the life of such buildings was comparatively short, they were constantly falling into disrepair and being replaced. The Sumerians liked to replace old temples with new ones on the same site, so the floor plans of current ruins are a mixture of original and later foundations. Archaeologists may distinguish different floor plans, but they often don't have much idea about what the original buildings actually looked like.

Art

Sumerian craftsmen were skilled in metalwork and engraving, making costly necklaces, head dresses, helmets and household ornaments in gold, silver and bronze. They also had a good knowledge of gems such as lapis lazuli and carnelian, and fashioned them into exquisite jewellery. A number of stone and wooden statues have been found, showing a high degree of sculpting skill.

Trade

The Sumerians were great traders. They exported grain, wool, oil, clothing and leather goods, and imported raw materials such as stone, metal and timber, and more exotic items like precious stones, pearls and ivory. Where possible, long-distance trade was conducted by river boats or sea-going ships. For the movement of goods overland, large donkey caravans were organised. Trade contacts extended as far west as Egypt and as far east as India.

Science

The Sumerians showed a keen interest in astronomy and mathematics. Astronomy was studied because it was a means to working out as accurate a calendar as possible. They had twelve months each of twenty-nine or thirty days, but each three years added an extra month to keep the calendar more in line with the movement of the sun. The need for mathematics probably came about because of the temples' needs to keep acurate accounts of their income and expenditure. The number system used was based on sixty, whereas our decimal system is based on ten. It is because of the Sumerians that we divide a circle into 360 degrees and an hour into sixty minutes.

Education

Only the sons of the wealthy received an education. They were taught to read and write, and this ability set them apart from the bulk of the population. With this knowledge, they entered the upper classes of priests and government officials, and so enjoyed privileges of rank and wealth. The actual process of education was harsh, however, with students being beaten if they could not remember what they had been taught.

AFTER THE DOWNFALL OF UR

Following the bloody destruction of Ur by the Elamites (see page 9), the Sumerian empire collapsed. In the south, a new Sumerian dynasty was started by Ishbi-Erra in the city of Isin. Although at first small and unimportant, this new kingdom slowly gained strength, and Ishbi-Erra eventually expelled the Elamites from the Sumerian cities of the south. However, he was not able to regain the territories of the north, for there his opponents the Amorites were too strong.

THE AMORITES

The Amorites (called *Martu*, or Westerners, by the Sumerians) were fierce tribesmen who came out of the western desert. A nomadic people of Semitic origin, they were held in fear by the more civilised people of the cities. Their entry into Akkad was not so much a concentrated invasion but a series of raids. Excellent fighters, they were more than a match for the local inhabitants, and gradually gained control over the land.

One group of Amorites made the village of

Babylon their capital, and gradually developed it into a large and important city. The name of this city, from the Akkadian *Bab-ilim*, meaning 'gate of god' was subsequently used to describe the region covering the whole of Sumer and Akkad: Babylonia. Historians describe the time from the fall of Ur (c. 2004) until the Hittite sack of Babylon in 1595 as the Old Babylonian period.

HAMMURABI

The first of the Amorite kings of Babylon was Sumu-abum, who established his dynasty around 1894. He and the four kings who succeeded him were unable to expand their kingdom, and it was not till the accession of Hammurabi in about 1792 that the established pattern changed. When he came to the throne, his kingdom was small and weak, and over-

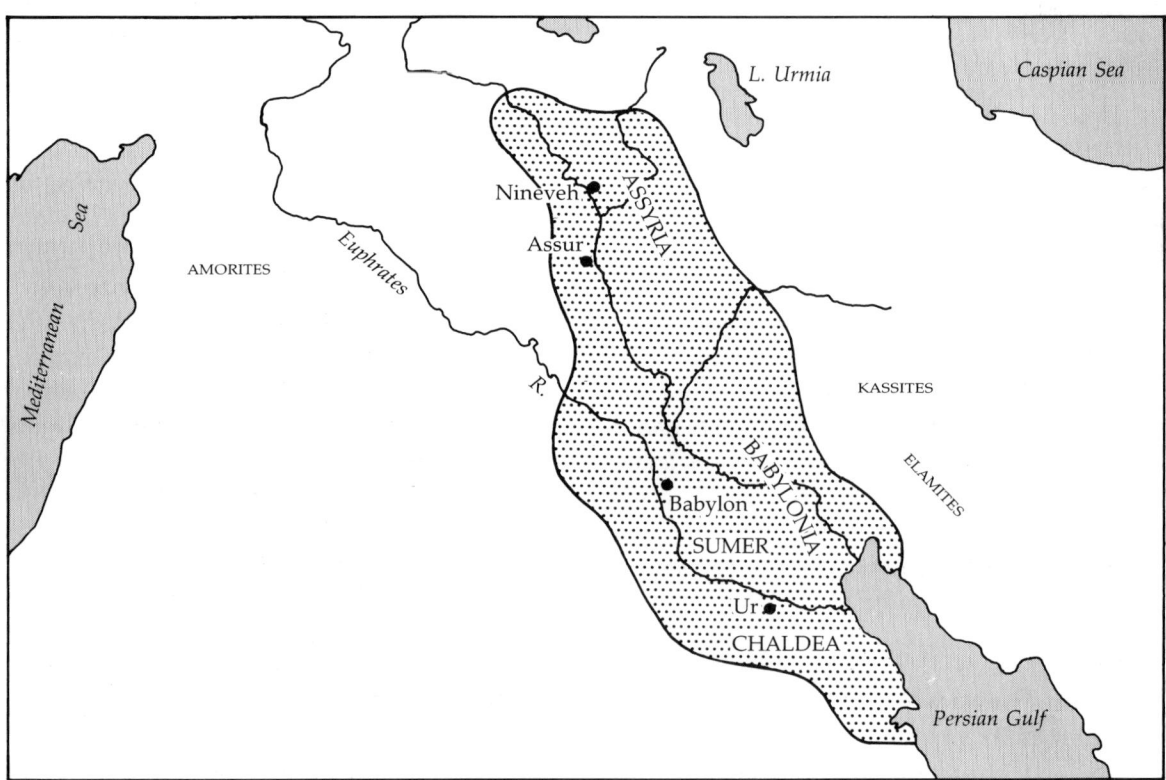

Fig. 1.10 *Old Babylonian Empire under Hammurabi.*

shadowed by much larger neighbours. This situation remained till the twenty-ninth year of his reign, when he suddenly adopted a more aggressive military policy. He defeated the Elamites in the south and so added Sumer to his domain, thus uniting Babylonia once again under a single ruler. He continued by moving north against Assyria and increasing his empire still further, now controlling all of Mesopotamia. His efforts made Babylon the seat of kingship in Mesopotamia, and this situation was to last for the next two thousand years.

Although renowned as a conqueror and empire builder, Hammurabi is generally better known because he drew up a code of laws to be used throughout the empire. These laws were not made up by Hammurabi personally, but were a summary of many that had been operating in the region for centuries. Hammurabi codified these laws, and made them applicable to all his subjects.

HAMMURABI'S CODE

We know so much about Hammurabi's Code because it was engraved on a stele that was discovered in Susa in 1901. On top of the stele is a carving of Hammurabi receiving the laws from Shamash, the sun-god and giver of justice. This was intended to convey to the people that the laws were the will of the gods, and must be obeyed (and, incidentally, not changed in the future). Some 8000 words were carved on the stele in cuneiform writing, setting out most of the Code.

Hammurabi stated his purpose in codifying the laws in these words which appear on the stele:

These are the laws of justice which Hammurabi the able king has established ... That the strong may not oppress the weak, to give justice to the orphan and the widow, I have inscribed my precious

words on my stele and established it in Babylon before my statue called 'King of Justice'.

The Code contains 282 laws. It covers such fields as family inheritance, land ownership, business practices, wages and debts. It also covers military service, marriage, slavery, false accusations, and responsibilities of doctors.

A radical change from the previous Sumerian laws was the appearance of what is called *lex talionis*, 'an eye for an eye and a tooth for a tooth'. This is certainly due to Amorite influence, and is seen in the list of penalties for those who broke the law. The lowest penalty was a fine, but others were much more severe. There were beatings, banishment and even slavery. Some offenders were mutilated by having a hand cut off, while others were killed by drowning or impalement on a sharpened stake thrust under the rib cage. To modern readers, the Code is a mixture of good common sense and harsh cruelty.

With its underlying theme that the strong shall not take advantage of the weak, the Code is very important because it became the model for similar codes throughout the region.

Some examples

If a man has committed highway robbery and has been caught, that man shall be put to death.

If a man has struck his father, his hands shall be cut off.

If a builder has made a house for a man, and has not made his work sound, and the house he has built has fallen and caused the death of its owner, that builder shall be put to death.

If a commoner has knocked out the eye of a noble, his eye shall be knocked out.

If a man has accused another man and has brought a charge of murder against him, but has not proved it, his accuser shall be put to death.

If a woman has brought about the death of her husband because of another man, they shall impale that woman on stakes.

BABYLON'S POWER

Under Hammurabi, Babylon grew rapidly in importance. Trade flourished, and many palaces and temples were built. A great deal of attention was given to the local god Marduk, and he was later promoted to an exalted position in the hierarchy of Mesopotamian gods, following closely behind Anu and Enlil.

Babylonian governors were sent to all the

Fig. 1.11 *The standing figure of Hammurabi faces the sun-god Shamash in an attitude of prayer and devotion. The seated god holds a ring and a staff, and rays can be seen emanating from his shoulders. This is only the top of the stele, which records Hammurabi's Code in detail.*

conquered cities, and Akkadian was made the official language of the empire. It displaced the original Sumerian language, which in time became a dead language.

Babylonian administration

Under Hammurabi, power slipped away from the temples and became more entrusted to the king himself. Hammurabi wanted to know everything that was going on in his kingdom, and insisted on being supplied with all manner of detail about even relatively minor matters. The result was a mass of clay tablets listing all sorts of information. Many of these have survived to the present day.

Since the empire's wealth depended on its crops and animals, much attention was given to the maintenance of canals. These were important not only for the water they provided, but as a means of transport as well. A strict account was kept of all crops and animals on the royal and temple lands, and negligent officials were called to account to explain any losses.

Palace officials were not paid in goods, but were granted land in return for specified days of service. The greater the service performed, the greater the amount of land allocated.

Hammurabi appointed many judges to administer the law, and these were widely respected as being his personal representatives. Sometimes, when no decision was reached in a difficult case, the matter was left to the gods through a 'trial by ordeal'. The accused person was thrown into the river to be judged by the river-god. If he sank and drowned, then he was guilty. If he floated and survived, then he was considered innocent.

Babylonian society

Babylonian society was made up of three classes. At the top were the nobles. These acted as priests and government officials, and were wealthy and privileged. Next were the commoners, who might be farmers, merchants, artisans or labourers. Finally there were the slaves. Most of these were people who had fallen on hard times and been forced to sell themselves to clear their debts. They were mainly engaged in domestic service. Slaves captured as the result of war were the property of the king. They lived in special barracks, and were forced to labour on laying roads, digging canals, and constructing all sorts of public buildings, from temples to fortifications.

THE EMPIRE COLLAPSES

Hammurabi's empire did not last long after his death. During the reign of his son Samsu-iluna (c. 1749–1712) some of the Sumerian cities of the south went into revolt. They were successful and established the so-called Sealand dynasty which soon controlled all the south as far as Nippur. Samsu-iluna's successors had no success against the Sealanders, and indeed their influence declined as their military position grew steadily weaker.

The Babylonians' worst blow came in 1595 when an Indo-European people known as Hittites swept in from southern Turkey. Led by the redoubtable King Murshili, the Hittite army overwhelmed the Babylonians and sacked their city. The Hittites soon withdrew, but their attacks so weakened the Babylonians that they were no match for a subsequent invading army of Sealanders led by Gulkishar. The Sealanders controlled Babylon for perhaps the next hundred years, when they themselves were threatened by the Kassites.

THE KASSITES

The Kassites were yet another Indo-European group from the north. They pushed the Sealand dynasty out of Babylon, and conquered Sumer as well. Once in command, the Kassites controlled Babylonia for the next 500 years. They did not tear down the cities, but tended to assimilate the Mesopotamian culture. In turn, their control of Babylonia came to an end about 910 when the fierce and warlike Assyrians conquered the land.

SUMMARY OF MAIN EVENTS

c. 5000	Beginning of Ubaid culture in Sumer
c. 3100	Invention of writing
c. 2500	Messalim of Lagash controls most of Babylonia
c. 2300	Sargon of Akkad defeats Lugal–zagesi and creates an empire
c. 2135	Start of the Third Dynasty of Ur
c. 1900	First Amorite dynasty at Babylon
1792–1750	Reign of King Hammurabi
1595	Hittites defeat the Babylonians
c. 1400	Kassites conquer Babylonia
c. 910	Assyrians conquer Babylonia

SUMMARY: MESOPOTAMIAN PEOPLES

Sumerians   The original inhabitants of Sumer. Probably descended from the Ubaid people, but some historians claim they came later, c. 3500.

Akkadians   People from Akkad, being of Semitic origin and originally desert nomads.

Gutians   Originally came from the central Zagros Mountains. Ruled Babylonia for about a century.

Amorites   A Semitic people who founded the first Babylonian dynasty.

Elamites   People from south-west Iran, later becoming part of the Persian Empire.

Babylonians   This term was at first reserved for the Amorite people who made Babylon their capital. Later it also applied to the peoples who formed part of the Babylonian Empire.

FEATURE

Cylinder seals

Fig. 1.7 on page 10 shows the impression of a cylinder seal. The seal itself consisted of a cylindrical piece of stone about three centimetres long. Usually it had a hole drilled through it so it could be attached to a cord. It could be made of various coloured stones such as rock crystal, agate, carnelian, lapis lazuli, marble and alabaster, and was decorated with an incised pattern. When it was rolled over soft clay, a raised pattern was left.

Important Sumerians used individual cylinder seals to identify their letters and documents, which were, of course, written in cuneiform on clay tablets. The example given here is a particularly fine one, and shows the intricate detail in which the artist had to carve to get the resulting picture in such clarity. The application of a seal to a tablet made it a legal document, and binding on the owner of the seal.

Seals first appeared in the Proto-Literate Period (3500–2800) and at first featured geometric, magical or animal patterns. Later, the owner's name was often incorporated somewhere on the seal.

Other civilisations such as those of Egypt and the Indus Valley in India followed the Sumerian lead in having cylinder seals to identify official documents.

Document 1.1

Fig. 1.12 shows a good example of cuneiform writing dating from Sumerian times.

Fig. 1.12 *Cuneiform writing on a clay tablet.*

1 The writing shown in the tablet is called cuneiform. How did it get this name? What sort of writing preceded it?

2 By inventing the art of writing, the Sumerians formed the first literate or historic society. Why is it easier for historians to learn more about the Sumerians than about the prehistoric peoples who came before them?

3 Why did the Sumerians choose to write on clay tablets and not on some other material? What were the advantages and disadvantages of using clay tablets?

4 The letter 'A' is wedge-shaped and thus had its origins in the cuneiform script. What other letters in our alphabet came from cuneiform writing?

Document 1.2

An unknown Sumerian poet wrote the following verse to describe the fall of Ur to the invading Elamites in about 2000.

> Dead men, not potsherds,
> Covered the approaches,
> The walls were gaping,
> the high gates, the roads,
> were piled with dead.
> In the side streets, where feasting crowds
>   would gather,
> Scattered they lay.
> In all the streets and roadways bodies lay.
> In open fields that used to fill with dancers,
> they lay in heaps.
> The country's blood now filled its holes,
> like metal in a mould;
> Bodies dissolved — like fat left in the sun.

1 Who was the king of Ur at the time of this attack by the Elamites? What other attacks were occurring at about the same time?

2 What can we learn about a Sumerian city from the description given in this poem?

3 How did the Elamites treat the Sumerians? What can you say about the nature of warfare at this period?

4 Which groups controlled Babylonia after the fall of the Third Dynasty of Ur?

Document 1.3

The following is an extract from the Code of Hammurabi.

> If a man has knocked out the eye of a noble, his eye shall be knocked out.
> If he has broken the limb of a noble, his limb shall be broken.
> If he has knocked out the eye of a commoner or has broken the limb of a commoner, he shall pay one mina of silver.
> If he has knocked out the eye of a noble's servant, or broken the limb of a noble's servant, he shall pay half his value.

If a noble has knocked out the tooth of a man that is his equal, his tooth shall be knocked out.

If he has knocked out the tooth of a commoner, he shall pay one-third of a mina of silver.

1 Under what circumstances is the law of 'an eye for an eye and a tooth for a tooth' invoked?
2 Under this Code, which class of society has an advantage in terms of penalties? Quote an example to illustrate your point.
3 Why do you think the Code was slanted to favour one particular class?
4 What objections to the Code could modern Australians make? In answering this question, note also the other laws of the Code quoted on pages 15–16.

Document 1.4

An extract from The Epic of Gilgamesh. Utnapishtim tells the story of the Great Flood.

I looked at the weather: stillness had set in,
And all of mankind had returned to clay.
The landscape was as level as a flat roof.
I opened a hatch and light fell upon my face.
Bowing low, I sat and wept,
Tears running down my face.
When the seventh day arrived,
I sent forth and set free a dove.
The dove went forth, but came back;
Since no resting place was visible, she
  turned round.
Then I sent forth and set free a swallow.
The swallow went forth, but came back;
Since no resting place was visible she
  turned round.
Then I sent forth and set free a raven.
The raven went forth and, seeing that the
  waters had diminished,

He ate, circled, cawed and turned not
  around.
Then I offered a sacrifice
And poured out a libation on top of the
  mountain.

1 What is meant by the expression 'all of mankind had returned to clay'?
2 Compare this extract with the account of Noah's ark in the eighth chapter of Genesis. In what ways are the accounts similar or different?
3 In the Genesis story, on what mountain did the ark finally rest?
4 Since the Epic of Gilgamesh pre-dates the Genesis story of the ark, which of the following statements may be true?
   a The author of Genesis used the Epic as a basis for his story.
   b There was a universal flood and the two accounts portray the same event.
   c There were two separate local floods, each being described by a different author.

CHECK THE FACTS

Write a sentence to answer each of these questions.
1 What is the region known as Mesopotamia? How was it named?
2 Into what regions was Mesopotamia divided 5000 years ago?
3 Why is the term 'Ubaid' used in relation to the early Sumerians?
4 What is the origin of the term 'Semites'? Who are the main Semitic peoples today?
5 What was the difference between an ensi and a lugal?
6 Which king started the Sumerian revival and founded the Third Dynasty of Ur?
7 What was a ziggurat? What was its function?

8 Who were the Amorites? What part of Mesopotamia did they invade?

9 Explain the term 'lex talionis' . What did this have to do with Hammurabi?

10 Which groups controlled Babylonia in turn following the sack of Babylon in 1595 by the Hittites?

GENERAL QUESTIONS

1 The Standard of Ur is a very important artefact because of the information it contains about life in Sumer. Study Fig. 1.6 on page 8 carefully, and say what the mosaic tells us about: *b.w.*
   a the kind of clothing worn
   b personal appearance, such as hair styles and beards
   c relaxation
   d furniture
   e musical instruments
   f domestic animals
   g food
   h transport techniques
   i art forms
   In what ways could this mosaic be more important than a written document?

2 Compile a brief report on cuneiform writing, showing how it developed from pictographs, and how it was actually written and preserved. Comment on what topics were written about, and how many examples have been recovered in modern times. How important has the development of writing been in informing people today about ancient times?

3 Imagine you are a Sumerian living in the city of Nippur. Explain how significant religion is in your life. Which gods do you worship, and how do you honour them? What religious significance does the Epic of Gilgamesh have for you?

4 If you were Hammurabi, how would you defend your Code against criticisms that it was too harsh and cruel? Find as many arguments as you can to justify your position.

5 Answer each of the following questions about life in Sumer with a paragraph.
   a What was the practice of divination? Why did the Sumerians take the matter so seriously?
   b Why have so few Sumerian buildings survived to the present day? What distinctive ideas did the Sumerians incorporate into their architecture?
   c In what ways did war stimulate the development of technology in Sumer?
   d How did the Sumerians conduct their trade? What goods did they buy and sell, and who were their trading partners?
   e What contributions did the Sumerians make to education and science?

6 Write an essay to compare and contrast the achievements of Sargon of Akkad and Hammurabi. *how long?*

2
THE RISE AND FALL OF ASSYRIA

THE ASSYRIANS: BACKGROUND HISTORY

Assyria occupied the northern part of Mesopotamia in the region of the Upper Tigris River. It was a land of hills, in contrast to the wide plains of Babylonia. Its people were mainly Semitic, and had ties with the Amorites.

The chief city of the Assyrians was Assur (also known as Ashur), inhabited since about 2000. In the early period of their history the Assyrians were great traders. They carried textiles and metals (especially tin) to Kanesh in Anatolia (modern Turkey) by donkey caravan and returned with copper. Those not engaged in trade were herders and farmers, a tough people accustomed to fighting enemies in time of war, and among themselves in times of peace. Their laws were based on Hammurabi's Code, but the penalties were much harsher.

The early kings of Assyria probably didn't rule over a very extensive region, but they considered themselves part of the old Babylonian and Sumerian culture. They founded libraries and stocked them with copies of old Babylonian documents, and these have proved invaluable to archaeologists in recent times. They compiled detailed king-lists, and these show that the same dynasty ruled continuously over Assur from about 1670 onwards.

Assyria came under the control of Babylonia during the reign of Hammurabi, but when the Babylonian empire collapsed, it became part of the empire of the Mitanni, an Aryan people who lived in northern Mesopotamia. This state of dependency continued till around 1350, when the Assyrian king Assur-uballit attacked and defeated the Mitannian king Tushratta. He was then able to establish a small independent kingdom of his own. Sympathetic to the Babylonians, he married his daughter to a Babylonian prince and adopted the Babylonian language for the inscriptions on his statues. A proud man, he called himself 'Great King' and sent envoys to King Tutankhamen of Egypt on equal terms. This drew a rebuke from the Babylonian king Burnaburiash, who sent a letter to Tutankhamen, complaining that the Assyrians were mere upstarts who should be ignored.

LATER KINGS

The kingdom established by Assur-uballit was later expanded by some of his successors, notably Adad-nirari I (c. 1305–c. 1274), Shalmaneser I (c. 1273–c. 1244) and Tukulti-ninurta (c. 1243–c. 1207).

Adad-nirari I defeated both the Kassites and the Mitanni early in his reign, and extended the borders of his kingdom extensively. He produced many public inscriptions in which he proclaimed that the gods called him to war, and he gave them the credit for his successes. To thank them, he greatly enlarged the temple in Assur. Later in his reign he lost much territory to the Hittites, and was largely forced on to the defensive.

Shalmaneser I had considerable success against the Mitanni, and claimed that he had blinded 14 400 prisoners in one eye. This bloodthirsty action was a kind of psychological warfare that was later widely followed. A great builder, Shalmaneser constructed a second capital at the junction of the Tigris and the Great Zab rivers. He called it Kalakh, but in the Bible it is known as Calah. Its modern name is Nimrud.

Tukulti-ninurta was a gifted but extravagant king who fought very successful wars against the Hittites and the Babylonians. When the Babylonians revolted, he plundered their temples. This was an extremely sacrilegious act which cost him the support of his own people, and he was eventually killed by his own sons. After his death, the empire broke up, and Assyrian power went into decline for several centuries.

THE EARLIER ASSYRIAN EMPIRE: 911–745

The start of a resurgence of Assyrian power came during the reign of Adad-nirari II (911–891). This eventually led to the establishment of an Assyrian empire which was to be the most extensive in the world up to that time. Under Adad-nirari and his successors, the Assyrian conquests came in two stages, the first ending in 745. In this earlier period the main kings were Adad-nirari II, Assurnasirpal II and Shalmaneser III.

ADAD-NIRARI II

Adad-nirari II fought mainly against the Aramaeans and the Babylonians. The former were nomadic invaders from northern Arabia who wanted to move into Assyria. Adad-nirari fought six campaigns against them and pushed them back deep inside their own territory. He also mounted two campaigns against the Babylonians, and won considerable territory from them. He left behind many documents which recounted his deeds. Although obviously proud of his military conquests, he was also apparently quite pleased with his efforts in improving agriculture. On the basis of these early conquests, succeeding kings were able to widen the Assyrian empire extensively.

ASSURNASIRPAL II (OR ASHURNASIRPAL II)

The greatest expansion was brought about by Assurnasirpal II (c. 885–860). He marched westwards towards the Mediterranean, conquering the Aramaean kingdom of Bit-Adini and the Hittite city of Carchemish on the way. He conquered Syria, and forced the cities of Phoenicia to pay tribute. All of Mesopotamia as far as the Euphrates came under his command.

His success was largely due to the military tactics that he employed. In addition to his infantry and war chariots, he organised large cavalry units, which had generally not been used before this time. Another novel tactic was the use of mobile battering rams and wall breakers in his sieges. His enemies recoiled before his new methods of warfare, and he met with success everywhere.

A NEW CAPITAL

It was Assurnasirpal II who, for strategic reasons, changed Assyria's capital from Assur

Fig. 2.1 *This winged, human-headed lion was part of a doorway of Assurnasirpal's palace. Carved in limestone and over four metres high, this creature was designed both to scare off evil spirits and to impress visitors with the king's grandeur.*

to the new city of Kalakh in 879. He built this city with captive labour on the site of the old city of the same name built by Shalmaneser I, which had long since crumbled and decayed. A stele was discovered on the site in 1951. It commemorated a great feast held over ten days with nearly 70 000 guests to celebrate the official opening of the city. Despite the building of the new city, Assurnasirpal retained Assur as the nation's religious capital.

The new capital was laid out on a grand scale, and no expense was spared to make it a city worthy of a great king. Special attention was paid to building a magnificent palace, which covered a space of 25 000 square metres. Some of the building blocks were inscribed with many details of the king's exploits. These

have become a valuable resource for historians, and have shown the ferocious nature of Assurnasirpal's attitude towards conquered people. Here is an example of the king's boasts about his enemies:

> I stormed the mountain peaks and took them. In the midst of the mighty mountain I slaughtered them, with their blood I dyed the mountain red like wool ... The heads of ... warriors I cut off, and I formed them into a pillar over against their city, their young men and their maidens I burned in the fire.

In like vein, there is this description of what happened to a city which rebelled against Assyrian rule:

> I built a pillar over against his city gate, and I flayed all the chief men who had revolted, and I covered the pillar with their skins; some I walled up within the pillar, some I impaled upon the pillar on stakes ...

Assurnasirpal also built many temples in honour of Ninurta, god of war and the hunt. The tower of the main temple in Kalakh doubled as an astronomical observatory.

SHALMANESER III

Shalmaneser III (c. 859–824) was Assurnasirpal's son and successor. He also had several conquests, notably in Syria, and forced King Jehu of Israel to pay tribute. In addition, he intervened in the affairs of Babylonia, helping King Marduk-zakir-shumi to retain his position against a palace revolt. This gave him considerable influence in Babylonian affairs. Despite these successes, he only had mixed fortune in his campaigns against the peoples of Cilicia and Urartu. An energetic king, Shalmaneser built many temples, palaces and forts and got his artists to create many statues and stelae.

Despite the successes of the three kings just mentioned, the Assyrians were on the defensive as this period of history ended. They were beset by enemies on all sides, and they had to give up many of their gains. But they were far from finished, as future events were to show.

THE LATER ASSYRIAN CONQUESTS: 745–612

Despite the setbacks suffered by the successors of Shalmaneser III, the Assyrian army remained strong, and only needed a capable leader before it became a force to be feared once again. This happened when a new series of strong kings revitalised the empire and pushed it to its greatest limits. The first of these kings was Tiglath-Pileser III (744–727), who came to power when the kingdom was threatened by external enemies and weakened by internal separatist movements.

TIGLATH-PILESER III

The new king first strengthened his position by subdividing some of the larger provinces which had tended to follow independent policies. The new, smaller provinces were given new governors who were all loyal to the king and who had to report to him regularly. They were made responsible for the collection of local taxes, the storage of military supplies, and the calling up of men for the new Assyrian army. Thus strengthened internally and militarily, Tiglath-Pileser was ready to face his external enemies.

His first moves were east and north against troublesome surrounding tribes. After defeating them decisively, he settled many thousands of his own people in the region, thus ensuring a firmer control for the future.

He next turned against his arch-enemy the King of Urartu, defeating him and his allies in 743. From there he pushed west into Syria and then south into Palestine till he came to the border of Egypt. In 734 he made Israel a vassal state and in the same year became

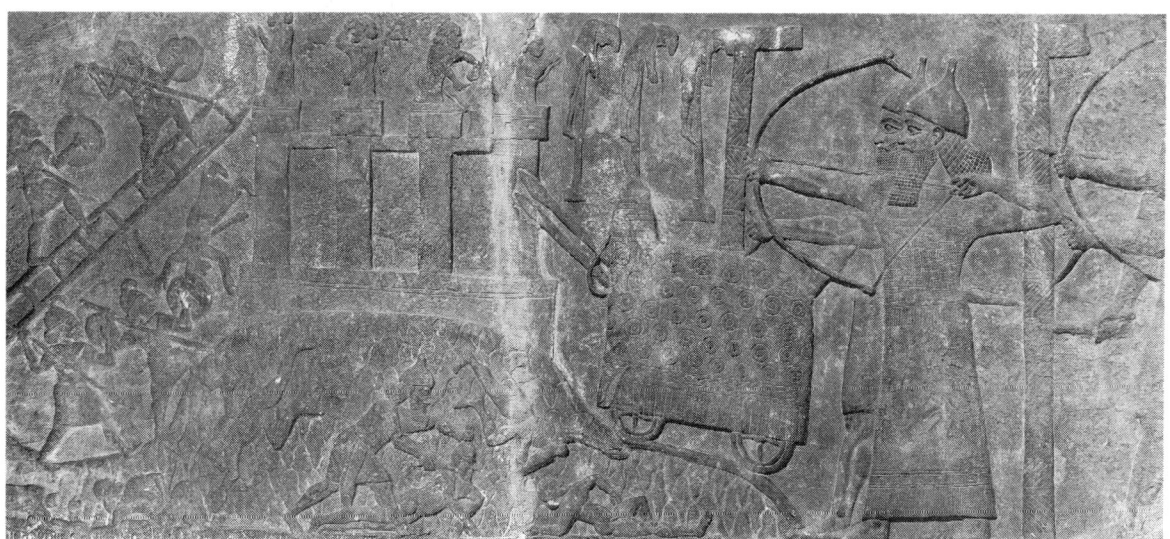

Fig. 2.2 *This relief shows the forces of Tiglath-Pileser III attacking a walled city. Note the mobile battering ram in the centre of the picture. Why do you think the figures of the archers are so large and out of proportion with the rest of the figures?*

King of Babylon. With the idea of keeping a firm control of the new territories, he set up a regular messenger service.

Archaeologists and historians have been able to reconstruct the events of Tiglath-Pileser's life fairly easily because much of his correspondence has been found, together with inscriptions on buildings. Perhaps most importantly, he was the first monarch to have historical records carved onto the stone walls of his palaces. These gave a history of his exploits year by year, and gave much more detail than the normal palace inscriptions that had preceded them.

SARGON II

The second of the Assyrian conquerors was Sharru-kin II, better known by the Hebrew name of Sargon II (721–705). Probably a younger son of Tiglath-Pileser III, his reign was one of almost relentless fighting and conquest. Almost from the start, he was faced with the rebellions of Babylon, Israel and Syria.

First he moved against Babylon, where an Aramaean prince named Marduk-apal-iddina had seized control. At first his efforts were unsuccessful, and he had to defer his plans for reconquest for another ten years. In the meantime, he put down the revolt of Israel, and converted it from a vassal kingdom to an Assyrian province. He also forced Judah to pay tribute as the only way of maintaining its independence. In 720 he crushed the Syrian revolt and four years later added the state of Carchemish to the empire.

The year 719 saw him campaigning in Persia, with parts of Media being added to the empire as a result. Five years later he was in Urartu, and won a crushing victory against King Rusas. This netted him immense booty, and the means to settle scores with Marduk-apal-iddina. Marshalling a great army, he

marched against his enemy, who fled without offering a battle. He was lenient towards the Babylonians, and refrained from the cruelties that marked his conduct elsewhere.

Sargon's new capital

In 713, Sargon decided to found a new capital north of Nineveh and assembled tens of thousands of labourers and hundreds of artists to build it. He called it Dur-Sharrukin (fortress of Sargon), but today it is known as Khorsabad. The city was roughly in the shape of a square and surrounded by a high wall incorporating seven gates. Its showpiece was the magnificent palace, enclosed within its own wall. The temples were incorporated into the palace complex, but they were considerably smaller, thus emphasising the importance of the king in contrast with the priests. At the entrance were two huge winged bulls with human heads, and the walls were covered with numerous reliefs showing scenes of war and a variety of religious processions. Because of the immense scope of the task, the city was never completed in Sargon's lifetime.

Writing

It was during Sargon's reign that the practice began of writing on a layer of beeswax spread on wooden boards. This form of writing was much less bulky than that written on clay tablets, but not as permanent, as it could be affected by extreme heat.

The death of Sargon

In 705 Sargon was fighting in north-western Persia when he was ambushed and killed. His son Sennacherib was on poor terms with his father, and apparently believed that the king's death came as a punishment by the gods for being too proud. The story goes that he allowed Sargon's body to remain unburied, and his bones were picked clean by the vultures.

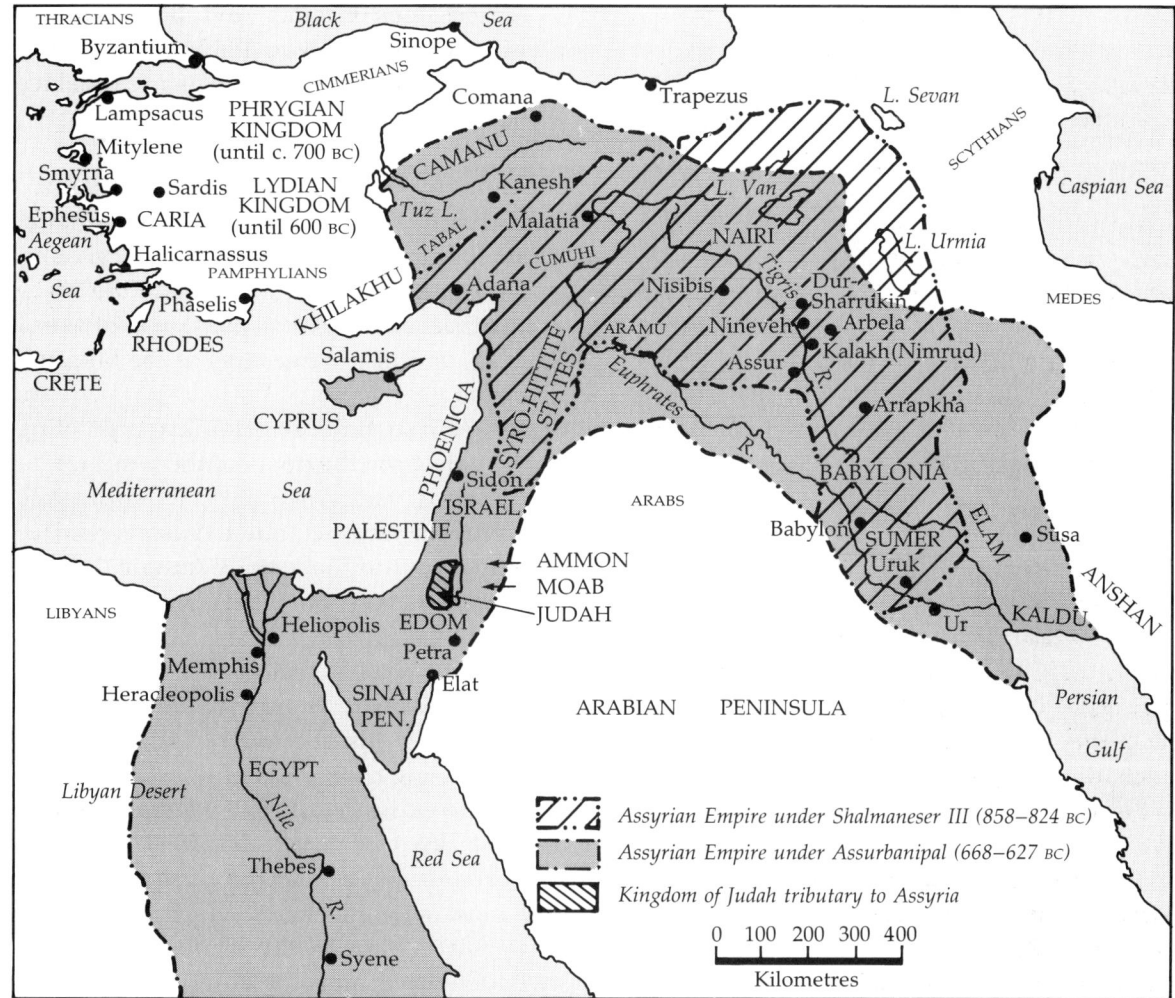

Fig. 2.3   *The Assyrian Empire, 858–627 BC.*

SENNACHERIB

Sargon's successsor was Sennacherib (704–681). Sennacherib, like his father, was at war for most of his reign. Some of the fighting was against rebellious subjects — for example, Babylon in 703 and again in 688. When Babylon rebelled the second time, Sennacherib destroyed the city as a warning to all other potential rebels against Assyrian rule. The destruction of Babylon also led to war against the Elamites, who had sided with the Babylonians. Sennacherib defeated the Elamites, but only at the cost of considerable losses to his own forces.

Further afield, Sennacherib attacked Jerusalem and made King Hezekiah of Judah pay tribute. He also conquered Cilicia, and added it to the empire. The biblical account of Sennacherib's success in Judah is found in II Kings 18, and reads as follows:

13   Now in the fourteenth year of the reign of King Hezekiah did Sennacherib king of Assyria come up against all the

Fig. 2.4 *This remarkable hexagonal clay prism records Sennacherib's victory over the Palestinian forces and their Egyptian allies. In referring to Hezekiah, Sennacherib said: 'like a caged bird, I shut up in Jerusalem, his royal city.' How was Hezekiah able to defend the city successfully?*

fenced cities of Judah, and took them.

14 And Hezekiah king of Judah sent to the king of Assyria to Lachish saying, I have offended; return from me: that which thou puttest on me will I bear. And the king of Assyria appointed unto Hezekiah king of Judah three hundred talents of silver and thirty talents of gold.

15 And Hezekiah gave him all the silver that was found in the house of the Lord, and in the treasures of the king's house.

16 At that time did Hezekiah cut off the gold from the doors of the temple of the Lord, and from the pillars which Hezekiah king of Judah had overlaid, and gave it to the king of Assyria.

Nineveh

While still crown prince, Sennacherib had begun a reconstruction of the ancient city of Nineveh. On his accession, he made it his capital. Using thousands of prisoners of war as labourers, he greatly extended and beautified the city. He laid out the streets, enlarged the squares and rebuilt the public buildings, the most magnificent of which was a vast new palace. Around the whole city he built two defensive walls, the inner one being thirteen kilometres long. They still stand today.

Outside the city he planted many groves of fruit trees and laid out numerous lush parks which included exotic plants and trees. One of his introductions was the cotton plant, described as 'the wool-bearing tree'. To irrigate these parks and groves he brought water in canals and aqueducts over distances of ten kilometres from springs in the nearby hills.

Technology

An extremely intelligent man, Sennacherib took a great interest in technology and supported those who were ready to experiment with new methods. Under his direction, improved methods of bronze casting were discovered, and better ways of raising water from wells. He also instigated searches for new supplies of building materials such as alabaster, stone and timber. These items were necessary, as they gave greater scope for constructing more elaborate buildings than the mud-bricks normally used.

Sennacherib was killed in 681, apparently by some of his sons who wanted to seize the throne.

ESARHADDON

Esarhaddon was one of Sennacherib's younger sons, but he had already been nominated as successor due to his undoubted ability. When he heard of his father's death, Esarhaddon moved swiftly against the assassins. They fled in disorder, and he was able to proceed to Nineveh and claim the throne without opposition. The Assyrian Empire was to reach its height under Esarhaddon, who ruled from 680 to 669.

A former governor of Babylonia, Esarhaddon had opposed his father's harsh attitude towards the Babylonians. As soon as he became king, he adopted a policy of reconciliation, and spent lavishly to restore the city of Babylon to its former glory. His policy paid dividends, as the Babylonians supported him enthusiastically, and he was spared the expense of keeping the land under military rule.

Esarhaddon now turned his attention to expanding the empire. Egypt had long been intriguing with some of Assyria's western vassal states, and Esarhaddon decided to stop this interference by invading Egypt. After two failed campaigns in 675 and 674, he finally defeated the Egyptian army in the Nile delta in 671 and captured Memphis. However, his forces were too few to provide an army of occupation. He had to withdraw, but appointed several Egyptian princes as vassal rulers. They revolted as soon as his back was turned, but he died before he could put down the rebellion.

ASSURBANIPAL

It was left to his son and successor Assurbanipal (668–627) to crush the Egyptian rebellion and leave behind Assyrian garrisons to maintain control. But Assyrian control was always shaky, given the size of Egypt and the hatred of the Egyptians for their conquerors. By 650 an Egyptian uprising had forced the Assyrians out, never to return.

When Assurbanipal first came to the throne, his half-brother Shamash-shum-ukin was made co-ruler, occupying the Babylonian throne. However, Assurbanipal was by far the dominant figure. He insisted that all Assyrian officials and garrisons stationed in Babylonia report to him personally, and it was he who appointed governors to the Babylonian provinces. Shamash-shum-ukin submitted to this subordinate role for sixteen years, but finally tried to assert his independence, and led a revolt against Assurbanipal in 652. It failed, and Babylon itself was besieged for two years. When it finally fell in 648, Shamash-shum-ukin committed suicide in the flames of his palace. The Assyrian army then exacted a terrible vengeance on the rebels. A victory inscription ascribes these words to Assurbanipal:

> As for those men ... who plotted evil against me, I tore out their tongues and defeated them completely. The others, alive, I smashed with the very same statues of protective deities with which they had smashed my own grandfather Sennacherib — now finally as a belated burial sacrifice for his soul. I fed their corpses, cut into small pieces, to the dogs, pigs, *zibu*-birds, vultures, the birds of the sky and to the fish of the ocean.

Fig. 2.5 *This figure is from a sandstone stele commemorating Assurbanipal's rebuilding of Esagila in Babylon. It shows the king carrying on his head a basket of earth which was used in the ritual moulding of the first brick. Why was Assurbanipal well disposed towards Babylon?*

Despite the troubles there, Assurbanipal himself always took a keen interest in Babylon, contributing heavily to the rebuilding of the temple at Esagila in 650. A sandstone stele has been found showing Assurbanipal carrying on his head a basket which contains earth for the ritual moulding of the first brick.

In 647 Assyrian troops pushed into Elam,

which had assisted the Babylonian rebels. The Elamite capital of Susa was sacked the following year, and its treasures plundered. The upper classes of the Elamites were sent in exile to Assyria, and Elam became an Assyrian province.

Assurbanipal's library

A highly intelligent man, Assurbanipal was perhaps the world's first 'scholar-king'. In an inscription, he describes his school days in which he learned 'the hidden treasure of all scribal knowledge. I solve complex mathematical reciprocals and products with no apparent solution; I read abstruse tablets whose Sumerian is obscure and whose Akkadian is hard to construe . . .'

His literary achievements led him to assemble at Nineveh the greatest library of the ancient world. His scribes and scholars collected or copied texts of all descriptions. There were literary epics such as Gilgamesh, folk tales, dictionaries, works on astronomy and mathematics, hymns, prayers, proverbs and fables. Since the library was first discovered in 1853, over 20 000 tablets or fragments have been recovered. These have been invaluable in constructing a picture of what Assyrian life was like during this period.

THE DECLINE OF ASSYRIA

Assurbanipal was the last of the great Assyrian kings, and the latter years of his reign saw the beginning of the empire's downfall. Although records of his last years are sketchy, it appears that he had twin sons who fought over the succession even while he was still alive. This greatly weakened the empire, and subject people such as the Medes were able to declare their independence. When Assurbanipal finally died in 627, the empire was in turmoil and headed for destruction.

Several weak kings followed Assurbanipal, and they saw the empire finally collapse. In

614 the Babylonians and the Medes invaded Assyria, and two years later captured Nineveh. A few Assyrians tried to maintain a resistance, using the old capital of Assur as their base. However, they were decisively defeated, together with their Egyptian allies, at the battle of Carchemish in 606 by Nebuchadrezzar, son of Nabopolassar, the new Chaldean king of Babylon. Most were wiped out, and only a few survived as slaves.

SOME ASPECTS OF ASSYRIAN SOCIETY

The Assyrian army

The Assyrian army was the terror of the Mesopotamian region. It was the first to use iron weapons, and the heavily armed and highly disciplined infantrymen struck terror into the hearts of their opponents. They devised a three-man war chariot for fighting on level ground, and invented a variety of war machinery to conduct sieges. These included battering rams, catapults and siege towers, and were most effective against walled cities.

Governing the empire

At the head of the Assyrian empire was the all-powerful king. If he was a strong ruler, his position was relatively safe, although there were always ambitious subordinates to be watched carefully. If he was weak, he was likely to be toppled by a usurper. The king guarded his position jealously, and gloried in exaggerated and exalted titles. As a gauge of their own self-importance, many kings built entirely new palaces, forsaking those built by their predecessors.

Helping the king to govern were the prime minister, military generals and provincial governors. These were the most important officials, and were assisted by a host of minor officials and scribes. Some conquered territories were allowed to keep their own ruler provided he remained loyal to Assyrian control and paid the required tribute on time. However, such vassal kings could expect torture and death if they defaulted on either count. Their lands would then be incorporated into the empire as a province, and they would be replaced by Assyrian governors. Frequently, mass deportations of troublesome populations were carried out in an effort to prevent further disturbances in the region.

Assyrian art and learning

The Assyrians were great builders, and their temples and palaces were the wonders of their day. They were extremely fond of decorating the interior walls of these buildings with paintings and relief sculptures. Popular themes were battle scenes, the punishment of enemies, the herding of captives, and violent hunting scenes involving lions.

The Assyrians had a keen interest in history. The kings appointed scribes to make detailed records of all their deeds, and these records have given modern researchers a valuable insight into the Assyrians' viewpoint of their times. They also ordered the copying of as many old Sumerian and Babylonian records as they could find, and stored them in great libraries. The greatest of these libraries was the one established by Assurbanipal at his palace in Nineveh (see page 30). Given the bulky nature of the tablets, any library needed a great deal of space.

THE CHALDEANS AND THE NEW BABYLONIAN KINGDOM

The Chaldeans were a powerful group who lived in Sumer on the coastal fringe near the Persian Gulf in a region formerly known as the Sea Lands (see page 17). They had long challenged Assyrian power, and the Assyrians had never been able to pacify them completely. When he saw the Assyrian power declining, a Chaldean chief named Nabopolassar seized power in Babylonia and challenged Assyria itself. As we have already seen, he formed an alliance with the Medes, and captured Nineveh in 612 (see page 31). His son Nebuchadrezzar routed the Egyptians at Carchemish in 606 and chased them right back to their borders. In his advance, he conquered both Phoenicia and Palestine.

Nebuchadrezzar could have invaded Egypt, but news reached him of his father's death and he had to return to Babylonia. Having established his right to the throne, Nebuchadrezzar was able to give thought to expanding the empire. He first turned his attention to the kingdom of Judah, which was intriguing with Egypt against Babylonia. Nebuchadrezzar captured Jerusalem in 597, and deported King Jehoiachim and some of the inhabitants to Babylonia. When the new king, Zedekiah, rebelled eleven years later, Nebuchadrezzar returned in a fury. He sacked the city and its temple, and carried most of the people into captivity in Babylon.

The Phoenician city of Tyre was another which challenged Babylonia's power. It was a great trading port, and heavily fortified. Nebuchadrezzar's army besieged Tyre for thirteen years, eventually capturing it in 571. With the fall of Tyre, Babylonian power extended to the borders of Egypt.

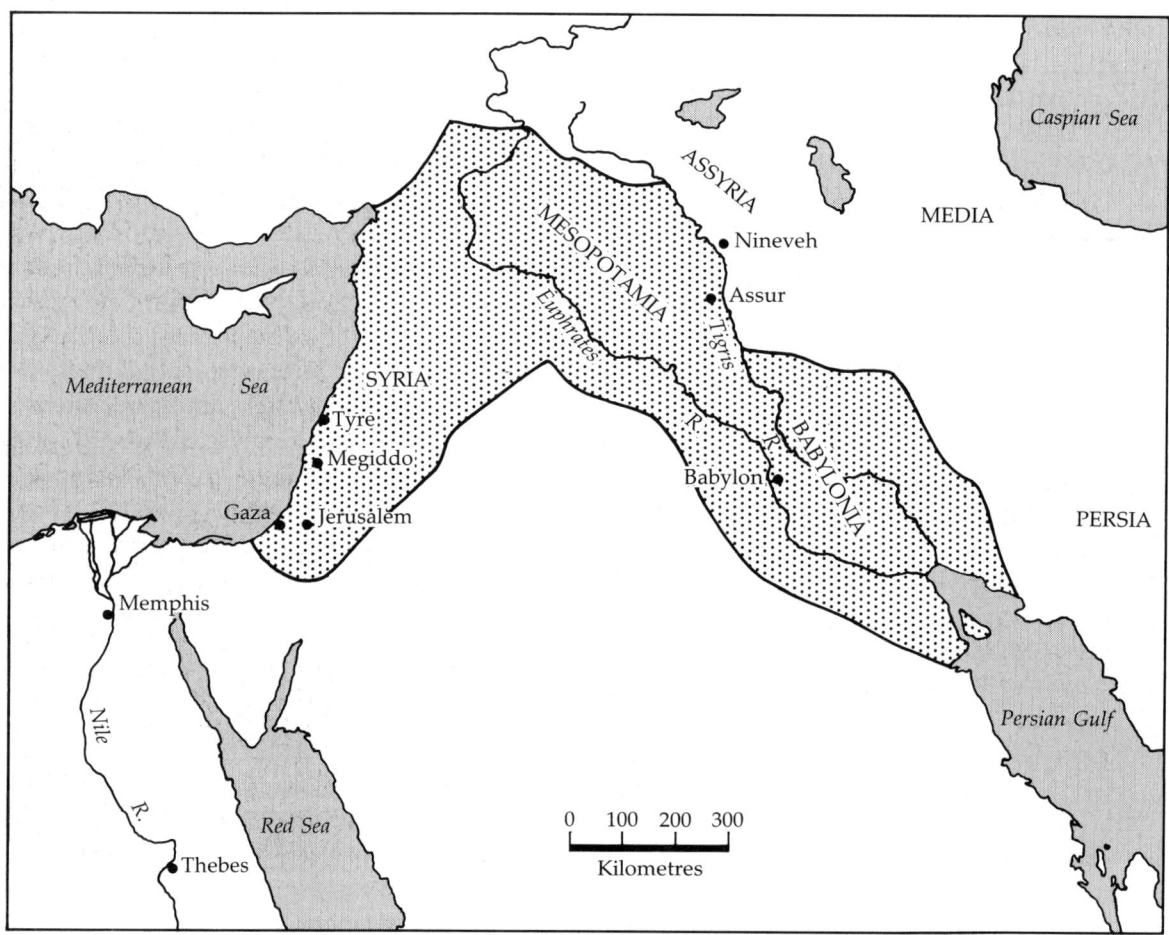

Fig. 2.6   *Chaldean Empire in the time of Nebuchadrezzar, c. 570* BC.

NEBUCHADREZZAR'S
BABYLON

Nebuchadrezzar was determined to make Babylon a city which reflected the greatness of its ruler. He built a huge temple to Marduk, and its ziggurat was probably the largest ever built. Very likely it was the original Tower of Babel mentioned in the Old Testament. His own palace was a marvel, and its famous ter-

Fig. 2.7 *This is the famous Ishtar Gate, built by Nebuchadrezzar II at Babylon. Ornamented with bulls and dragons, this gate is Babylon's only well-preserved monument.*

raced roof gardens planted with a profusion of lush tropical plants became one of the seven wonders of the ancient world.

In addition to these and other lesser temples and palaces, Nebuchadrezzar built numerous roads, bridges, walls and gates. The most spectacular of the surviving gates is the Ishtar Gate, lavishly decorated with lions and dragons. Its foundations were as deep as the wall was high. Surrounding the entire city was a high wall which was believed to be impregnable. Babylon was indeed a marvel in its own time, as was stated by the Greek historian Herodotus, who visited it at a later period.

RELIGION AND ASTROLOGY

The Chaldean rulers of Babylonia followed the ancient Sumerian religion in which the gods were all-powerful but uncaring about human welfare. The gods gave no commandments for the people to follow, but were quick to punish any unwitting offences committed by luckless individuals. The people could do nothing but accept whatever fate the gods decreed. They could try to propitiate the gods by building temples and making offerings, but they could never be sure of the results. Some priests turned to a study of the stars as a means of determining the will of the gods, and this led to a belief in astrology.

The Chaldean interest in astrology led to the more precise study of astronomy. Chaldean astronomers made accurate star charts and named all the planets. They were so precise in their observations that they were able to calculate the length of the year to within twenty-six minutes.

NABONIDUS

Nebuchadrezzar died in 562. In the space of the next six years three kings came and went, and it wasn't till Nabonidus seized the throne in 556 that stability returned to the government. But Nabonidus was soon in trouble with the priests of Marduk because he devoted so much attention to the moon-god Sin. As well, the neighbouring Persians under Cyrus were becoming menacing as they expanded their empire westwards. In 539 Cyrus eventually moved against Babylon, and the city fell without a struggle.

SUMMARY OF MAIN EVENTS

The early period

c. 2000	Foundation of the city of Assur
c. 1350	Assur-uballit establishes a small kingdom
c. 1305–c. 1207	Early kings: Adad-nirari I, Shalmaneser I, Tukulti-ninurta

Early Assyrian Empire

911–891	Adad-nirari II starts the Assyrian Empire
883–859	Assurnasirpal II greatly expands the empire
879	Foundation of Kalakh by Assurnasirpal
858–824	Reign of Shalmaneser III

Later Assyrian Empire

744–727	Reign of Tiglath-Pileser III
721–705	Reign of Sargon II
713	Sargon starts construction of Dur-Sharrukin
704–681	Reign of Sennacherib
680–669	Reign of Esarhaddon
668–627	Reign of Assurbanipal
648	Babylon falls: Shamash-shum-ukin suicides

The Chaldeans

606	Assyrians defeated at Carchemish by Nebuchadrezzar
597	Nebuchadrezzar captures Jerusalem
562	Death of Nebuchadrezzar
539	Cyrus the Persian captures Babylon

IMPORTANT CITIES OF THE ASSYRIAN PERIOD

Assur   Also known as Ashur, was the original city of the Assyrians and was named after the god Ashur. Capital of Assyria till 879, but remained religious capital till its destruction in 614. Modern Qal At Sharqat in Iraq.

Kalakh   Known also as Kalhu, was founded in 879 to replace Assur as Assyria's capital. Remained capital till Sargon moved the government to Dur-Sharrukin. Known today as Nimrud in Iraq.

Babylon   Capital of Babylonia, but part of the Assyrian Empire. Destroyed by Sennacherib after a rebellion, but restored by Esarhaddon. Greatly enlarged and beautified by Nebuchadrezzar. Only ruins remain today.

Jerusalem   Capital of Judah. Attacked by Sennacherib and forced to pay tribute. Twice captured by Nebuchadrezzar (597 and 586). On the second occasion, the people were taken to Babylon as captives.

Susa   Capital city of the Elamites. Captured by Assurbanipal in 646.

Nineveh   Became capital of Assyria under Sennacherib. It was the location of Assurbanipal's magnificent library. Captured by Nabopolassar in 612. Near Mosul in modern Iraq.

FEATURE

Assyrian palaces

Assyrian kings were very keen to build palaces as a clear demonstration of their power and prestige. Some kings refused to live in palaces built by their predecessors, and insisted on building completely new edifices of their own. Others built more than one palace, glorying in their ability to display their wealth and prestige in such a highly visible manner.

Royal palaces generally had three main functions. The first was to provide a splendid residence for the king and his family, and a place where he could conduct the business of government. The second function was to house the offices of the royal bureaucracy. Finally, there was always a large storage area for a huge variety of taxes in kind. The treasures stored here were used to pay for the running expenses of the empire.

One of the best-preserved of the Assyrian palaces is the one built by Sargon II at Dur-Sharrukin (Khorsabad). Spread out over ten hectares, it contained more than 200 courtyards and rooms. It was built on a large raised area which stood sixteen metres above the surrounding buildings of the city. This heightened location served two purposes. One was to keep the palace well above flood level. The second was meant to emphasise the importance of the king, who lived midway between the people and the gods.

The building is a stretched-out rambling

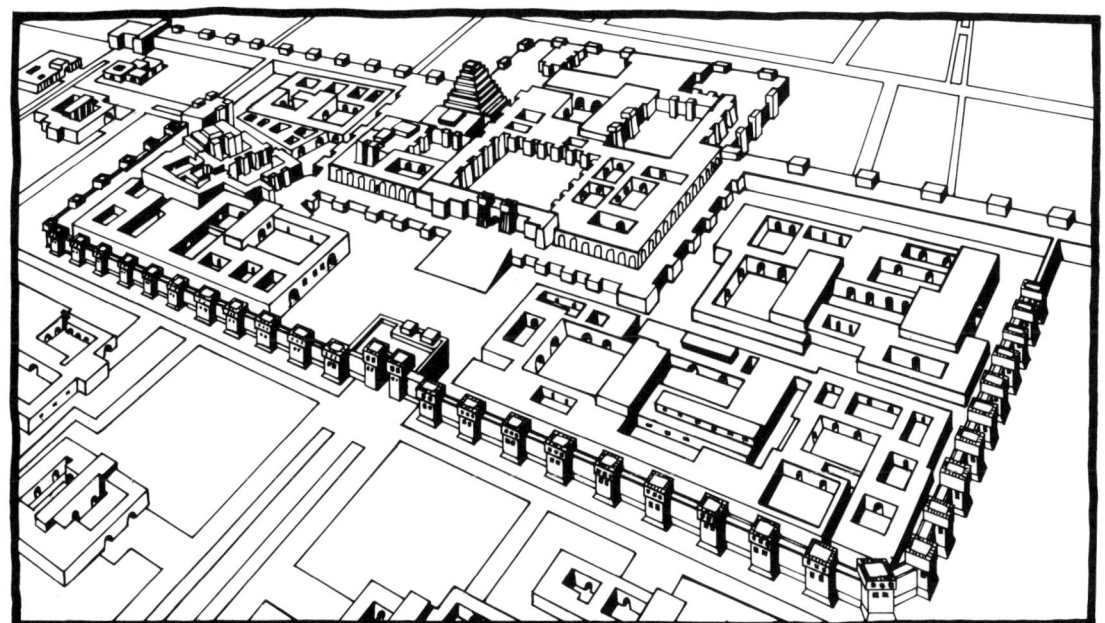

Fig. 2.8 *Reconstruction drawing of the citadel of Sargon II, Khorsabad, c. 720 BC.*

affair incorporating long rectangular rooms around square courtyards. The shape of the long narrow rooms and the incredible thickness of the walls suggests that the rooms were covered by brick barrel vaults. These were necessary because mud bricks were easily obtainable, while good timber was not.

The main courtyard was square, and measured 100 metres along each side. The rooms to its right were mainly used by the king's high officials as offices. The block to the left comprised a group of temples dedicated to the national gods. Although they are part of the palace complex, they are clearly not as important as the bureaucrats' offices. The ever-present ziggurat was located in this area as well. It may have had as many as seven stages, each over five metres in height and painted in a different colour, but only four remain.

To the left of the smaller rectangular courtyard were the living quarters of the king and his family, and are obviously very extensive. They included bedrooms, state chambers, a harem, service quarters and guard rooms. The king himself held court in the throne room, measuring forty by ten metres. Entrance to this room was through two open doorways which were guarded by colossal winged bulls with human heads. (Fig. 2.1 on page 24 shows a similar figure from a doorway of Assurnasirpal's palace).

Sargon was extremely proud of his palace. One of his inscriptions reads like this: 'Sargon, King of the World, has built a city. Dur-Sharrukin he has named it. A peerless palace he has built within it.'

Document 2.1

The Assyrian King Shamshi-Adad V, who reigned between 823 and 811, had this account of his attack on the Babylonian fortress of Dur-Papsukal included in the royal annals.

13 000 of their warriors I cut down with the sword. Their blood like the waters of a stream I caused to run through the squares of their city. The corpses of their soldiers I piled in heaps ... His [the Babylonian king's] royal bed, his royal couch, the treasure of his palaces, his property, his gods and everything from his palace, without number, I carried away. His captive warriors were given to the soldiers of my land like grasshoppers. The city I destroyed, I devastated, I burned with fire.

1 Which other Assyrian kings wrote similar bloodthirsty accounts of their conquests?
2 Why do you think Assyrian kings displayed such ferocious attitudes towards their enemies?
3 What was their purpose in recording such violent scenes of bloodshed? Do you think they were proud of their deeds, or perhaps wanted to cast fear into the hearts of potential enemies?
4 If you were a Mesopotamian ruler faced by an invading Assyrian army, would you fight against them or surrender to their demands? Give reasons for your answer.

Document 2.2

Sennacherib's attack on Jerusalem has already been referred to (see page 27). The following account from II Kings 19 tells of the epidemic that struck Sennacherib's forces when he persisted in besieging Jerusalem even after he had received the promised tribute. The words are those of the Lord, given to King Hezekiah through the prophet Isaiah.

32 Therefore thus saith the Lord concerning the king of Assyria, He shall not come into this city, nor shoot an arrow there, nor come before it with shield, nor cast a bank against it.
33 By the way that he came, by the same shall he return, and shall not come into this city, saith the Lord.
34 For I will defend this city, to save it, for mine own sake, and for my servant David's sake.
35 And it came to pass that night, that the angel of the Lord went out, and smote in the camp of the Assyrians an hundred four score and five thousand: and when they arose early in the morning, behold, they were all dead corpses.
36 So Sennacherib king of Assyria departed, and went and returned, and dwelt at Nineveh.
37 And it came to pass, as he was worshipping in the house of Nisroch his god, that Adrammelech and Sharezer his sons smote him with the sword: and they escaped into the land of Armenia. And Esarhaddon his son reigned in his stead.

1 What do you think is meant by the expression 'nor cast a bank against it'?
2 How many Assyrians died in the epidemic? Many historians claim that this number is greatly exaggerated; what are your thoughts on this matter?
3 What light does this extract throw on the eventual fate of Sennacherib?
4 Would you consider this passage to be a reliable source of ancient history? Give reasons for your answer.

Document 2.3

The Greek writer Herodotus lived during the fifth century BC and travelled widely in the ancient world. Because of his account of the Persian invasions of Greece, he is generally known as 'the Father of History'. In this extract from his work, he describes the city of Babylon.

The city is divided into two portions by the river which runs through the midst of it. This river is the Euphrates, a broad, deep, swift stream, which rises in Armenia, and empties itself into the Red Sea. The city wall is brought down on both sides to the edge of the stream: thence from the corners of the wall, there is carried along each bank of the river a fence of burnt bricks. The houses are mostly three and four storeys high; the streets all run in straight lines, not only those parallel to the river, but also the cross streets which lead down to the waterside. At the river end of these cross streets are low gates in the fence that skirts the stream, which are, like the great gates in the outer wall, of brass, and open on the water.

The outer wall is the main defence of the city. There is, however, a second inner wall, of less thickness than the first, but very little inferior to it in strength. The centre of each division of the town was occupied by a fortress. In the one stood the palace of the kings, surrounded by a wall of great strength and size: in the other was the sacred precinct of Bel (Baal), an enclosure 400 metres square, with gates of solid brass; which was also remaining in my time. In the middle of the precinct there was a tower of solid masonry, 200 metres in length and breadth, upon which was raised a second tower, and on that a third, and so on up to eight. The ascent to the top is on the outside, by a path which winds round all the towers. When one is about half way up, one finds a resting-place and seats, where persons are wont to sit

some time on their way to the summit. On the topmost tower there is a spacious temple, and inside the temple stands a couch of unusual size, richly adorned, with a golden table by its side. There is no statue of any kind set up in the place, nor is the chamber occupied of nights by any one but a single native woman, who, as the Chaldeans, the priests of this god, affirm, is chosen for himself by the deity out of all the women in the land.

Herodotus, *The Persian Wars*: 1:180, 181 (translated by George Rawlinson) The Modern Library, New York, 1942, pp. 97, 98.

1 Describe the layout of the city. What provisions were made for its defence?
2 What part of the passage indicates that Herodotus actually visited the city? What does this do for the extract's credibility?
3 What is the 'tower of solid masonry' that Herodotus describes?
4 What points about the city's religion can you gain from this extract?

Document 2.4

Fig. 2.9 shows Assurbanipal hunting lions.
1 Why do you think the king would risk his life in such a dangerous undertaking? Did the lion have any special significance as far as kings were concerned?
2 What purpose was served by commemorating such an event in stone?
3 What does this relief and the one on page 25 (Fig. 2.2) tell you about Assyrian attitudes towards life, both animal and human?
4 How does the image of Assurbanipal the slayer of lions sit with his other image as the scholar-king, the founder of libraries? What is your opinion of his character?

Fig. 2.9 *This picture of a relief carving in alabaster shows Assurbanipal hunting lions. It was found in Nineveh, and dates around 650 BC. The lions, which had previously been caged, were released into a large enclosed area where they could give battle to the king.*

CHECK THE FACTS

Who am I? Which people who were prominent in Assyrian history could have made comments such as these?

1 I assembled the world's greatest library at Nineveh.

2 I was the first Assyrian king to claim the title of King of Egypt.

3 My conquests against the Aramaeans and the Babylonians started the nucleus of the earlier Assyrian empire.

4 I got into trouble with the priests of Marduk because I paid too much attention to the moon-god Sin.

5 By defeating the Assyrians, I started the New Babylonian Kingdom.

6 Many of my men were killed by a plague while I was besieging Jerusalem.

7 I built a new capital for the empire at Dur-Sharrukin.

8 I freed my people from the domination of the Mitanni and formed the first independent Assyrian kingdom.

9 My conquests, which began soon after my accession in 744, started the resurgence of the Assyrian empire.

10 Because I introduced large cavalry units and mobile battering rams into the army, I had great success in battle.

GENERAL QUESTIONS

1 Study Fig. 2.5 on page 30 and answer the following questions. The first four need only one or two sentences, but the last requires a paragraph.

   a What is Assurbanipal doing? What is the political significance of his action?

   b How did the predominant use of baked mud bricks affect the style and durability of Mesopotamian buildings?

   c What does this picture tell you about the kind of writing used by the Assyrians, and the fashions of their kings?

d What events led to the destruction of Babylon which Assurbanipal is now trying to rectify?

e Make an assessment of the achievements of Assurbanipal. In what ways might his character appear somewhat conflicting to the modern mind?

2 Assyrian kings often proclaimed their military victories on stone stelae. Imagine you are Assurnasipal II, and compose a text to announce your achievements in general. Read the accounts from other stelae that appear in the chapter, and try to model your statement along the same lines.

3 Make brief summaries of the achievements of Tiglath-Pileser III, Sargon II, Esarhaddon and Nebuchadrezzar. Which king do you admire the most, and why?

4 Imagine you are Sennacherib, and write an account of your dealings with King Hezekiah of Judah. Make a special refer-

ence to the biblical claim that the angel of death killed so many of your men while you were besieging Jerusalem.

5 The following questions refer to the achievements of the Assyrians. Answer each one with a paragraph.

a Why was the Assyrian army able to achieve such widespread successes in battle?

b What was the role of the king in the Assyrian form of government? Who did he get to assist him, and how did he safeguard his position?

c What sort of buildings did Assyrian kings like to construct? Describe the construction of just one example.

d What was the attitude of Assyrian kings towards education? What was Assurbanipal's particular contribution in this regard?

e What factors led to the final downfall of the Assyrian empire?

3
THE PREDOMINANCE
OF PERSIA

IRAN

Lying to the east of Mesopotamia is the country we now call Iran. Most of it consists of a plateau 1200 metres high surrounded by rugged mountain ranges. The highest of these, the Zagros Mountains, form a massive natural barrier between Iran and Mesopotamia.

We don't know who were the first inhabitants of the region, but archaeological evidence suggests that humans lived there as early as 100 000 BC. These people were wandering food gatherers. Very few in number, they lived in small groups widely spread over a large area. Their culture fitted into the pattern we now call Paleolithic (Old Stone Age).

THE NEOLITHIC AGE

By about 10 000, some people had begun to adopt a more settled existence. They began to domesticate plants and animals and to settle down to a life in villages. They made and used simple hand tools to their advantage. Most of these developments were in the west, and some were even in the Zagros Mountains themselves. Those villages from that era which have been found up till now all date from around 8000. With the passing of time the population increased, and many more villages have been found which date from

around 6000. Due to the rugged nature of the countryside, most of these settlements developed in isolation, and there was no sign of their having developed a common culture as was the case in Mesopotamia.

THE ELAMITES

The first people to develop an urban civilisation similar to that of the Mesopotamians were the Elamites. They lived in the south of the region, close to the Persian Gulf, and were separated from Mesopotamia by the Zagros Mountains. Their capital was Susa.

The earliest Elamite kings date back to approximately 2700, and after several centuries they were at odds with the Mesopotamians. King Shulgi (2094–2047) of the Third Dynasty of Ur overran them for a time, but the Elamites regained their freedom when the Third Dynasty collapsed soon after. Some 200 years later they suffered again, this time at the hands of King Hammurabi of Babylon (1764). However, their loss of freedom did not last long, for they regained their independence during the time of Hammurabi's son.

Elam came into conflict with the Assyrians during the reign of Tukulti-Ninurta, but its army was no match for their enemies. After the death of its king, however, Assyria went into decline. The Elamites took advantage of the situation and struck into the centre of Babylonia. Their king, Shutruk-Nahhunte, captured Babylon and carried Hammurabi's famous law-giving stele back to Susa in triumph. But this period of military ascendancy did not last long, and the Elamites were barely able to fend off the attacks of Nebuchadrezzar less than a century later. A second Babylonian attack was successful, and the Elamites were once more subject to their conquerors.

There was some recovery for the Elamites in the centuries to follow, but their final downfall came through Assurbanipal, whose armies utterly destroyed Susa. The Assyrians plundered and looted at will, and sowed the land with salt so that it could never be used again.

THE INDO-EUROPEANS

At this stage it is necessary to refer more specifically to the Indo-European peoples who made such an important contribution to the history of the world. Reference has already been made to the Hittites, the Kassites, and the people of Mitanni, who were all Indo-Europeans (see pages 17, 23).

The Indo-Europeans are thought to have originated in eastern Europe, and to have begun migrating south and east about 2500. They apparently split into two main groups, eastern and western, and are identified by their languages. The eastern group, sometimes known as Aryans (from a Sanskrit word meaning 'noble'), moved into Iran and on as far as north-west India. Their main languages were Iranian and Sanskrit. The western group stayed in Europe and their language was the forerunner of Latin, Greek, Celtic and the Germanic tongues.

The Hittites, the Kassites and the Mitannians were all from the eastern group. So too were the Medes and the Persians, who moved into Iran about 1000.

Fig. 3.1 *This relief shows a Mede and a Persian in conversation. What similarities and what differences can you see in their dress and hairstyles?*

THE MEDES

The Medes inhabited what is today the northernmost Iranian province of Azerbaijan. Their eastern border was the Caspian Sea while the Zagros Mountains formed the western boundary. To the north lay Armenia; to the south, Persia.

The traditional founder of the first Median kingdom was Deioces. The Greek historian Herodotus claimed that Deioces reigned from 728 to 675 and that he founded the Median capital of Ecbatana (modern Hamadan). The

Assyrian records show no such name, and it is now assumed that Herodotus probably only recorded a Median legend about their origins. For the moment, Deioces remains a shadowy and unsubstantial figure.

Herodotus claimed that Deioces' son and successor was Phraortes. Although Herodotus used this name, the king may well have been Kashtariti, a name found in Assyrian texts. Phraortes came to power in 675, and soon afterwards subjugated the Persians. He then organised a great alliance with his people and the Scythians to fight against Assyria. However, he was killed in battle, and the kingdom was apparently taken over by the Scythians.

CYAXARES

His son and successor Cyaxares later rallied the Medes and pushed the Scythians out of Media (625). A successful ruler, Cyaxares reorganised the Median army, dividing it into spearmen, bowmen and cavalry. With this improved force he extended south into Persia, and by 614 was strong enough to ally himself with the Babylonians and attack Nineveh.

Nineveh fell in 612, and Assyria was divided between the Medes and the Babylonians. Following this success, Cyaxares pushed north against the kingdom of Mannai and conquered it. Then he moved west into Asia Minor and took over some of the lands that had once belonged to Urartu. This eventually brought him into conflict with Alyattes, the king of Lydia, and a five-year war was fought between the two sides. Finally, in 585 Cyaxares and Alyattes were able to agree that the Halys River should be their common border. Cyaxares died the next year and was succeeded by his son Astyages, who ruled for thirty-four years. Not much is known of his rule, but we know that in 550 he was overthrown by Cyrus of Persia, who up to that time had been his vassal. It was Cyrus who later overthrew Nabonidus and captured Babylon in 539.

THE KINGDOM OF LYDIA

Little is known about the early history of Lydia (in what is now western Turkey), although it may have been part of the Hittite empire. One of the earliest records about Lydia tells of how in 667 its King Gyges asked for help from King Assurbanipal against the invading Cimmerians. Apparently that help was given, for the Cimmerians were defeated.

The people of Lydia were farmers and herders, and excellent horsemen. Their national wealth mostly depended on agriculture, but was enhanced by large deposits of the metal electrum, a natural mixture of gold and silver. Since the kings controlled all the metal deposits, they became very wealthy. One of their number, King Croesus, was so wealthy that even today we use the expression 'as rich as Croesus'. The Lydians were the first people to use coins. Called *staters* and made of electrum, the coins were bean-shaped and bore a punchmark to certify their weight.

Many Greeks lived on Lydia's Aegean coastline, and a strong relationship sprang up between them and the Lydians. They accepted the overlordship of King Croesus (560–547), and some even served in the Lydian army. Greek merchants were vital to Lydia's economy, exporting their agricultural products and importing luxury goods from Phoenicia and Egypt.

During Croesus' reign Lydia's power reached its height, but its capital Sardis fell to the invading Persians under Cyrus in 547, and the kingdom was incorporated into the Persian empire.

THE FIRST PERSIAN KINGDOM

The first Persian kingdom was formed in Fars (or Parsa) in south-western Iran about 700 by King Achaemenes. Called Parsumash by the Assyrians, it bordered on the territory of the Elamites. When in time the Elamites became weak, the successors of Achaemenes (known as the Achaemenid dynasty) expanded at their expense. Despite their improved position, the Persians had to acknowledge control first by the Assyrians, and later the Medes.

CYRUS

The Persians first became a really strong power under Cyrus. Born between 590 and 580, Cyrus was the son of King Cambyses of Persia and Mandane, the daughter of King Astyages of Media. He came to the throne of Persia c. 559, while his country was still under the control of the Medes. An extremely talented ruler, he soon extended his control over several Persian and Iranian groups who had not previously supported his father, and even made overtures to King Nabonidus of Babylon. His growing strength worried his grandfather Astyages, who started to prepare an army against him. This led Cyrus to rebel against Astyages in 550. The Persian won convincingly, as many of the Median troops deserted to him in battle.

Cyrus and Lydia

Cyrus' victory over the Medes marked the start of the Persian empire. The next territory to be added was Lydia, then ruled by Croesus. After first assuring the Babylonians that they had nothing to fear from him, Cyrus led his army across the southern regions of Anatolia and acquired Cilicia peacefully. In addition to gaining new territory, he also cut Lydia off from any possible assistance from Babylonia. He then struck north, capturing Harran from Babylonia before confronting the Lydian army at the Halys River. There, an inconclusive battle was fought. Croesus then withdrew to Sardis, and dismissed most of his troops, thinking that Cyrus would not fight any more that winter. But Cyrus surprised him by continuing the war and finally captured Sardis in 547. There are conflicting reports about the fate of Croesus. Some say that he was killed, others that he either burned himself to death or was taken prisoner by Cyrus and well treated.

Now firmly in control of Lydia, Cyrus demanded that the Greek cities on the Aegean coast submit to Persia as their new overlord. Only Miletus complied peacefully. The rest had to be forced, and this was done over the next seven years by one of Cyrus' generals.

Cyrus in the East

After his victory over Croesus, Cyrus turned his attention to the lands east of Persia. He was worried about attacks from this quarter by nomadic tribes, and was determined to get in first and secure his eastern borders. He therefore led his army as far east as the Indus River in India, and as far north as the Jaxartes River, which runs into the Aral Sea. After conquering the land, he set up many fortified towns to keep the nomads under control.

Cyrus and Babylonia

Babylonia was the next prize for conquest. Cyrus noted that Nabonidus was not a popular king and that he had alienated the priests of Marduk. He therefore gained their support before moving against Babylon in October 539. His victory was easy, as he promised to give honour to Marduk, and not rule as a foreign conqueror. He was true to his word, and he made Babylon one of several capitals of his growing empire. The Babylonians enjoyed peace under Persian rule, but were required to pay taxes as a subject people. The Jews who had been brought to Babylon by Nebuchadrezzar were well treated by Cyrus. He allowed them to return to Jerusalem and build their temple.

As conqueror of Babylonia, Cyrus inherited its empire in the west. Both Syria and Palestine supported the new ruler. Cyrus responded by not interfering with their local customs and religion.

Fig. 3.2 *This is the tomb of Cyrus the Great, built in the gardens of his palace at Pasargadae. The Roman writer Plutarch says that the tomb had this inscription on it: 'Oh man, whoever you are and wherever you come from, for I know that you will come, I am Cyrus, and I won for the Persians their empire. Do not, therefore, begrudge me this little earth which covers my body.' What are the main differences between this tomb and that of Darius?*

The death of Cyrus

Although Egypt was now vulnerable to Persian attack, Cyrus left this task to his son Cambyses, instructing him to organise an invasion as soon as possible. He then returned to the east, where he was killed in 530 while fighting the nomads.

Cyrus was an outstanding leader who was able to inspire strong devotion among his followers. He was also a military genius, leading his army to success against many enemies in widely diverse battle conditions. In victory he was considerate of defeated kings and tolerant of the local beliefs of his new subjects. Indeed, he was not afraid to adopt local practices which he felt might be useful in the administration of his empire. Such was his prestige that he is often referred to in historical records as Cyrus the Great.

He was greatly revered by the Persians, just as the Romans honoured Romulus and Remus and the Israelites, Moses. Many stories were told about his childhood, and how he had been favoured by the gods. He was viewed not just as a great conqueror, but as a man who had all the magnificent qualities of generosity, tolerance, bravery and daring. He was greatly admired by the Greeks, and by Alexander the Great in particular. It is interesting to note that Iran celebrated the 2500th anniversary of his death in 1971.

CAMBYSES

Cambyses was one of the two sons of Cyrus; Bardiya (or Smerdis to the Greeks) was the other. He apparently enjoyed the confidence of his father, as he governed Babylonia for

Cyrus, and was made regent when Cyrus set out on his last campaign in 530. He succeeded to the throne the next year. There may have been some ill-feeling between him and Bardiya, and it is alleged that he had Bardiya secretly killed so that there would be no challenge to his position.

Cambyses invades Egypt

Cambyses is best known for his successful invasion of Egypt, a campaign originally planned by his father. Gathering a large army, he set out in 525, and was guided across the Sinai Desert by the Arabs, who also supplied water. Once in Egypt, he received help from Polycrates of Samos, and military advice from Pharnes, a Greek officer in the Egyptian army. He brought Pharaoh Psamtik III to battle at Pelusium in the Nile Delta and had a convincing victory. From there he took both Heliopolis and Memphis, and the Egyptians were then forced to surrender, the Pharaoh being taken back in captivity to Susa. Cambyses stayed for three years in Egypt, and generally adopted a conciliatory attitude towards his new subjects. However, Herodotus, who considered that Cambyses was mad, accused him of the most dreadful atrocities.

Plans that failed

While in Egypt, Cambyses conceived three new plans of conquest, all of which went horribly wrong. The first was a march to the oracle of Amon in the Libyan Desert, but this was defeated by a massive sandstorm. Then there was a projected invasion of Carthage, but the Phoenicians in his fleet refused to man the ships against their home colony. Finally there was the planned conquest of Ethiopia. This succeeded only in part, and was a wasteful use of resources. Clearly Cambyses was not comparable with his illustrious father.

In 522 news reached Cambyses that a major rebellion had broken out at home. It

was led by a man named Gautama, who was impersonating the dead Bardiya. Cambyses at once made for home, but died on the way. Herodotus said that he committed suicide, but it is more likely he died from an infection caused by an accidental sword wound. The army soon chose as his successor an officer named Darius, a distant relative of the royal family and a member of the royal bodyguard.

DARIUS

Darius was the son of Hystaspes, the *satrap* (provincial governor, see page 51) of Parthia. He returned with all speed to Persia, where he crushed the rebellion and put Gautama to death. Becoming king, he began a long reign of thirty-six years in which he extended the empire to its greatest limits and brought it to the peak of its glory.

Information about these early events mainly comes from the inscriptions Darius had carved in three languages on a huge rock at Bisitun. Some scholars have suggested that he made up the story about Gautama, and that the man he killed was really Bardiya. This is something we will never know, but it is interesting to be aware of the two main versions of his accession to the throne. It took some time for him to be fully accepted as the new king, however, and he had to deal with no less than nine separate uprisings. By 518 he was no longer challenged.

The conquests

Darius disagreed with Cambyses' ideas about expansion in Africa, and instead looked to Asia. He completed the conquest of northwest India started by Cyrus, and encouraged trade between India and Persia both by land and by sea. Around 513 he changed direction and looked towards Europe. He led a great expedition against the Scythians in southern Russia, going well beyond the Danube River. However, he did not try to incorporate the

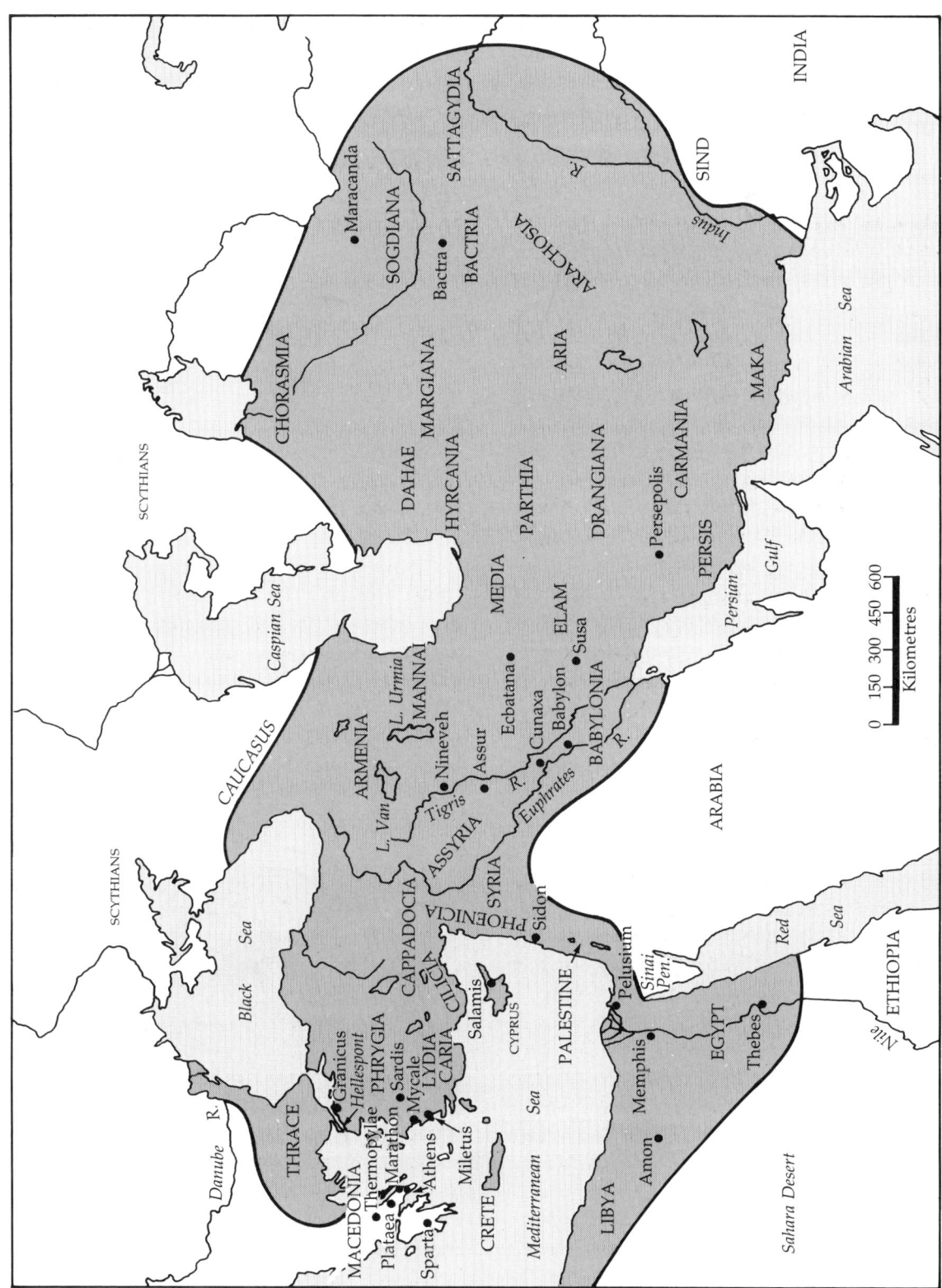

Fig. 3.3 *The Achaemenid Empire in the sixth and fifth centuries* BC.

land into his empire. He was content merely to conquer Thrace, a country renowned for its rich silver mines, and to receive the submission of Macedonia.

Darius and Greece

Soon after, the Aegean islands of Lemnos and Imbros fell into his hands, and this meant that he now controlled the grain trade from the Black Sea region to Greece. With this command of the route to Greece, it was logical that he should consider adding it to his empire.

His excuse came in 499, when the Greek states of Athens and Eretria sent ships to help the Ionian Greeks (those living on the coast of Asia Minor) when the Ionians rebelled against Persian rule. When this rebellion was finally put down, Darius sent his son-in-law Mardonius with an army to punish Athens and Eretria for their interference in Persia's affairs. However, the Persians had to abandon their invasion plans when much of their fleet was sunk in a furious storm off Mt Athos in 492.

Two years later, a second Persian force under the command of Datis sailed directly across the Aegean. It captured Eretria and enslaved its people, then turned its attention to Athens. Datis landed his troops on the plain of Marathon where he was soon confronted by the Athenian army under Miltiades. The Athenians defeated the Persians, and so saved their city for the time being. Darius made preparations for a third expedition against Greece, but he died before they could be completed.

SOME ASPECTS OF PERSIAN SOCIETY

Organisation of government

The Persian empire was so huge and widespread that careful organisation was needed to govern it effectively. In this regard Darius completed the work started by both Cyrus and Cambyses.

At the head of the empire was the 'Great King' himself. The security of his position depended on his ability to inspire and dominate the nobles who might have latent ambitions to replace him one day. In this regard, Darius was supreme. He stressed the appropriate pomp associated with his office, and its hereditary nature. He also maintained a council of leading nobles to advise him, but was not obliged to follow their advice.

Fig. 3.4   *This relief from the palace complex at Persepolis shows Darius on his throne receiving a foreign dignitary who is holding his hand in front of his mouth as a sign of respect. Darius holds a sceptre in one hand and a lotus blossom in the other. Directly behind the king is Xerxes the crown prince. Of the two, who had the greater success for Persia?*

At the start of his reign Darius made Susa his capital, and built an impressively huge palace. In 512, however, he moved the capital to a new site closer to the Persian heartland. Called Istakhar by the Persians, it is now known by its Greek name, Persepolis, which means 'City of the Persians'. Here another great palace was built and lavishly decorated with tribute from all over the empire.

The empire was divided into approximately thirty provinces, each governed by a satrap. Satraps were inevitably Persians of royal or noble blood. Their responsibility was to administer the province smoothly and to collect taxes for remittance to the capital. While they were generally given a free hand, satraps were subject to periodic inspections by officials sent by the king to check on their efficiency. Satraps were sometimes removed from office for not performing their duties satisfactorily.

Realising the importance of communication between the different parts of the empire, Darius developed the so-called Royal Post Road which ran 2500 kilometres from Sardis to Susa. A series of staging posts was built along the road, each equipped with a plentiful supply of horses for the king's special messengers who could cover the entire route in seven or eight days. The road was also used by merchant caravans, and so had commercial significance as well.

As another means of unifying his diverse empire, Darius introduced a common system of weights and measures. He also began minting gold coins, which were called *darics* in his honour.

The army

The Persian army had several components. Firstly there was the elite corps known as the 'Ten Thousand Immortals', of whom a thousand formed the king's personal bodyguard. Then there was the main body of Persian and Median troops, tough and disciplined soldiers who were the backbone of the army and its main strength. In time, soldiers from among

Fig. 3.5 *This picture shows the remains of the great palace of Darius I at Persepolis. Beyond it you can see the columns of the great audience hall (apadana) of Darius. Why is the palace now in ruins?*

the subject peoples were also recruited into the army to serve under Persian officers. They were generally not as enthusiastic or as valiant as the Persian soldiers, and their loyalty was sometimes suspect. Lastly there were the mercenaries, troops who fought purely for money and without any considerations of patriotism. Many of these were Greeks. The various components of the army were scattered all over the empire, and it was often difficult to get them all together quickly in times of national emergency.

Religion

The chief god of the Persians was Ahura Mazda, the sky-god. Others of importance were Mithras, a sun-god, and Anahita, a fertility goddess. These and other gods were served by a class of priests called *Magi*. The Magi were powerful people in society because the ceremonial rites they alone could perform were considered essential to the prosperity of the state.

Sometime in the sixth century BC a religious reformer named Zoroaster (sometimes also known as Zarathustra) appeared. Because of his teachings, Persian religion changed significantly. Zoroaster taught that Ahura Mazda was all-powerful and that the other gods were as nothing compared with him. Having thus promoted Ahura Mazda to being the one true god, Zoroaster proclaimed that Ahura Mazda was the source of all justice and truth and that he was willing to help mortals in their constant battle against the forces of evil. This teaching was extremely

Fig. 3.6 *Tomb of Darius the Great in the famous Valley of the Tombs where many of the Achaemenid kings were buried. Note the cruciform shape of the façade. Why do you think Darius had such a magnificent tomb?*

important because it took the Persians away from the concept of gods who were powerful, but capricious in their attitudes to humans.

At first the Magi were totally opposed to Zoroaster's teachings, but he was protected from their anger by the kings. In time the Magi came to accept the new beliefs, and eventually compiled a book about them called the *Zend-Avesta*. This included not only Zoroaster's doctrines but other ancient religious traditions handed down by word of mouth over many centuries. The book is very complex, and it is impossible to distinguish between Zoroaster's ideas and the other additions. It predicts that at the end of time, Zoroaster will return to the earth as a Saviour, and prepare men and women for the Last Judgment.

The religion of Zoroaster appealed to many people because it taught there *was* a life after death. Also, this life could be a joyous one provided a person accepted Ahura Mazda's help against the forces of evil led by Ahriman. Zoroastrianism influenced the ideas of later religions such as Judaism and Christianity.

XERXES

The son and successor of Darius, Xerxes is best remembered in history as the king who was defeated by the Greeks at the battle of Salamis. He was born about 519, and his mother was Atossa, the daughter of Cyrus. Although he was not Darius' eldest son, he was obviously made the heir apparent quite early in his life. At the early age of about twenty-three he was appointed satrap of Babylonia, and held that position for twelve years, up to the time he succeeded his father in 486.

Early troubles

Xerxes was faced with a rebellion in Egypt as soon as he ascended the throne. He marched there in 485, and crushed the rebels in the Delta early the next year. Whereas Darius had tended to respect the special nature of local conditions and to govern in a fairly lenient manner, Xerxes took the exact opposite course. He treated the Egyptians with great severity, and built up a hatred of the Persians which was always likely to break out in further rebellion and violence.

About 482, Xerxes had to face another uprising, this time in Babylonia. Once more his response was swift and harsh: he tore down Babylon's walls, plundered the temples and destroyed the statue of Marduk. This latter action had important repercussions, as it insulted the Babylonians and filled them with resentment. Xerxes justified his action by claiming that only Ahura Mazda should be worshipped, but this made little impression with the Babylonians, who preferred their own god.

Xerxes invades Greece

Having finally established peace within the empire, Xerxes was now persuaded by his cousin and brother-in-law Mardonius to avenge the Persian defeat at Marathon. He started preparations for a major campaign in 484, and was busily engaged in assembling ships, troops and supplies for the next three years. His plan was for a military invasion of Greece, with ample support from a large fleet of ships.

When he reached the Hellespont (modern Dardanelles) in 480, he got his engineers to build two bridges of boats for the troops to cross the narrow strait. Before they could be used, however, a storm sprang up and wrecked them. Furious with rage, Xerxes had the waters given 300 lashes with a whip and the engineers beheaded. The bridges were then rebuilt, and the troops crossed over. We don't know the exact size of his army. Herodotus said it numbered over 5 000 000, but this is an exaggeration. A more likely figure is around 350 000.

Xerxes met his first real opposition at Thermopylae when a combined Greek force under the Spartan Leonidas made a stand in August. It was soon overwhelmed by the Persians, and Xerxes then marched on to Athens, which he reached in September. Although its people had all fled to safety, the Athenian fleet under the command of Themistocles was more than willing to try itself out against the invading fleet. Themistocles tricked Xerxes into fighting a sea battle in the confined waters around the island of Salamis. Here the superior Greek tactics made up for inferiority of numbers, and Themistocles won a crushing victory over the Persians.

Xerxes retreats

With no fleet to keep his troops supplied, Xerxes had no choice but to retreat. However, he left Mardonius in Thessaly with a large army with orders to renew the campaign the next year. Mardonius moved south again in 479, but was killed at the battle of Plataea in August. Thereafter all the Persians returned home, and Xerxes' plans to become master of Greece ended forever.

Xerxes spent the rest of his life at Susa and Persepolis. His main interest was at Persepolis, where he finished his father's palace, and made extensive additions of his own to the palace complex (see page 60). In 465 he and his eldest son were both assassinated in a palace revolt by Artabanus, commander of the guard. He was succeeded by another son, Artaxerxes. With the death of Xerxes, the Achaemenid dynasty gradually went into decline.

ARTAXERXES I

Although Artaxerxes ruled for forty years (465–425), he is generally considered to be a weak and ineffective ruler. He tried to follow a policy of peace for the empire, but was faced with several rebellions. The first was a

challenge from one of his brothers, who was satrap of Bactria. Much more serious was a revolt in Egypt (459), in which the rebels received help from the Athenians. Persian authority over Egypt was only restored after a six-year struggle by the Persian forces under Megabyzus, satrap of Syria.

The state of hostility between Athens and Persia continued for many years, but in 448 an agreement was reached between the former enemies. Under the terms of the Peace of Callias, Athens agreed to stay out of Asia Minor, while Persia agreed not to interfere in the Aegean region. Athens broke this agreement in 439 when it attacked Samos, and in the ensuing skirmishes Persia had something of an advantage.

Artaxerxes died in 425, but his successor Xerxes II ruled for less than two months before he was killed in a drunken brawl. Darius II was the next king, ruling from 424 to 404.

DARIUS II

Darius was keenly interested in regaining Persian control of Ionia (the west coast of Asia Minor) from the Athenians. He did this by financially supporting Athens' enemy Sparta in the famous Peloponnesian War. His efforts, however, were frustrated by the personal ambitions of his two most important satraps in the region, Tissaphernes and Pharnabazus. They seemed more interested in pursuing their own careers than in coordinating their resources against a common enemy. Disappointed and resentful of his weakness, Darius died of natural causes in 404.

ARTAXERXES II

The reign of Artaxerxes spanned sixty-five years. Full of incident, it started with a rebellion in Egypt and ended with a major revolt of some of his satraps.

Fig. 3.7 *An inscription from the palace of Darius. Can you identify the style of writing?*

Egypt

The long-smouldering Egyptian discontent with Persian rule broke out into yet another rebellion in 405, but there was little that Artaxerxes could do to retain control. From this point on, Egypt remained free from Persian domination for over sixty years. True, Artaxerxes mounted two campaigns to regain his lost territory in 385 and 374, but both operations were complete failures. The loss of Egypt was one of the great disappointments of Artaxerxes' reign.

The rebellion of Cyrus

Soon after the loss of Egypt, Artaxerxes faced further trouble when his younger brother Cyrus led a rebellion against him. Commander of the Persian forces in Asia Minor, Cyrus added to his army some 10 000 Greek mercenaries, and thus had a mighty force to be reckoned with. The armies of Cyrus and Artaxerxes finally clashed at Cunaxa in 401, and although the Greeks were undefeated on the field of battle, Cyrus himself was killed. This meant that the rebellion was over, but there was still the problem of the Greeks. Too strong to be overwhelmed but not strong enough to win the empire for themselves, they then had to make their own way home. Under the leadership of Xenophon, they struggled through difficult terrain and fought against hostile tribes till they finally reached a Greek settlement on the Black Sea. Xenophon wrote an intriguing account of their adventures in his *Anabasis*, a book still widely read today.

The success of the Greek soldiers at Cunaxa and their later ability to survive under such perilous conditions had important political results. It gave the Spartans the belief that their fighting men were vastly superior to the Persians, and that the Persian empire was weak and ripe for plunder. As a result, Sparta broke off diplomatic relations with Persia in 400, and its army plundered Anatolia for the next five years. As a means of self-defence, Artaxerxes had to subsidise Sparta's old enemy Athens, and only achieved some relief when the Spartan navy was defeated at Cnidus in 394.

The King's Peace

Artaxerxes continued to support Athens with funds for several more years until he realised that Athens would soon be strong enough to try itself out against Persia as Sparta had done. He therefore withdrew his subsidies, and got the warring Greek states to make peace. Under the terms of the so-called King's Peace of 386, the Greeks and the Persians agreed not to interfere in the other's spheres of influence. Thereafter, the Greek states each sought the aid of Artaxerxes in their unending quarrels, and this gave the king considerable influence in Greek politics.

The revolt of the satraps

Some of Artaxerxes' western satraps grew increasingly frustrated with the continued weakness of the king, and his inability to maintain Persia's prestige. Therefore, in about 366 they staged a rebellion against his authority. One of them, Aroandas of Armenia, even went so far as to mint his own coinage. Unfortunately for the rebel satraps, they were unable to co-ordinate their efforts, and moreover they were divided by conflicting personal ambitions. As a result, Artaxerxes was able to move against them one by one and defeat them before they could organise a united front against him.

Religion

Under Artaxerxes, an important change was made in the nation's religion. Whereas previous kings had been loyal only to Ahura Mazda, Artaxerxes raised statues to Anahita and Mithra in some of the largest cities of the empire. These were deities of the old Iranian religion, and had been neglected for a long time. Anahita was the goddess of waters, fertility and procreation, and in Greece was identified with Athena and Aphrodite. Mithra was known as the creator of life, the giver of fertile rain and the god of sunlight. He was Ahura Mazda's chief helper in the fight against Ahriman.

ARTAXERXES III

Artaxerxes III came to the throne in 359. A cruel and ruthless man, he at once put to death any relative thought to be a possible challenger to his position. He tried to reconquer Egypt in 351, and his failure eventually sparked off a series of rebellions in Sidon, Phoenicia, Palestine and Cilicia in 345. He crushed these uprisings the same year, then moved on against Egypt once more. In 343 he defeated the Egyptians at Pelusium in the Delta, and made Egypt a satrapy once more. The Egyptians were sorely punished for their rebellion of 404.

In 340 King Philip of Macedonia attacked the cities of Perinthus and Byzantium, preparatory to an invasion of Asia Minor. Artaxerxes sent support to these cities. Soon after, both Artaxerxes (338) and Philip (336) were dead, the victims of assassination.

Arses succeeded Artaxerxes, but his reign was less than two years old before he too was assassinated.

DARIUS III

The last of the Achaemenian dynasty, Darius III came to the throne in 336. It was his misfortune to face the all-conquering Alexander the Great, and his unhappy reign lasted for only six years.

It was Philip who planned the original invasion of Asia Minor, and his advance force crossed into the territory early in 336. Soon after, he was assassinated, and his young son Alexander took his place. After spending some time in consolidating his position, Alexander finally crossed the Hellespont in the spring of 334. Soon after, he defeated a Persian army at the River Granicus, not far from the Hellespont. From there he pressed on into Asia Minor and the next year faced Darius at Issus. A cowardly man, Darius fled before the Greek onslaught, leaving his mother, wife and children to be captured by the victorious Alexander.

Over the next two years, Darius sent two letters to Alexander, asking for the return of his family and offering many concessions in return for an alliance. Alexander rejected these offers out of hand, and continued his relentless march deeper into Persian territory. Finally, at Gaugamela in Mesopotamia just east of the Tigris River, he met Darius in battle once more in October 331. Darius again fled in terror, and continued his flight ever eastwards. Eventually he reached Bactria where the satrap, Bessus, deposed and killed him. With his death, the Achaemenian dynasty ended, and the affairs of Persia fell firmly into the hands of foreigners.

SUMMARY OF MAIN EVENTS

Early history

c. 8000	First villages formed in Persia
c. 2700	First Elamite kingdom established
c. 2500	Indo-Europeans begin migrations south and east
c. 700	First Persian kingdom founded by Achaemenes
614	Cyaxares the Mede attacks Nineveh

Cyrus the Great

550	Cyrus of Persia overthrows the Medes
547	Cyrus overthrows Croesus and conquers Lydia
539	Cyrus captures Babylon
530	Cyrus killed in battle; succeeded by Cambyses

Cambyses

525	Cambyses enters Memphis
522	Death of Cambyses

Darius

512	Darius moves his capital to Persepolis
492	Mardonius' fleet sunk off Mt Athos
490	Athenians defeat Persians at Marathon

Xerxes

484	Xerxes crushes rebellion in Egypt
482	Xerxes crushes rebellion in Babylonia
480	Xerxes' invasion of Greece; disaster at Salamis

Artaxerxes II

404	Egypt successfully rebels against Persia
401	Cyrus killed at Cunaxa; Xenophon leads Greek mercenaries home
386	The King's Peace
c. 366	Revolt of the satraps

Darius III

336	Darius comes to the throne
334	Alexander invades Asia Minor; victory at Granicus River
333	Darius defeated at Issus
331	Darius defeated at Gaugamela; killed by Bessus; end of the Achaemenian dynasty

FEATURE

Herodotus on Croesus

In his famous history of the Persian Wars, Herodotus tells the following stories about Croesus, King of Lydia. The first, involving Solon, certainly never happened, but was probably included on ethical rather than on historical grounds. The second is debatable, but follows on logically from the first.

According to Herodotus, the great Athenian lawgiver Solon visited Croesus at his magnificent palace in Sardis. Immensely proud of his enormous wealth, Croesus took Solon for a long tour of the palace and its many fabulous treasures. At the end of the tour, Croesus asked Solon whom he thought was the happiest man on earth. Naturally he thought that Solon would name *him* because of his great possessions. He was therefore both surprised and disappointed when Solon gave the name of Tellus of Athens, a man who had had a loving family, and had died with honour on the field of battle.

Pressed for a second choice, Solon quoted two brothers named Cleobis and Bito who had been famous athletes, had honoured their mother and who had died at the height of their careers. By now quite angry, Croesus asked why *he* hadn't been named the happiest of men, given his great wealth. Solon replied that although Croesus was indeed extremely rich, there was always the chance that he might lose his wealth through a change of fortune. He continued by saying that a man could only be considered truly happy if his good fortune continued right up to the time of his death. Croesus was unhappy with this answer, and dismissed Solon as a fool.

Herodotus continued that after the fall of Sardis, Croesus was condemned by Cyrus to be burnt alive on a huge funeral pyre. As the flames began to take hold of the wood, Croesus remembered the words of Solon, and cried out in anguish: 'Solon! Solon! Solon!' This aroused Cyrus' curiosity, and he had Croesus taken down from the pyre. When he heard the full story of Solon's wisdom from Croesus, Cyrus cancelled the execution order. He realised that he too was vulnerable and that pity was better than vengeance. Croesus was spared, and he gave valuable advice to Cyrus in the years to come.

FEATURE

Persepolis

The great palace at Persepolis was started by Darius in 512 and mostly completed by Xerxes around 460. Built in a remote and

mountainous region, it was the centre-piece of a somewhat inconvenient capital, and was used mainly in the spring. The

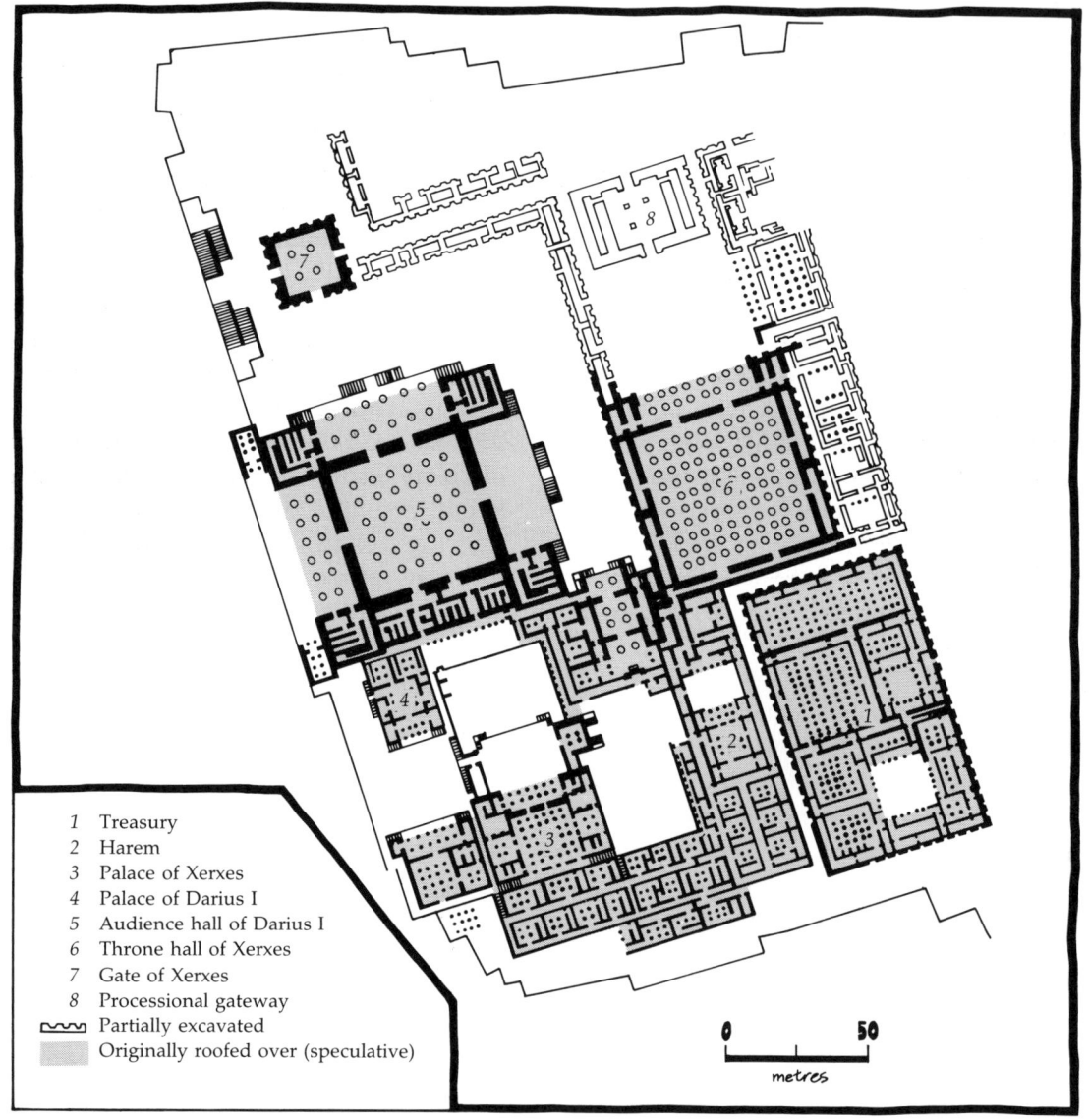

1 Treasury
2 Harem
3 Palace of Xerxes
4 Palace of Darius I
5 Audience hall of Darius I
6 Throne hall of Xerxes
7 Gate of Xerxes
8 Processional gateway
〰 Partially excavated
▨ Originally roofed over (speculative)

0   50
metres

Fig. 3.8 *Plan of the palace at Persepolis.*

effective administration of the empire was carried on from Susa, Babylon or Ecbatana. The palace was destroyed by Alexander the Great in 330 as an act of revenge for the Persian invasions of Greece 150 years earlier.

Unlike the Assyrian palaces which were centred around courtyards, the buildings at Persepolis were more loosely grouped, and separated by streets and irregular open spaces. Dominating the complex was the huge audience hall (*apadana*) of Darius. Raised three metres above ground level, it was some sixty metres square. Its roof was supported by thirty-six columns over twelve metres high. Adjoining the apadana was Darius' palace, and some distance to the south-east, a treasury. These buildings were started by Darius, but not completed.

It was Xerxes who finished off his father's projects and built several of his own. These included his own palace and a mysterious building near it. Although it has been called 'the harem' by archaeologists, it may have been Xerxes' treasury. He also made a start on the throne room, or 'the Hall of One Hundred Columns', but never finished it, the task being completed by his son Artaxerxes.

Since there was plenty of stone available near the site, it was used widely used for platforms, stairs, gateways and columns. Brick was mainly used for the walls, and timber for the ceilings.

The gigantic scale of the palace complex was meant to reflect the grandeur and magnificence of the Persian empire. The kings held court in the apadana amid brilliant and colourful ceremonies, and there received gifts and tribute from the empire's subject peoples. Many of the wall carvings with which the palace is richly decorated show envoys bringing tribute to the king. It is likely that at least some of these carvings were coloured.

Despite the destruction caused by Alexander, sufficient remains still stand to show something of the wonderful and imaginative architecture created by the ancient Persians.

Document 3.1

The Greek historian Herodotus believed that Cambyses was completely mad. This is one of the many stories he tells about him. Cambyses has just asked his adviser Prexaspes what the Persians think of their king, and is highly offended when Prexaspes tells him they think he drinks too much.

Recollecting these answers, Cambyses spoke fiercely to Prexaspes, saying, 'Judge now, Prexaspes, whether the Persians tell the truth, or whether it is not they who are mad for speaking as they do. Look there now at your son standing in the vestibule — if I shoot and hit him right in the middle of the heart, it will be plain the Persians have no grounds for what they say: if I miss him, then I allow that the Persians are right, and that I am out of my mind.' So speaking he drew the bow to the full, and struck the boy, who straightway fell down dead. Then Cambyses ordered the body to be opened, and the wound examined; and when the arrow was found to have entered the heart, the king was quite overjoyed and said to the father with a laugh, 'Now you see plainly, Prexaspes, that it is not I who am mad, but the Persians who have lost their senses. I pray you tell me, did you ever see a man send an arrow with a better aim?' Prexaspes, seeing that the king was not in his right mind, and fearing for himself, replied, 'My lord, I do not think that god himself could shoot so dextrously.' Such was the outrage which Cambyses committed at this time: at another, he took twelve of the noblest Persians, and, without bringing any charge worthy of death against them, buried them all up to the neck.

Herodotus, *The Persian Wars* III: 35, pp. 227, 228.

1　On the evidence Herodotus gives, what is your opinion of Cambyses' state of mind?

2　Why do you think Herodotus was so hostile to Cambyses? What are his sources likely to have been for such a story?

3　Do you find Herodotus' story credible? Could a man command an army successfully and still be mad?

4　What sort of emotions would a king like Cambyses inspire in his subjects, both of high and low birth?

Document 3.2

The edict of Cyrus the Great, allowing the Jewish exiles living in Babylon to return to their homeland in Judea.

So speaks Cyrus, King of Persia: Jehovah, God of Heaven, gave me all the kingdoms of this earth, and has Himself commanded me to build for Him a mansion in Jerusalem, which is in Judea.

Who amongst your people wish to perform this task? May God go with them, and may they go to Jerusalem, which is in Judea, and may they there rebuild Jehovah's mansion.

And may those others who cannot go, wherever they might live, assist with money, gold and beasts, those who wish to be present with the Elohim who reside in Jerusalem.

J. A. de Gobineau, *The World of the Persians*, Minerva, Geneva, 1971, p. 48.

1　How do you know that Cyrus considers himself a great king? Give two examples from the document.

2　Under what circumstances were the Jews taken to Babylon in the first place?

3　Why do you think Cyrus quotes Jehovah as God of Heaven, and not a Persian deity?

4　What is 'the mansion in Jerusalem' and 'the Elohim' referred to in the passage?

Document 3.3

Early in his reign, Darius had a record in three languages carved on a huge rock at Bisitun (or Behistun) near Kermanshah. This told of how he overcame the evil imposter Gautama to become the rightful king. Here are some extracts from the carvings.

I am Darius the Great King, King of Kings, King in Persia, King of countries, son of Vishtapsa, grandson of Arshama, an Achmaenid ...

Saith Darius the King: For this reason we are called Achaemenids. From long ago we have been noble. From long ago our family was noble. Saith Darius the King: Eight of our family were previously kings. I am the ninth. Nine kings we have been in succession.

Saith Darius the King: By the will of Ahuramazda I am king. Ahuramazda gave me kingship ...

A certain Cambyses by name, son of Cyrus, (King of Persis, King of Lands), of our family, was king here. That Cambyses had a brother called Bardiya, of the same mother and the same father. Then Cambyses slew that Bardiya. After Cambyses slew Bardiya, it was not known to the people that Bardiya had been slain. Then Cambyses went to Egypt (with an army) ...

Then there was a man a Magian (a Mede), Gautama by name. He rose up (and) lied to the people thus: 'I am Bardiya, son of Cyrus, brother of Cambyses.' Afterwards all the people revolted from Cambyses and went over to him ... He seized the kingship. Then Cambyses died by his own hand.

Saith Darius the King: The kingship which that Gautama took away from Cambyses, this kingship had belonged to our family from long ago. Then Gautama the Magian took [the kingship] from Cambyses. He made his own Persis, Media and other lands. He became king.

Saith Darius the King: There was no man ... who might take the kingship from that Gautama the Magian. People feared him greatly, that he might slay in great numbers the people who had known Bardiya previously ... No one dared say anything about Gautama the Magian until I came. Then I prayed to Ahuramazda; Ahuramazda bore me aid ... I slew that Gautama the Magian ... I took the kingship from him. By the will of Ahuramazda I became king. Ahuramazda gave me the kingship.

Richard N. Frye, *The History of Ancient Iran*, Verlag C. H. Beck, Munich, 1984, pp. 363, 364.

1 Why do you think Darius is so keen to stress that he is a member of the Achaemenid family?

2 What is the crime that Gautama the Magian has committed? How does Darius justify his action in killing Gautama?

3 Is it possible that there was no such person as Gautama? If so, whom might Darius really have slain?

4 To whom does Darius give credit for his becoming king? What is the importance of having such an ally?

Document 3.4

In addition to starting the great palace complex at Persepolis, Darius also built a splendid palace at Susa. He had many texts carved on marble and clay tablets and placed in different parts of the building. One such text was discovered in 1898, and has been called the Susa Magna Carta. Here is what was written on it.

The Great God is Ahuramazda, who has created this earth, who has created yonder sky, who has created mankind, who has created welfare for man, who has made Darius king, the one king of many, one lord of many.

I am Darius, Great King, King of kings, king of peoples, king of this earth, son of Hystaspes, an Achaemenian.

And Darius the King says: Ahuramazda, the greatest of the gods, he created me; he made me king; he granted to me the kingdom that is great, with good horses, with good men.

By the grace of Ahuramazda, my father Hystaspes and Arsames my grandfather, they were both living when Ahuramazda made me king on this earth. It was the wish of Ahuramazda to make me alone king and he made me king on this earth. I worshipped him: Ahuramazda brought me aid. What I commanded to be done, that he made successful. What I did, I did it all by the grace of Ahuramazda.

This palace which I erected at Susa, its materials have been brought from afar. The earth was dug deep until bedrock was reached. When the earth had been thoroughly excavated, the rubble was packed in, one part forty cubits, one part twenty cubits deep. On that rubble the palace was erected. That the earth was thoroughly excavated, and that the rubble was packed in, and that unbaked bricks have been moulded—all this was the work of Babylonians.

And timber, cedar, this was brought from a mountain named Lebanon; the Assyrian folk, they brought it to Babylon and from Babylon Carians and Ionians brought it to Susa. *Yaka*-wood [teak?] was brought from Gandara and Carmania. Gold was brought from Sardis and from Bactria and wrought here. And precious stones—lapis lazuli and carnelian [?] which were worked here, these were brought from Sogdiana, and turquoise [?] was brought from Choresmia. And silver and ebony were brought from Egypt. And the material with which the wall of the palace was painted, that was brought from Ionia. And the ivory which was wrought here, that was brought from Ethiopia and from Sind and from Arachosia. And the stone pillars which were fashioned here, these were brought from a palace called Abiradus in Elam.

The masons who wrought the stones, they were Ionians and Sardians. The goldsmiths who wrought the gold, they were Medes and Egyptians. And the men who worked on the wood, they were Sardians and Egyptians. The men who worked on the baked bricks, they were Babylonians. And the men who adorned the wall, they were Medes and Egyptians.

And Darius the King says: At Susa splendid things were ordered and splendid things were achieved. Me may Ahuramazda protect, and Hystaspes who is my father and my people.

W. Culican, *The Medes and the Persians*, Thames & Hudson, London, 1965, pp. 103–5.

1   In what ways is this document similar to the preceding one?
2   If Darius is king by the grace of Ahuramazda, what responsibilities do the common people have towards Darius?
3   From what places were the raw materials and the craftsmen gathered to work on the palace? What does this extract tell about regional products and skills?
4   Why was so much effort and expense incurred in building this palace? Why did it have to be so splendid?

CHECK THE FACTS

Are the following statements true or false?

1   The first people to form a kingdom in Persia were the Elamites.
2   The Medes and the Persians were Aryans.
3   Herodotus' account of Croesus' meeting with Solon of Athens is historically accurate.
4   The eastern conquests of Cyrus extended as far as India.
5   Both Herodotus and the rock carvings at Bisitun state that Cambyses committed suicide.
6   Datis won a great victory over the Athenians at Marathon in 490.
7   The chief gods of the Persian religion were Mithras and Anahita.
8   A satrap was a Persian provincial governor.
9   Xerxes was forced to retreat from Greece following his defeat at the disastrous sea battle at Salamis.
10 King Darius was responsible for building most of the palace complex at Persepolis.

GENERAL QUESTIONS

1   Fig. 3.9 shows part of the palace complex at Persepolis as viewed from the east. After checking with the plan of the complex (Fig. 3.8 on page 60), answer the following questions. The first four need only one or two sentences, but the last needs a paragraph.

    a   What is the building in the foreground? Who built it? How are you able to identify it?
    b   What is the large building behind the first one? How many columns did it have originally? Who built it?

Fig. 3.9 *Ruins at Persepolis.*

c What building was originally on the site of the mound to the left rear of the picture? Why do you think it was raised above the levels of the other buildings?

d What buildings are *not* visible from this viewpoint? Describe where they should be.

e Why did the Persian kings build palaces on such a grand scale? Who destroyed the palaces and why?

2 In your opinion, was Cambyses mad? Read the account of his life in the text, and see what was written about him by Herodotus and on the Bisitun rock carvings. Defend your conclusion with as many arguments as you can.

3 Imagine you are a soldier in the army of Xerxes. You have served with him in Egypt, Babylonia and Greece. Give an account of some of the actions in which you were involved, and make an assessment of Xerxes' character.

4 If you were Artaxerxes, how would you describe the achievements of your long reign? Discuss your successes, and show some of the problems with which you had to contend.

5 The following questions refer to the career of Darius. Answer each one with a paragraph.

a Under what circumstances did Darius come to the throne? What steps did he take to justify his accession?

b What conquests of foreign lands did Darius achieve? Why did he attack Greece, and with what success?

c How did Darius organise the government of his vast empire? What steps did he take to ensure a fast communication service?

d How was the Persian army organised in the time of Darius? What were its strengths and weaknesses?

e What was Darius' attitude towards religion? What did the Persians think about Ahura Mazda?

6 Why was Cyrus called 'the Great'? Write an essay to examine his achievements in detail and say whether you agree with the awarding of this title.

4

KINGDOMS OF THE NEAR EAST

THE PHOENICIANS

In writing about the kingdom of Lydia, reference was made to Phoenicia (see page 45). This land, situated on the eastern seaboard of the Mediterranean Sea, corresponds with modern Lebanon and parts of Syria and Israel. It was originally known as Canaan, and its people as Canaanites. Later, the Greeks called them Phoenicians because of the Greek word *phoinix* meaning 'purple red'. This referred to the cloth dyes which they were so expert at producing from the murex shellfish. In this discussion the Greek term will be used to refer to these people.

The Phoenicians were a Semitic people, related to the Babylonians, the Assyrians and the Hebrews. They probably arrived in the area about 3000, possibly from the Persian Gulf region. They settled mainly on the coast and organised themselves into several petty states, each centred on a port city. The first of these to achieve importance was Byblos, which prospered because of its trade with Egypt. Later, Tyre and Sidon passed it in importance. Under King Hiram, Tyre became a strongly fortified city, well and truly able to defend itself against the strongest assaults.

Phoenician trade

Because they lived near the sea they became a maritime people, and for about 300 years (from about 1100 onwards) completely dominated sea trade in the Mediterranean. Their geographical position was of great importance in this regard. They bought jewels, silver, ivory and spices from the caravan trade coming overland from the East, and sold them to the lands bordering the Mediterranean. As well, they traded extensively in the goods they

Fig. 4.1 *Phoenician glass vessels from Camirus (left) and from Tharros (right) inlaid with threads of different colours.*

produced themselves, such as fine cloth, furniture, glass and jewellery.

In later years they suffered from increasing competition from Greek merchants, and their influence further declined when much of their trade profit had to go to the Assyrians as tribute. Despite their fall from a leading role, they were always noted for their skills at sea. They supplied ships for the Persian navy, and played a prominent part in Mediterranean trade under both the Greeks and the Romans.

The Phoenicians as sailors

The Phoenicians made their place in history as the most daring of the ancient Mediterranean sailors. They were expert boat builders, and their sturdy craft were powered both by sails and by tiers of slave-rowers. At first they sailed north along the coast of Asia Minor and across to the islands of the Aegean Sea. Mostly they engaged in legitimate trade, but some apparently resorted to piracy when they could get away with it. The Greek poet Homer described them in these words: 'Thither came Phoenicians, men famed for their ships, greedy knaves, bringing countless trinkets in their black ship.'

Later, around 800, they pushed ever further west, establishing colonies at Utica and Carthage on the north African coast, and on the island of Sardinia. Although their most western permanent colony was at Gades (now modern Cadiz) in Spain, they are generally believed to have sailed all the way up to Cornwall in search of tin.

The alphabet

In addition to their contribution to the economic and cultural life of Mediterranean lands through trade, the Phoenicians are also credited with inventing the alphabet. Although at first they used the Mesopotamian cuneiform method of writing, they later devised a script of their own, with an alphabet comprising twenty-two letters. Although it had no symbols for vowels, the alphabet was extremely useful in writing. The Greeks got *their* alphabet from the Phoenicians. The earliest examples of inscriptions in the Phoenician alphabet were found at Byblos. Incidentally, the word 'Bible' comes from Byblos, which was a famous exporter of papyrus, the Egyptian writing material.

In the early period of their history the Phoenicians were independent, each city state ruled by a king and controlling its own affairs. From about 850, however, the Phoenician cities came under the sway of the Assyrians. At first they were merely forced to pay a hefty tribute, but less than a century later formally became part of the Assyrian Empire as a province.

THE PHILISTINES

No history of the eastern Mediterranean region would be complete without reference to the Philistines. Indeed, one of the best-known stories of the Bible tells of the fight between the shepherd boy David and the Philistine giant Goliath.

The Philistines (at first called Peleset) originated somewhere in the Aegean or Asia Minor region and were among the so-called Sea Peoples who attacked Egypt during the reign of Ramses III (1198–1167) . Beaten off by the Egyptians, they settled on the coastal plain of southern Canaan where they formed five city states: Gaza, Ashkelon, Ashdod, Gath and Ekron. Although each was under its own king, they formed a strong confederacy in time of war and were formidable opponents because of their temporary monopoly of iron weapons. Their control of the land gave it the name of Philistia: land of the Philistines. The Greeks later changed the name to Palestine and that is the term we will use here.

In time, the Philistines came into conflict with a Semitic people called the Hebrews

Fig. 4.2 *This picture, from the wall of an Egyptian temple at Medinet Habu near Thebes (Luxor), shows some of the Sea Peoples defeated by Ramses III. The captives are tightly bound and tied together by a rope around the neck. They are, in order, a Libyan, a Syrian, a Hittite, a Philistine and another Syrian. Where did the Philistines end up after their defeat by the Egyptians?*

over the occupation of Palestine. This conflict is covered on page 71. Without going into any detail now, all that needs to be said here is that although the Philistines were at first successful, they were eventually defeated by the Hebrews. For a time they retained their· own identity, but after conquest by the Assyrians, they gradually became completely merged with the local peoples.

THE HEBREWS

In their day, the Hebrews did not exercise much influence on the peoples of the surrounding regions. They were relatively few in number, and exercised little political power. Yet they are generally better known to the modern Western world than any other ancient people. This is because of their religious writings, which have influenced Western culture for nearly two thousand years. These writings are in the Old Testament part of the Bible.

In considering the Old Testament as a reliable historical record, some caution must be exercised. To start with, many of the events written about occurred centuries before they were recorded. With such a passage of time, it is difficult to be sure what was fact and what was legend. Stories and beliefs from other cultures may well have been absorbed by early Hebrew writers and then portrayed as fact. As an example, the Hebrew story of

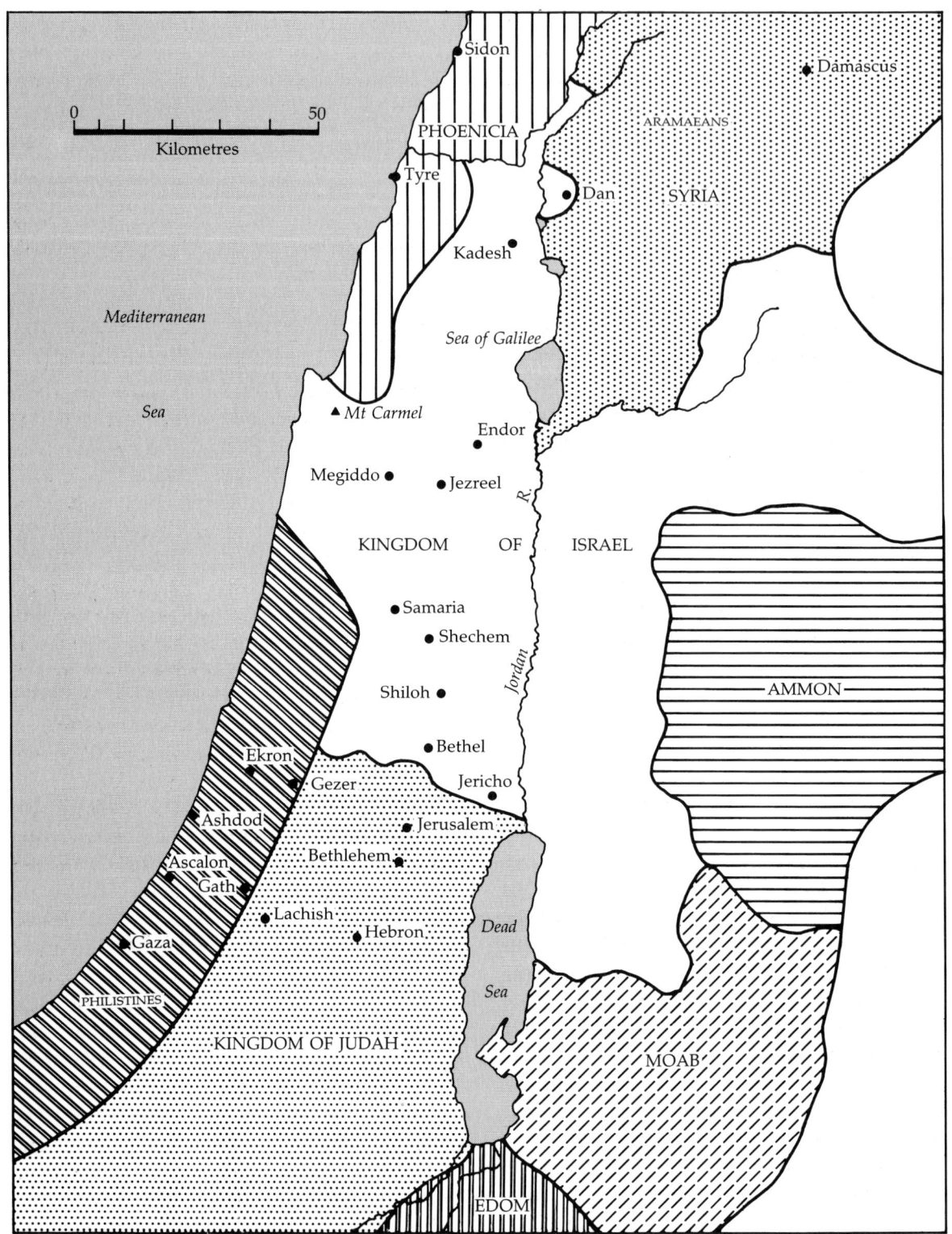

Fig. 4.3 *Palestine c. 800* BC.

Noah's Ark has parallels in both Sumerian and Babylonian lore (see pages 11 and 12).

The Hebrews believed that their god Yahweh (or Jehovah) was directly involved in human affairs, personally rewarding virtue and punishing sin. They therefore wrote their history in religious terms, crediting divine intervention into all sorts of political, social and economic activities. Modern histories are not written in this vein.

History as portrayed by early Hebrew writers could be better verified if it could be matched against other accounts of the same events recorded by writers from other cultures. Take for example the Old Testament account of the flight of the Children of Israel from Egypt under the leadership of Moses. This is recorded in great detail in the book of Exodus, but there is no corresponding account in Egyptian records. The Egyptians did refer to a desert people known to them as Habiru (or Apiru), but this term may well have referred to all aliens, and not a specific group such as the Hebrews.

In summary, the Old Testament is an extremely valuable source of information about the Hebrew people, but the interpretations of its writers about various events may have been overly influenced by religious considerations.

The Old Testament account

According to the Hebrews, their history began with the patriarch Abraham who originally came from Ur of the Chaldees. This is probably not the original Sumerian city, but one of its colonies. Abraham migrated into Palestine in the fifteenth century BC with his flocks, and introduced the worship of Yahweh into the land. He became prosperous, as were his son Isaac and grandson Jacob (who was also known as Israel). One of Jacob's sons, Joseph, was sold into slavery in Egypt, but rose to become the Pharaoh's trusted vizier. When famine later swept Palestine, Joseph arranged for his family to migrate to Egypt, where conditions were better. In time, the family multiplied greatly, but were later forced into slavery by a new Pharaoh and compelled to work as builders. After many years, a leader named Moses led them out of Egypt. They stayed in the Sinai Desert for forty years before finally re-entering Palestine (their 'promised land') under their new leader Joshua.

The settlement of Palestine

Historians currently believe that the Hebrews were a nomadic group who came out of the Arabian Desert, drawn by the fertile lands of Mesopotamia and Palestine. A Semitic people, they eventually settled in Palestine, coming in several waves. The period of greatest migration was probably around the thirteenth century BC.

At first the Hebrews faced strong opposition from both the Canaanites (Phoenicians) and the Philistines who were already in control of the fertile plains and sea coasts. They were forced to remain in the hilly country west of the Jordan River. Although they displaced some Canaanites, the Hebrews did not come as overwhelming conquerors. They settled quietly down beside the Canaanites, and learned much from them that was useful in changing from a nomadic to a settled people.

The twelve tribes

The early Hebrews were by no means united into a nation. Instead, they were divided into twelve tribes, a feature accentuated by the geographical conditions of the land they occupied. Each tribe tended to look to its own affairs, and concerted action by all tribes was rare. Despite this apparent lack of cohesion, the tribes were united in their worship of Yahweh, and had a common shrine at Shiloh, where the Ark of the Covenant (see page 81) was kept. Although the Hebrews were devoted to Yahweh, many were also influenced by the religious practices of their Canaanite neighbours.

Warfare was a constant occupation of the early Hebrews as they struggled to hold their place against the attacks of aggressive neighbours such as the Canaanites, the Philistines and the Midianites. It was during this period that Hebrew leaders such as Gideon and Samson became famous in defeating their enemies from time to time. But the period ended in the defeat of the Hebrews by the better armed and disciplined Philistines at the battle of Aphek about 1050. The Philistines humiliated the Hebrews by carrying off the Ark of the Covenant as a war trophy (see page 81) and by establishing garrisons in Hebrew territory to keep them under control.

SAUL AND THE KINGDOM OF ISRAEL

The defeat at Aphek demonstrated to the Hebrew tribes that they needed to combine into one nation if they were to end domination by the Philistines. Consequently Samuel, the respected religious judge, proposed that Saul from the tribe of Benjamin be made king of a new, united nation, to be called the Kingdom of Israel. Samuel's advice was accepted, and Saul became king (c. 1020–1000). This was despite misgivings from some of the Israelites that a monarchy was not in the best interests of the nation. However, the immediate effect was beneficial. At once the newly unified Israel had a victory when Saul's army defeated the Philistines and forced them to withdraw their garrisons from Israel. Saul followed this up with another victory over the Amalekites in the south and firmly established his position.

In time, however, Saul's leadership came under threat. Apparently rather unstable and given to violent rages, he alienated many of his former supporters, including Samuel. Samuel withdrew his support from Saul after several disputes over religious matters, and this was a severe blow to Saul's position. Embittered and frustrated, Saul became very jealous of the young hero David (who had slain Goliath) and threatened to kill him. Alarmed, David had to flee into exile to Philistia for safety.

In about 1000 Israel was again under threat from the Philistines. Saul took to the field against them at Esdraelon, but was defeated after a bitter and hard-fought battle. In despair, he took his own life, and left Israel without a king.

DAVID

David was of the tribe of Judah, and soon after the death of Saul was elected King of Judah. This had the effect of splitting Israel into two parts, since Saul's son Ishbaal had succeeded his father as King of Israel. After several years, Ishbaal was murdered by his own courtiers. The northern tribes then accepted David as Saul's true successor, thus making him king of a reunified Israel.

David was a vigorous and successful ruler who soon broke the Philistine bond over Israel forever. After a series of victories, he pushed them back to the coastal fringes where they ceased to be a threat. One of the cities he captured on his campaign was Jebus, which he renamed Jerusalem and made his capital. With the Philistines effectively contained, David gradually took over the remaining cities of Palestine peacefully, and exacted tribute from them. Then he turned against the people of Ammon, Moab and Edom, and brought them under his control. Finally he moved north and subdued the Arameans, capturing their chief city of Damascus. He hesitated to move against the Phoenicians, choosing instead to conclude treaties of

Fig. 4.4 *Modern Jerusalem, the domes being those of mosques. Originally called Jebus, Jerusalem was renamed after its capture from the Jebusites by King David. To what three religions is Jerusalem a holy city?*

friendship with them. In extending his nation's frontiers so effectively, David was the real founder of the Kingdom of Israel.

Under David, Jerusalem became both the political and religious focus of Israel. David had his court there, and the city had the advantage that it was easily defensible because it was located on a great rock almost surrounded by deep ravines. The Ark of the Covenant was taken back from the Philistines and housed in Jerusalem, and it was guarded by a priesthood who supervised the religious affairs of the kingdom.

As David's kingdom increased in size, he was forced to place less emphasis on personal rule, and more on government through a bureaucracy. The demands of the new nation meant that its citizens had to pay more taxes, provide labour for public buildings and be more liable for military service. These demands created some unrest from a people accustomed to a minimum of government intervention in their lives.

David's family

In an attempt to tie together the various groups that made up his kingdom, David took wives from each group and so created a harem. This was far from the traditional family structure, and was in time to cause trouble. For example, there was disharmony between the wives and the children, and no clear precedent as to who was to succeed David when he eventually died. Toward the end of David's reign, his third son Absalom led a rebellion against him, and David was forced to flee. Eventually, however, the rebellion was crushed, with Absalom being killed by

Joab, David's general. Finally David chose Solomon, the son of his favourite wife Bathsheba, as his eventual successor. In the last years, Solomon acted as co-ruler with David, and succeeded him on his death in 961.

David was Israel's first successful king. He united the nation, removed the Philistine menace, extended the nation's borders and established an enduring dynasty. Under David, Jerusalem became the holy city of the Jews, and the king was considered the mediator between Jehovah and the people. David was thus the first of a line of priest-kings, a line that lasted some four centuries. The belief later grew up that the messiah of later times was due to be born of the House of David. The New Testament proclaimed Jesus was a direct descendant of David, thus reinforcing his claims to be the messiah.

THE REIGN OF SOLOMON

Solomon has been traditionally recognised as Israel's greatest king. Although the exact dates of his reign are not known, he ruled unchallenged for about forty years in the middle of the tenth century BC. During his long reign, Solomon had two main preoccupations : raising the prestige of the monarchy and prospering the kingdom through the extension of trade and diplomacy.

In pursuing his first aim, Solomon established a luxurious court life with himself as centre and star. His models seem to have been the great kings of Babylonia and Assyria. He ordered a huge new palace, and filled it with a harem of seven hundred wives and three hundred concubines. Many of these marriages were a form of diplomacy, cementing alliances with a wide variety of foreign kings. Within the palace precincts he built a new and glorious temple, emphasising how religion and state were closely combined.

Solomon encouraged intellectual pursuits

and as a result, there emerged at court a class of educated men who became administrators and priests. Their activities gave rise to a new interest in literature, based on national pride at the achievements of David and Solomon. Attempts were made to distinguish between fact and legend, and historical records became more objective.

Solomon and trade

Solomon was a great believer in the benefits of trade, especially with Phoenicia. He sent wheat, olive oil and wool to Phoenicia and in return imported cedar and craft products. He frequently hired Phoenician craftsmen, ship builders and sailors to work on a variety of schemes of his own. His ships often sailed on joint trading expeditions together with those of his friend and ally, King Hiram of Tyre.

Solomon traded widely in other regions as well. He built a port called Ezion-Geber at the head of the Gulf of Aqaba to be the centre of a thriving trade route along the coast of Arabia as far as the fabled land of Ophir. In addition, he sent overland caravans to the south of Arabia to pick up spices and incense from India. These trading ventures and others brought great wealth to the kingdom, and glory to Solomon for his guidance and enterprise.

A well-known episode of Solomon's reign was the visit of the fabled Queen of Sheba. Her southern Arabian kingdom was rich in gold, frankincense and myrrh and moreover was strategically placed along the Red Sea route into the Indian Ocean. Solomon needed her products and her trade routes for maintaining his commercial networks. She in her turn needed his help to market her products in the Mediterranean via Palestine.

The army

Like his father before him, Solomon had a large army. It included not only the traditional infantry, but cavalry and chariots as well. The discovery of 450 horse stalls at Megiddo show that the claim found in I Kings that he had 1400 chariots and 12 000 horses was probably not exaggerated. Despite its strength, Solomon's army was not used to expand the kingdom, but to defend it against enemies. The soldiers were conscripted, and stationed at fortified bases scattered throughout the land. The army was expensive to maintain, and not always successful in its main role. For example, it was unable to quell a revolt by the Edomites, and lost Damascus to the Aramaeans. Nevertheless, its existence was essential for national survival.

Solomon's government

Solomon divided his kingdom into twelve regions which were independent of the old tribal areas. Over each region he placed a governor responsible for the provision of tax money for the central government. Much money was needed for Solomon's elaborate schemes and building programmes, and the demands on the citizens rose steadily. For example, men had to put in one month out of every three in forced labour on crown projects, and this caused a steady grumbling among the people. Solomon was able to maintain his position while he was alive, but when he died in 922, he left a legacy of discontent for his successor Rehoboam.

THE KINGDOM DIVIDES

Rehoboam's accession to the throne was accepted by the people of Judah (comprising the tribes of Judah and Benjamin), but the northern tribes would not have Rehoboam unless he promised to reduce taxes. When he refused point blank, the northerners broke away, proclaiming themselves to be the nation of Israel and appointing Jeroboam as their king. Thus was the Hebrew nation again divided into two parts. This disunity was soon to have drastic results. Neither Israel nor Judah could hang on to the outlying territories, and denied income from these sources, both suffered a severe reduction of power and influence.

EVENTS IN ISRAEL

Jeroboam's rule over Israel was not successful, one of the factors being religion. There were many Canaanites living in Israel, and when Jeroboam made concessions to *their* religious practices and beliefs, he infuriated the Hebrews who accused him of betraying his own faith. The result of this religious discord was instability of government.

The dynasty had more success later, first under King Omri and then his son King Ahab. Keen to cement good relations with the Phoenicians, Ahab married Jezebel, daughter of the King of Tyre, and moved the capital from Shechem to Samaria. Here he established a brilliant court modelled on Solomon's lines. But he soon faced trouble on two counts. Firstly, the high cost of running the court led to heavy taxation, which was bitterly resented. Secondly, Jezebel was a devotee of the god Baal, and her attempts to get him recognised in Israel led to even more religious strife.

In an effort to please his wife and satisfy the Canaanite element of the population, Ahab built a temple for Baal in Samaria. This led to a severe reaction from the Hebrews, and the prophets Elijah and Elisha called for Ahab's removal. Their words were heeded by a general named Jehu, who in 842 overthrew Ahab and made himself king.

JEHU

As the new king, Jehu acted in a vigorous and ruthless fashion to exterminate all the non-believers in Yahweh. He threw Jezebel to the dogs, and slaughtered the priests of Baal. Although this action was applauded by

Fig. 4.5 *The Black Obelisk of Shalmaneser III.*

the Hebrews, it ended the alliance with Tyre, and made Israel weak and isolated. Israel was soon threatened with invasion by King Hazael of Syria. To prevent this happening, Jehu voluntarily paid tribute to King Shalmaneser III of Assyria in return for his protection. Although this act is not mentioned in the Old Testament, a record of it exists on the famous Black Obelisk of Shalmaneser III.

The Black Obelisk

Sometimes also known as the Jehu Stele, this obelisk was discovered at Nineveh in 1846. Two metres in height, it is made of black stone and shows five different nations bearing tribute to Shalmaneser.

In Fig. 4.5 the obelisk has five carved panels on the side shown. Similar carvings occur on each of the obelisk's four sides. The carving which is second from the top depicts Jehu, and the other three on the same level form a frieze which deals with the submission of Israel to the Assyrian king. The writing under the panels refers to Shalmaneser as 'the mighty king, king of the universe, king without a rival, the autocrat, the powerful one of the four regions of the world', and records that Jehu offered gold and silver ornaments, a staff and some fruit as his contribution.

In Fig. 4.6 we see Jehu kneeling before Shalmaneser, who has a bowl in his hand. Behind Shalmaneser is an attendant bearing a parasol, and a guard carrying a club and a sword. Two more guards are behind Jehu. In the complete frieze, no less than thirteen Israelites are shown carrying a variety of gifts for presentation to the Assyrian king.

As a matter of interest, the inscriptions refer to Jehu as 'the son of Omni', but this is incorrect. Jehu overthrew the house of Omni when he took the throne from Ahab.

Jehu's submission to the Assyrians gained Israel some breathing space, but towards the end of his reign Hazael was again threatening

Fig. 4.6 *A close-up of the second panel from the top of the obelisk.*

Israel's independence. Israel was finally forced in 734 to become a vassal state under the Assyrian Tiglath-Pileser III, and thirteen years later was made a province of Assyria by Sargon II.

EVENTS IN JUDAH

The smaller of the two Hebrew states, Judah had to struggle to maintain its independence. It fell to an Egyptian attack in 918, and for a time was forced to pay tribute to Egypt. When the Assyrian Tiglath-Pileser III entered the region in 734, Judah became a vassal state without a struggle.

HEZEKIAH

Hezekiah became king in c . 715 and reigned for approximately thirty years. He is noted as a great religious reformer who cleansed Judah of many of the pagan practices that had gradually attached themselves to the Hebrew religion. For example, he did away with many of the local shrines and altars that reflected the religious influences of the Canaanites in the community.

Hezekiah was also a great patriot. Under his rule Judah grew resentful of Assyria's domination, and in about 712 joined Egypt and some of the Philistine cities in rebelling against it. King Sargon of Assyria soon put down the rebellion, but was surprisingly lenient with Judah. In 705 Hezekiah led his country into another rebellion against Assyria, which was then led by Sennacherib. We have already seen (on page 27) that Sennacherib overran Judah and forced Hezekiah to pay tribute. The Assyrian besieged Jerusalem too, but eventually raised the siege, presumably due to an outbreak of plague.

The Siloam water tunnel

Before his rebellion against Sennacherib, Hezekiah ordered the construction of a long tunnel to bring water from the Spring of Gihon outside the city to the Pool of Siloam inside the city wall. This tunnel was designed to save the city from being deprived of water during sieges. A remarkable engineering feat, it travelled for over 500 metres via a winding route through solid rock and was cut by workmen using picks, hammers and wedges. The workers started from both ends simultaneously, and finally met in the middle. To commemorate the completion of the tunnel, an inscription was carved into the rock at one end. It tells the story of the work involved, and records that 'while there was yet three cubits to be bored through, there was heard the voice of one calling to another'. The tunnel still exists today, and visitors can walk along it through the knee-deep cold spring water.

LATER KINGS

Hezekiah's successor was Manasseh, who became co-ruler in c. 697, but who ruled

alone from c. 687 to c. 642. Under Mannasseh, Judah was a submissive ally of Assyria, and supported the campaigns of Esarhaddon and Assurbanipal. As a result of this support, Judah became prosperous through trade, but it also came under the influence of many Assyrian religious ideas. Manasseh himself supported many foreign gods, and neglected the sole worship of Yahweh.

Under King Josiah (reigned c. 640–609) an attempt was made to clean up the Hebrew religion from outside influences. This task was made easier after the death of Assurbanipal in 627, but the nation's status as an Assyrian vassal state remained till the final collapse of the Assyrian Empire in 612.

Although at last freed from the domination of Assyria, Judah soon had to contend with the rising power of Babylonia under Nebuchadrezzar. Its fate was finally sealed, however, when its kings intrigued with Egypt against Babylonia. Nebuchadrezzar captured

Fig. 4.7   *The Babylonians often took conquered peoples off into exile. Here, in a scene from the palace of Tiglath-Pileser III, Babylonian soliders take Hebrew prisoners away from a captured city. What was the fate of such prisoners?*

Jerusalem in 597 and again in 586 and carried most of the people to captivity in Babylon (see page 32).

HEBREW CONTRIBUTIONS TO RELIGIOUS THOUGHT

Religion was of vital importance to the Hebrews, and their adherence to it kept them apart from the peoples with whom they mingled who had competing faiths. The Hebrew religion contained several ideas that were quite contrary to the religious thought of the day, and that have affected later religions such as Christianity and Islam.

In the first place, they introduced the idea of monotheism (the worship of one god) in opposition to polytheism (the worship of many gods). In the early period of their history when they were still a nomadic people, the Hebrews worshipped Yahweh as their own special god. He would look after and protect them if they kept his commandments. At this stage there was no suggestion that there were *not* any other gods; it was just that they were not to be acknowledged. In later years, Hebrew writers progressed to the concept that Yahweh was not just a local god, but a universal god who controlled the destinies of all people all over the world.

Hand in hand with the concept of monotheism was the idea of morality, that is, that Yahweh gave his children a set of laws to live by. If they kept the laws they would be rewarded, and if they disobeyed the laws they would be punished. This idea was in stark contrast to the Mesopotamian idea that people could offend the gods unwittingly and would be punished severely even though they had no deliberate intent to give any offence whatsoever. The Hebrews replaced the idea of a range of capricious and wilful gods with a single just god who dealt fairly with his people.

SUMMARY OF MAIN EVENTS

The Phoenicians

c. 3000	Phoenicians reach the east Mediterranean coast
c. 1100–800	Phoenicians dominate Mediterranean sea trade
c. 850	Phoenicia comes under Syrian control
c. 800	Phoenicians found colonies

The Philistines

12th century	Philistines settle in southern Canaan
c.1050	Philistines defeat Hebrews at Aphek

The Hebrews

15th century	Abraham migrates into Palestine
c. 1021	Saul becomes King of Israel
c. 1000	Death of Saul; eventual succession of David

David

c. 1000–c. 961	Reign of David over Israel
	Defeated Philistines; extended the frontiers
	Increased taxes; trouble with large family

Solomon

c. 961–922	Reign of Solomon over Israel
	Established luxurious court; encouraged learning
	Traded extensively with great profits
	Maintained large army

The divided kingdoms

918	Judah forced to pay tribute to Egypt
842	Jehu overthrows King Ahab
734	Israel a vassal state of Assyria
586	Hebrews carried off to Babylon by Nebuchadrezzar

FEATURE

The Ark of the Covenant

The Ark of the Covenant was an oblong chest made of wood. It measured roughly just over a metre in length and two-thirds of a metre in width and height. Made by Moses at Yahweh's express command, it was the oldest and most sacred of the Hebrew religious symbols. The Mercy Seat which formed its covering was regarded as the earthly dwelling place of Yahweh. The Ark was fitted with rings and staves, by which it was carried, and prayers were always offered before it was moved or rested. Whenever it was on the move, the people treated it with great reverence. Some sources say it contained only the Tables of the Law, but others say it also held a pot of manna and Aaron's rod that budded. The Ark was frequently carried on military campaigns, presumably to gain Yahweh's assistance in battle. On one such campaign, it was captured by the Philistines, only to be rescued on a subsequent occasion. When not travelling, the Ark was located in the Holy of Holies inside the Tabernacle. Its last known location was in Solomon's Temple, but it was lost when Nebuchadrezzar's troops captured Jerusalem in c. 586. The last Biblical reference to it is in Revelation 11. 19. Its whereabouts today is unknown.

FEATURE

Baal

It was Jezebel's attempt to introduce the worship of Baal into Israel that led to her overthrow and death. Baal was a god very much in favour with the Phoenicians. He was a fertility god, and his titles included Prince, Lord of the Earth, Lord of Rain and Dew, and Lord of the Heavens.

Increased knowledge about Baal came to light from 1929 onwards when several tablets were found at Ugarit (modern Ras Shamra) in northern Syria. The texts indicated that fertility was looked at in seven-year cycles. The belief was that every seven years, Baal had a great struggle against Mot, the god of death and sterility. If Baal won, a seven-year cycle of good times eventuated. If he lost, then there would be seven years of drought and famine.

The worship of Baal was very popular in Egypt from the fourteenth century BC. He later became known to the Babylonians as Bel, and later still became known as the Greek Belos, identified with Zeus.

FEATURE

Solomon's Temple

Although King David first conceived the notion of building a temple, it was left to Solomon to put the idea into practice. It was part of Solomon's incredibly ambitious twenty-year building programme. The site selected was on a ridge which David had previously bought for an altar. It is likely that the site is now occupied by the Mosque of Omar (the Dome of the Rock). Although not very large by modern standards (about thirty metres by ten metres, and fourteen metres high) it was considered a marvel in its day. It was designed and built by Phoenician architects and craftsmen, and construction started around 950. It took seven years to complete.

Only priests could enter the temple; the congregation worshipped in the courtyard outside. Here there was a large bronze container for the worshippers to cleanse themselves, and a large altar where animal sacrifices were made all year round.

The temple itself had three parts, the vestibule (*Ulam*), the sanctuary (*Hekal*) and the inner shrine (*Debir*). Entry to the vestibule was up a flight of ten steps and through two richly decorated cypress doors. From here, the priest entered the sanctuary through two similar doors. The sanctuary was the largest room in the temple and contained seven-branched golden candlesticks (*menora*), the table of showbread, and a small altar. The walls were panelled with cedar and richly ornamented with carvings. At the end of the temple was the inner shrine, the Holy

Fig. 4.8 *Reconstruction drawing of Solomon's temple.*

of Holies. It contained two large carved olive-wood cherubim about five metres high, whose outstretched wings covered the Ark of the Covenant (see page 81), which was considered to be Yahweh's throne. It was the Ark of the Covenant which made the temple such a holy place. The high priest entered the Holy of Holies once a year to perform the ritual of Yom Kippur (Day of Atonement).

The temple was destroyed about 586 when Nebuchadrezzar captured Jerusalem and hauled many of its citizens off to captivity in Babylonia. Another temple was later built on the same site about 520 on the orders of Zerubabbel, the Persian governor. It was not as elaborate as Solomon's temple, however, and did not contain the Ark of the Covenant, which was long since lost.

Document 4.1

Fig. 4.9 is a detail from an Egyptian tomb painting of the Eighteenth Dynasty. It shows slaves making bricks for the Pharaoh.

1 Describe what is happening at the bottom left and centre top of the picture. How do you think the bricks were made?
2 What is the kneeling figure in the centre doing? Do you know what form of writing the symbols behind him belong to?
3 What role do you think the seated figure at the top right of the picture has? What makes you think this?
4 Do you think that the slaves might be Hebrews? Why do you think so?

Document 4.2

King David of Judah is offered the kingship of Israel as well. This account is found in II Samuel 5.

1 Then came all the tribes of Israel to David unto Hebron, and spake, saying, Behold, we are thy bone and thy flesh.
2 Also in time past, when Saul was king over us, thou wast he that leddest out and brought in Israel: and the Lord said to thee, Thou shalt feed my people Israel, and thou shalt be a captain over Israel.
3 So all the elders of Israel came to the king to Hebron; and King David made a league with them in Hebron before the Lord: and they annointed David king over Israel.
4 David was thirty years old when he began to reign, and he reigned forty years.
5 In Hebron he reigned over Judah seven years and six months: and in Jerusalem he reigned thirty and three years over all Israel and Judah.
6 And the king and his men went to Jerusalem unto the Jebusites, the inhabitants of the land: which spake unto David, saying, Except thou take away the blind

Fig. 4.9 *Slaves making bricks for the Pharaoh.*

and the lame, thou shalt not come in hither: thinking, David cannot come in hither.

7 Nevertheless David took the strong hold of Zion: the same is the city of David.

1 What do you think the Israelites meant by the expression 'we are thy bone and thy flesh'?
2 What reasons do they advance for wanting David to be their king?
3 What are three names for Jerusalem mentioned in this passage?
4 Give your opinion about whether or not this passage is easy to understand. Explain the reasons for your opinion as clearly as you can.

Document 4.3

This passage, quoted from I Kings 10, describes Solomon's meeting with the queen of Sheba.

1 And when the queen of Sheba heard of the fame of Solomon concerning the name of the Lord, she came to prove him with hard questions.

2 And she came to Jerusalem with a very great train, with camels that bare spices, and very much gold, and precious stones: and when she was come to Solomon, she communed with him of all that was in her heart.

3 And Solomon told her all her questions: there was not any thing hid from the king, which he told her not.

4 And when the queen of Sheba had seen all Solomon's wisdom, and the house that he had built,

5 And the meat of his table, and the sitting of his servants, and the attendance of his ministers, and their apparel, and his cupbearers, and his ascent by which he went up unto the house of the Lord; there was no more spirit in her.

6 And she said to the king, It was a true report that I heard in mine own land of thy acts and of thy wisdom.

7 Howbeit I believed not the words, until I came, and mine eyes had seen it: and, behold, the half was not told me: thy wisdom and prosperity exceedeth the fame which I heard.

8 Happy are thy men, happy are these thy servants, which stand continually before thee, and that hear thy wisdom.

9 Blessed be the Lord the God, which delighteth in thee, to set thee on the throne of Israel: because the Lord loved Israel for ever, therefore made he thee king, to do judgment and justice.

10 And she gave the king an hundred and twenty talents of gold, and of spices very great store, and precious stones: there came no more such abundance of spices as these which the queen of Sheba gave to king Solomon.

1 Why did the queen of Sheba come to visit Solomon? Did she find what she was looking for?
2 Show evidence that the writer believed that God had a hand in appointing the king to his position.
3 Explain the expression, 'there was no more spirit in her'.
4 Quote verses to show how both Solomon and the queen of Sheba were rich and powerful.
5 Read I Kings 3 : 16–28 as an example of Solomon's wisdom. Write a brief account of the incident.

Document 4.4

This passage from II Chronicles 32 tells of King Hezekiah of Judah's preparations to withstand the siege of Jerusalem by King Sennacherib of Assyria.

1 After these things, and the establishment thereof, Sennacherib king of Assyria came, and entered into Judah, and encamped against the fenced cities, and thought to win them for himself.

2 And when Hezekiah saw that Sennacherib was come, and that he was purposed to fight against Jerusalem,

3 He took counsel with his princes and his mighty men to stop the waters of the fountains which were without the city: and they did help him.

4 So there was gathered much people together, who stopped all the fountains, and the brook that ran through the midst of the land, saying, Why should the kings of Assyria come, and find much water?

5 Also he strengthened himself, and built up all the wall that was broken, and raised it up to the towers, and another wall without, and repaired Millo in the city of David, and made darts and shields in abundance.

6 And he set captains of war over the people, and gathered them together to him in the street of the gate of the city, and spake comfortably to them, saying,

7 Be strong and courageous, be not afraid nor dismayed for the king of Assyria, nor for all the multitude that is with him: for there be more with us than with him:

8 With him is an arm of flesh; but with us is the Lord our God to help us, and to fight our battles. And the people rested themselves upon the words of Hezekiah king of Judah ...

32 This same Hezekiah also stopped the upper watercourse of Gihon, and brought it straight down to the west side of the city of David.

1 Why did Hezekiah's men take the action as described in verses 3 and 4? How could it help in securing Sennacherib's defeat?

2 What preparations did Hezekiah make to protect Jerusalem for the siege to come?

3 What psychological methods did Hezekiah employ to lift up the people's hearts?

4 Explain the significance of verse 32.

CHECK THE FACTS

Match the following list of famous people with the appropriate descriptions from the second list.

People: Abraham; Ahab; Bathsheba; David; Hezekiah; Jehu; Jezebel; Samuel; Saul; Solomon.

Descriptions: respected religious judge of the Hebrews; first king of a united Israel; at first king of Judah, but later king of a reunited Israel; David's favourite wife, mother of Solomon; builder of the great temple at Jerusalem; king of Israel who married Jezebel; daughter of the king of Tyre, devotee of the god Baal; overthrew Ahab and sought help from Shalmaneser III; introduced the worship of Yahweh into Palestine in the fifteenth century BC; built Siloam water tunnel.

GENERAL QUESTIONS

1 Look at Fig. 4.5 on page 76 and answer these questions. These first four need only one or two sentences. Write a paragraph for the fifth.

   a Shalmaneser III was a king of Assyria. What does this obelisk have to do with Israel?

   b Why did Jehu need to pay tribute to Shalmaneser? Did this action do him any good?

   c What error did the Assyrians make in their inscription?

   d Why did Assyrian kings raise stelae such as this one? What other kings followed the same practice?

   e Explain how the stele was organised, and why there were five levels of carving on each of the four sides. As well, indicate the historical significance of such a stele.

2   Imagine you are a Phoenician living in Tyre around 800 BC. Give a brief account of the history of your people, and explain what contributions they have made to the economic and cultural life of the Mediterranean region in the last 300 years. Also indicate any fears you may have for the future.

3   What is your opinion of the Old Testament as a reliable source of history? Do you think its authors were over-influenced by religious considerations? Take a story from the Old Testament, say the creation of the world and the placing of Adam and Eve in the garden of Eden, and comment on your acceptance or otherwise of this story. Make sure you give adequate reasons for making your decision.

4   Read the story of the contest between Elijah and the prophets of Baal (I Kings 18: 17–40), and write a summary in your own words. Show how this story depicts divine intervention into everyday events. What is your own opinion of this story — is it credible? Give reasons for your answer. Criticise or defend Elijah's actions in slaying the prophets of Baal.

5   The following questions refer to the career of Solomon. Answer each one with a paragraph.

a   In what ways was Solomon's court different from those of his predecessors? What models did he follow in organising it?

b   Why was Solomon so keen to expand Israel's trade as widely as possible? What was the extent of his trade contacts, and how did they benefit the kingdom?

c   Why did Solomon need such a large army? Was it successful in the role planned for it?

d   How did Solomon organise his government? Was it successful? What demands did it place on the people?

e   Why did Solomon build his famous temple in Jerusalem? Describe the temple and explain how it was used.

6   Why did Israel split into two separate kingdoms after the death of Solomon? What were the results of this split on the Hebrew people? Who were the outstanding kings of both Israel and Judah and what were their most important achievements?

5
EGYPT: THE GIFT OF THE NILE

THE NILE

While one civilisation was developing in Mesopotamia, another was emerging in Egypt along the banks of the Nile River. This Egyptian civilisation was totally dependent on the Nile, and all aspects of Egyptian life were influenced by the flow of this mighty river.

The Nile has two sources: the Blue Nile, which rises in Ethiopia, and the White Nile, which rises in Uganda. They join at Khartoum, and from there a single mighty river rolls three thousand kilometres north to the Mediterranean Sea. Just north of Khartoum is a series of rapids known as the Sixth Cataract. There are five more of these rapids. The last one, called the First Cataract, occurs near Aswan, just inside the Egyptian border. From here, the Nile flows without further interruptions to the Mediterranean Sea, some 1200 kilometres away. About 150 kilometres from the sea, it spreads out into a triangular marshy area known as a delta. This delta area is known as Lower Egypt. The remainder of the country is called Upper Egypt.

The benefits of the Nile

The Nile benefited the Egyptians in many ways. To start with, it flooded its banks every year and dumped tonnes of fertile black silt over a wide area. This enriched the soil annually and brought the farmers excellent crops. Secondly, the Nile was the nation's main source of water, as rainfall was so light. Its water, drawn up by means of a *shaduf*, irrigated the fields, enabling the farmers to grow wheat, barley, grapes, dates, sesame, castor oil and flax.

Growing wild in the Nile's marshy areas was a tall reed called the papyrus. Boats, paper, rope, baskets, mats and footwear were all made from this remarkable plant.

The last gift of the Nile was transportation. Since the prevailing wind blew from the north to the south, a boatman could drift downstream, then have the wind obligingly blow him back upstream. The river was thus a unifying factor, enabling the people to communicate fairly readily.

The Egyptians appreciated all the blessings given them by their beloved river, and composed many hymns of praise to it. One such appears on page 99 as Document 5.2.

The seasons

The Egyptians based their seasons on the recurring cycles of the Nile. Firstly, there was Flood Time, running from approximately June to September. No work could be done in the fields then, so the farmers were expected

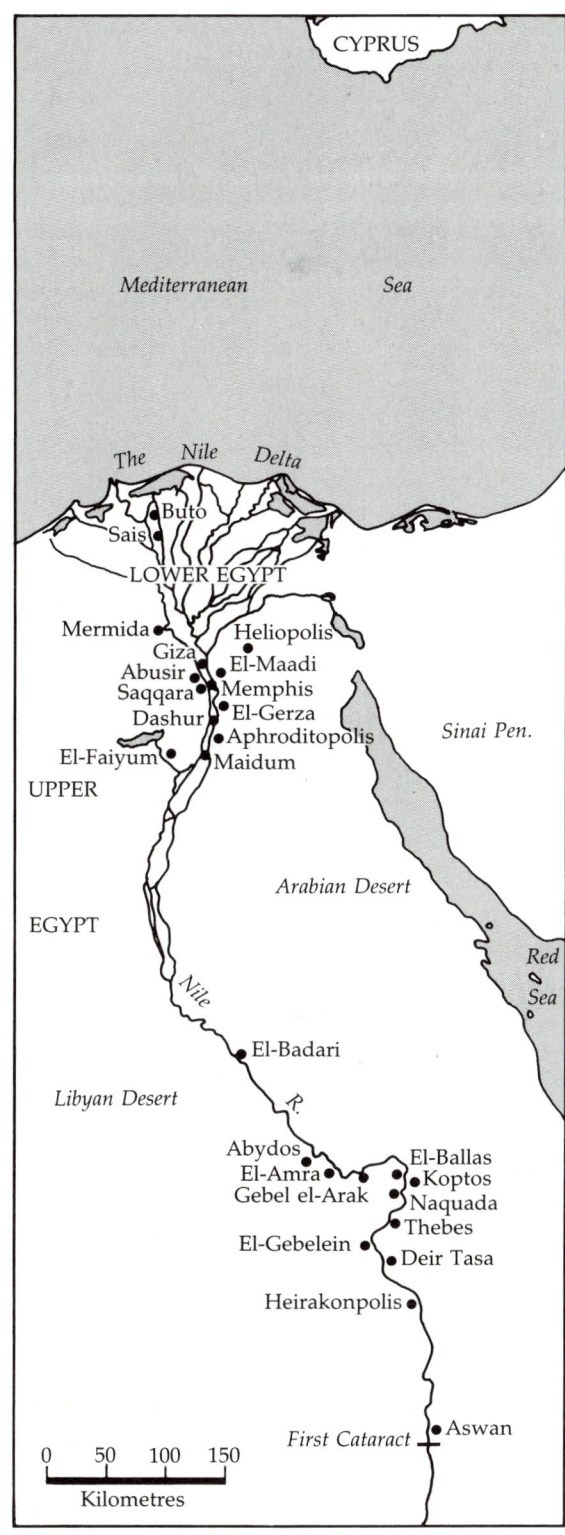

Fig. 5.1 *Egypt.*

to labour on the king's building projects. Next there was Seed Time, from October through till about February. This was a busy time when farmers trapped water for future irrigation and planted crops in the mud. Finally there was Harvest Time, when the crops were gathered and stored.

The kings (later called Pharaohs) were always concerned about the annual floods, and dreaded the onset of dry years, which would result in famine. They devised gauges called Nilometers which would measure the rise of the river at various places along its length. Should the Nilometers show that a dry year was apparent, renewed efforts had to be made to conserve as much of the available water as possible.

The flooding of the Nile determined the value of land. Land that would always receive the benefit of flooding was considered better than land that only got it sometimes. The annual flooding also led to a study of geometry and arithmetic, as surveyors had to redraw farm boundaries every year after the floods had subsided.

GEOGRAPHY AND DEFENCE

Egypt's geographical setting contributed substantially to its defence. Both its eastern and western flanks were bounded by desert which was difficult to penetrate. To the north lay the Mediterranean Sea, and this too proved a formidable obstacle to invaders till comparatively late in the nation's history. The only real avenues of invasion were across the Isthmus of Suez on the north-east, and from the lands of Nubia (Sudan) and Kush (Ethiopia) to the south. The early Egyptians met the latter threat by establishing forts along the Nile and pushing deep into Nubian territory themselves. It was across the Isthmus of Suez that they were at their most vulnerable, as their later history was to show.

Generally safe from potential enemies and insulated from external influences, the Egyptians developed a civilisation that endured for over 2500 years. Their great discoveries were accomplished within the first few centuries of their civilisation. Thereafter, seemingly quite content with what they had achieved, they looked on change with disfavour and seemed to spurn new ideas. Changes did indeed come, but only very slowly during this long period.

PREHISTORIC EGYPT

This is the earliest period of Egypt's history, and refers to the time before the recording of human affairs by the use of writing. It is also sometimes known as the Predynastic Period, the time before rule by kings. This prehistoric era is generally divided into two parts: the Paleolithic period, or Old Stone Age, and the Neolithic period, or New Stone Age.

Paleolithic Egypt

Although precise dates for early events are virtually impossible to obtain, it is generally believed that the first people in Egypt arrived before 12 000 BC. They were hunters and gatherers who used hand axes and choppers skilfully. Leading a nomadic life, they hunted lions, goats, wild cattle and sheep on dry land, and ventured into the marshy areas for crocodiles, hippopotami, water birds and fish. Archaeologists have found remains of their occupation in the gravel terraces of the Nile Valley and in the nearby desert.

Neolithic Egypt

By about 4500, human occupation had entered the Neolithic period. People now lived in permanent houses and they grew crops such as barley, emmer (a variety of wheat) and an edible grass called vetch. As well, they raised domesticated animals. Their first houses were just crude mud huts, but later they prog-

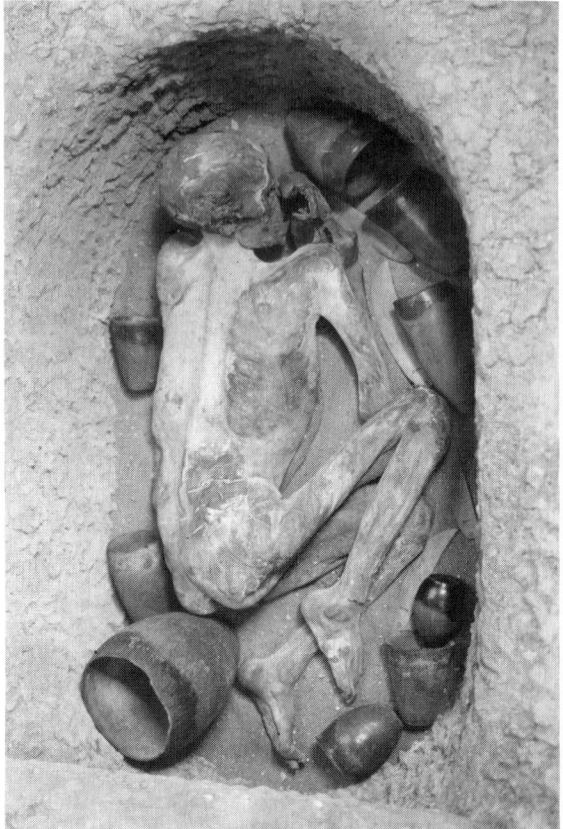

Fig. 5.2 *This well-preserved body is shown crouched in its sand grave. The preservation is due to the action of the hot sand on the body, which effectively dried it out. Why are the utensils buried in the grave?*

ressed to building homes with mud bricks. They wore clothes made of linen (from the flax plant) and used wooden hoes to cultivate their gardens. They made attractive pottery, but were ignorant of the potter's wheel.

TASIAN CULTURE

Evidence of human settlement in the Neolithic period has been found in the Faiyum district, a large lakeside region about 100 kilometres south of Cairo, and near Deir Tasa, 500 kilometres further south. Here the people did a lot of fishing and hunting, but also grew grain and stored it in containers made of woven straw. Having no metal, they made their tools from stone, flint and bone. Their pottery was rather crude, but it served its purpose reasonably well.

Especially interesting are the graves which show that even at this early stage, the people believed in a life after death. The dead were buried in shallow sand graves, usually wrapped in a reed mat, and in a crouched or bent position. With them were buried pots, food, drink, stone tools and jewellery made of bone, ivory and shell. Also included were palettes on which pigment was ground, and later mixed with animal fat to make eye shadow. These remains have been designated the Tasian culture because they were found at Deir Tasa on the east bank of the Nile.

BADARIAN CULTURE

A later and somewhat more advanced culture that is believed to have followed the Tasian is the Badarian. It is so named because its artefacts were first found at El-Badari, some 200 kilometres north of Deir Tasa. British archaeologists excavated Badarian settlements and cemeteries in the 1920s, and dated them around 4000, thus making them some 500 years later than the Tasian finds. However, while most archaeologists support this view, it *is* possible that the two cultures may have been contemporary.

The Badarians were much more skilful than the Tasians in their artistic and technical skills. Their pottery, for example, was infinitely superior to the somewhat clumsy efforts of the Tasians. Often distinguished by a black top, it was very thin-walled and well baked. Frequently it was decorated with a burnished ripple, the favourite colours being red and brown. Other Badarian artefacts to be discovered were ivory combs and spoons, slate palettes and copper beads. There were

also necklaces made from a soft soapstone called steatite.

AMRATIAN CULTURE (NAQADA I)

A still further development was the Amratian culture, which dates around 3600. It was named by the famous archaeologist Sir William Flinders Petrie, after El Amra, a village near Abydos in Upper Egypt. It is also known as Naqada I, after the modern village of Naqada.

The Amratian culture progressed further than the Badarian. Its people developed improved techniques for the working of raw materials, and their pottery and stonework were better designed and made. Their pottery mainly featured black-topped red ware and a dark-red burnished ware and was often decorated with human and animal figures painted on in white. They were skilled in fashioning disc-shaped stone maceheads and flint javelin heads, and so had some experience in war. We do not know, however, if these weapons were used for attack or defence.

The people buried their dead in simple round holes which were lined with woven mats. The corpse, often wrapped in animal skins or placed in a wicker basket, was placed on its left side with its face to the west. With it were buried pottery, palettes, combs, armlets, beads, and sometimes small statues of men and women. An examination of skeletons has shown that the people tended to be short, of slim build and with delicate features.

GERZEAN CULTURE (NAQADA II)

Following the Amratian culture came the Gerzean. It too was named by Petrie, this time after the village of El-Gerza, some distance to the north of El Amra. Dating from c. 3400 to c. 3100, it is also known as Naqada II. Many archaeologists believe that the

Gerzean culture originated in Lower Egypt, and gradually made its way south, where in time it replaced the older Amratian culture. Others, however, maintain that it was a natural development of the Amratian.

Whatever its origin, the Gerzean culture was a great improvement on its predecessor in terms of technology and artistic achievement. For example, its people had better houses. Instead of small round houses with roofs made of straw, the Gerzeans had larger, rectangular mud-brick houses with proper doors and window openings featuring timber supports.

The pottery produced during this period was usually buff coloured and decorated with dark red paint. The designs featured animals, trees and humans, with the female figure usually larger than the male. The people also made stone vases, elaborately carved palettes, pear-shaped maceheads, ripple-flaked flint knives and beads made of iron, copper and gold.

The graves of the Gerzean people were different from those dug during the Amratian period. To start with, they were rectangular instead of round, and had a shaft that led down to the actual burial chamber, which was lined with mud bricks. The graves of the obviously important people were more elaborate than normal, and were kept separate from the simpler graves of the average person.

NOMES

With the passing of time, numbers of village communities gradually welded together to form larger territorial units (later known by the Greeks as *nomes*). Each had its own religious traditions, local gods and rulers. The

Fig. 5.3 *Excellent examples of Gerzean artefacts.*

rulers had religious responsibilities, and were often blamed when the community was suffering hard times. On such occasions they were likely to be sacrificed.

It was during this time that migrants from Palestine and Syria entered Lower Egypt. They brought with them a knowledge of metalworking, and certain Sumerian cultural traits. These included the use of cylinder seals, the practice of burial in tombs lined with bricks, and the concept of writing. The Egyptians adopted these ideas, but developed them in their own way. In the process, they advanced the pace of their civilisation.

POLITICAL DEVELOPMENT

It is apparent that the various Egyptian nomes eventually consolidated into two separate kingdoms. One was in Upper Egypt, with its capital at Naqada and the god Seth as its special deity. The king wore a white crown. The other kingdom was in the Delta, with

Fig. 5.4 *This palette is the most important single monument to have survived from the Archaic Period of Egyptian history. On the obverse side, Narmer is preceded by a priest and four standard bearers carrying fetishes. Behind him is his sandal bearer and foot washer. They are inspecting rows of beheaded corpses who represent his defeated enemies. At the bottom of the palette the king is represented as a strong bull breaking down a township and trampling a foreign rebel, probably a Libyan. Note how on the reverse side, Narmer is represented as being much larger than his enemy. This was a typical representation of a successful Pharaoh when defeating his enemies, who are here described as 'marsh-dwellers'.*

Behdet as capital and Horus as chief god. Its king wore a red crown. There was rivalry between the two kingdoms, and war broke out about 3100. By this time, new capitals had been established in both kingdoms—Hierakonpolis in Upper Egypt and Buto in the Delta.

The Egyptian historian Manetho, a high priest in the temple at Heliopolis in the third century BC, wrote that King Menes of Upper Egypt was the victor, and thus the first king of a fully united kingdom. Most historians now believe that the conqueror's real name was Narmer and that he and Menes were one and the same person. In 1898 an archaeologist digging at Kom-al-Ahmar unearthed a slate palette. On one side was King Narmer, wearing the crown of Upper Egypt, striking a defeated enemy. We know his name because it was written above him between the two horned heads. On the reverse side was Narmer again, this time wearing the crown of Lower Egypt. Below him were two snake-necked leopards symbolising the union of the two kingdoms. After Narmer's success, Egyptian kings wore a double crown to show the union of Upper and Lower Egypt.

UNCERTAINTIES IN EGYPTIAN HISTORY

Starting with Narmer, Egypt was ruled by a series of dynasties (government by members of a royal family). Unfortunately, we do not know who *all* the kings were because full and reliable records have not been found. Such records may well have been made, but many have been lost or destroyed, and only a few fragments remain. We have, for example, the king lists from Abydos, which record the names of seventy-six kings on stone, and similar records from Karnak and Saqqara. Probably, however, the best record is the Palermo Stone, which gives information about

Fig. 5.5 *The Palermo Stone, one of the basic sources of ancient Egyptian history. What form of writing is there on the stone?*

the first five dynasties. Although it is in fragments, the Palermo Stone not only gives the names of the rulers, but some details about each reign.

Manetho's history of Egypt was written 3000 years after the period of Narmer. Apparently basing his work on reasonably reliable sources, Manetho claimed that up to the conquest of Egypt by Alexander the Great in 332 BC, there were thirty dynasties. Manetho's work has not survived, although parts of it have been included in the works of other writers such as Josephus and Eusebius. Today, scholars still accept Manetho's assessment of thirty dynasties, even though there are so many gaps in the record.

Modern historians have divided Egyptian history into several time periods. In general terms, these are:

The Archaic Period (c. 3100–2686)
The Old Kingdom (c. 2686–2180)
The Middle Kingdom (c. 2040–1786)
The New Kingdom (c. 1570–1085)

It should be noted here that all these dates are only tentative. They are not necessarily accepted without reserve by all authorities. At best they can be described as a general guide only.

THE ARCHAIC PERIOD
(c. 3100–2686)

As first king of a united Egypt and founder of the First Dynasty, Narmer established his capital at Memphis. The name means 'White Walls', and comes from the fact that Narmer fortified the city and had the walls white-washed. The city was near the apex of the Delta, and its site was chosen because of its proximity to both Upper and Lower Egypt. Narmer's queen was Neithotep, who came from the Delta. This indicates that it was likely that Narmer deliberately chose a Delta prin-cess for his queen so as to consolidate his position by marriage. It is also likely that future kings of the First Dynasty married princesses from the Delta for the same reason.

Narmer and the seven kings who succeeded him all mounted military expeditions abroad and extended their authority as far south as the first cataract. Here they fought success-fully against the Nubians. They also sent expeditions eastward to the Sinai to protect trade routes, and in the west had some vic-tories over the Libyans. Their success justified the belief that each king was divine, and the

embodiment of the god Horus. More about the divinity of Egyptian kings is to be found on page 103.

ROYAL TOMBS

As a sign of their divine status, Narmer and his successors were accorded great honour when they died. They were buried either at nearby Saqqara or further south in Abydos. Since tombs connected with these kings have been found at both places, it is not known at present which of these places was considered the *principal* burial site. Having two tombs would, of course, be in keeping with the status of a monarch who claimed to be ruler of two kingdoms. The tomb at Saqqara would be for the people of Lower Egypt; the one at Abydos for the people of Upper Egypt.

The lavish tombs in Saqqara were dug deep in the earth. The richly decorated main chamber was reserved for the body of the king, and contained all sorts of treasures and artefacts that he would need in the next life. Surrounding the main chamber were a whole series of lesser graves. These contained the bodies of servants slain so as to accompany and serve their master on his journey to the next world. Remains show that most of these unfortunate servants were women. The whole complex was covered by a block-shaped building made of bricks. This was called a *mastaba*, a name deriving from the Arabic word for 'bench'.

THE END OF THE DYNASTY

The kings of the First Dynasty made use of the invention of writing to establish a bu-reaucracy to help them govern the land. They also encouraged the arts of calculation and surveying, and a more accurate reckoning of time.

It is not known why the dynasty collapsed, but evidence suggests that towards the end there was a lot of internal dissension and that the kings were not strong enough to solve the problems that faced them.

THE SECOND DYNASTY

Not a great deal is known about the kings of the Second Dynasty. The first was Hetepsekhemui, who came to the throne about 2890. Since he plundered and burned the tombs of his predecessors, he apparently came to power only after a violent struggle against the previous dynasty. Five other kings followed him, the last being Khasekhemui. Little was written about the dynasty. Their mastaba tombs were discovered by Petrie at Abydos, but there were no human remains in them. This has led to the speculation that they may have been buried at Saqqara, where remains *were* found in larger and more elaborate mastabas. If this was the case, then the mastabas at Abydos may have been merely cenotaphs, and not tombs (refer to page 116).

The period of the First and Second Dynasties was a great formative time for Egypt. The skills of government, administration, technology, writing and building were all fostered and developed at this time. They later flowered during the period of the Old Kingdom.

THE HEB-SED FESTIVAL

At this stage, mention should be made of the *Heb-Sed* festival. This was a special festival held for any king who had occupied the throne for thirty years and was repeated every three years after that. The festival was in the nature of a jubilee and was meant to ensure the renewal of his powers. There were great public celebrations, and as part of the festival, the king made offerings to a series of gods. He was then crowned, first with the white crown of Upper Egypt, then with the red crown of Lower Egypt. Finally, clad in a short kilt with an animal tail at the back, he was required to run four laps of a ritual course. This presumably was to demonstrate his physical energy and his continued ability to control the nation.

Numerous wall reliefs and paintings about the Heb-Sed festival have been found in the complex of King Djoser's Step Pyramid. This is one of the main sources of our information about the ceremony that took place.

SUMMARY OF MAIN EVENTS

Paleolithic period

Pre- 12 000   First people arrive in Egypt—nomads and hunters

Neolithic period

c. 4500   People started to settle down in villages; start of Tasian culture at Deir Tasa

c. 4000   Start of Badarian culture

c. 3600   Start of Amratian culture (Naqada I)

c. 3400   Start of Gerzean culture (Naqada II)

First Dynasty

c. 3100   Union of Upper and Lower Egypt under Narmer; start of the First Dynasty
Eight kings comprised the First Dynasty

Second Dynasty

c. 2890   Hetepsekhemui starts the Second Dynasty

c. 2686   End of the Second Dynasty

FEATURE

Papyrus

The Egyptians made the world's first paper, using the papyrus plant which grew in plenty along the marshy banks of the Nile. To start the process, they cut the long stems of the plant into thin slices. They then laid these strips crosswise in a double layer on a flat stone. A cloth was laid over the strips, which were then beaten with a wooden mallet. This beating continued for an hour or so. When it ended, the strips were joined together in a single sheet which was then pressed under a heavy weight. It was then polished with a smooth stone, and its edges were trimmed.

Because the time involved in its manufacture was so long, papyrus was very expensive and was used only by priests, nobles and wealthy people. It provided a very convenient medium for the writing of official documents, certainly much simpler than the laborious carving of characters on stone monuments. The recovery in modern times of many ancient papyrus scrolls helps historians enormously in determining what life was like in Ancient Egypt.

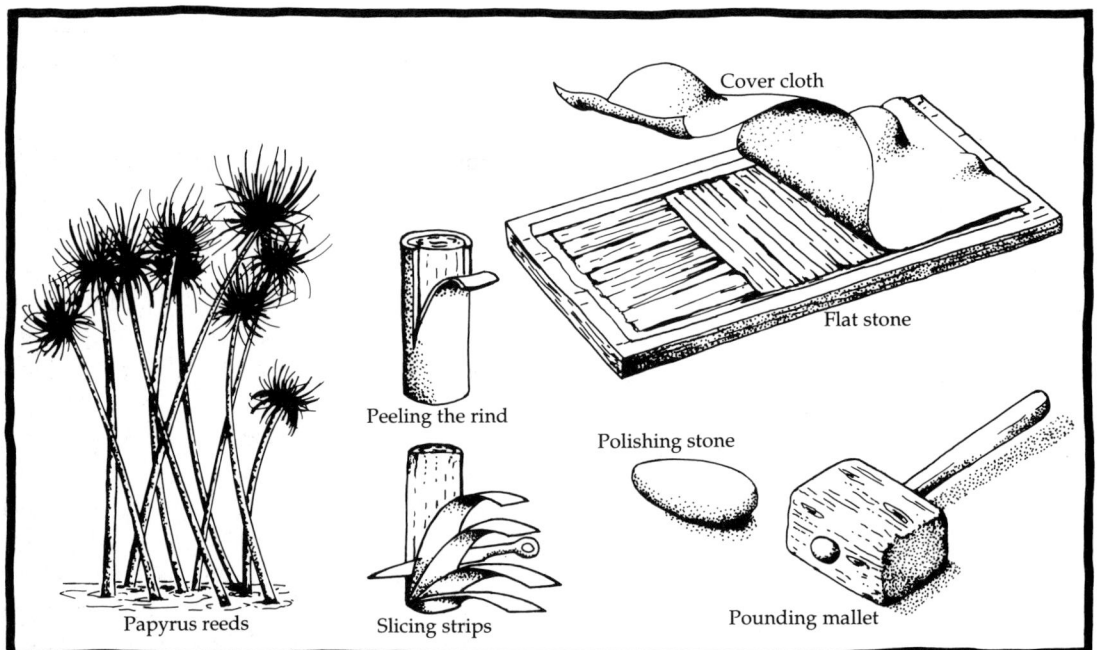

Fig. 5.6 *It was a long process to make paper from the papyrus plant.*

Document 5.1

The following extract comes from the writings of the Greek historian Herodotus, whose work has appeared earlier in the book. Here he discusses the early history of Egypt and the building of Memphis.

The priests said that Min was the first king of Egypt, and that it was he who raised the dyke which protects Memphis from the inundations of the Nile. Before his time the river flowed entirely along the sandy range of hills which skirts Egypt on the side of Libya. He, however, by banking up the river at the bend which it forms about eighteen kilometres south of Memphis, laid the ancient channel dry, while he dug a new course for the stream half-way between the two lines of hills. To this day, the elbow which the Nile forms at the point where it is forced aside into the new channel is guarded with the greatest care by the Persians, and strengthened every year; for if the river were to burst out of this place, and pour over the mound, there would be danger to Memphis being completely overwhelmed by the flood. Min, the first king, having thus, by turning the river, made the tract where it used to run, dry land, proceeded in the first place to build the city now called Memphis, which lies in the narrow part of Egypt; after which he further excavated a lake outside the town, to the north and west, communicating with the river, which was itself the eastern boundary.

Herodotus, *The Persian Wars* II: 99, pp. 99, 100.

1 Why do you think Herodotus calls the first king by the name of Min? Does it sound like any name you have already heard? What do modern scholars call this king, and why?

2 What do Min's exploits tell you about the following?
   a Egyptian capacity to plan large-scale public works
   b the labour force available to complete those works
   c the power or wealth of the king to organise and pay for these works
3 Who are the Persians mentioned by Herodotus? Look back at Chapter 3 and see if you can identify who they were, and what they were doing in Egypt.
4 How reliable do you think Herodotus is as a historian? What factors add to or detract from his reliability? To answer this question properly, you may need to do some research on the life of Herodotus.

Document 5.2

This hymn to the Nile was probably written sometime between the Middle and New Kingdoms for an inundation festival held at Thebes.

Hail to thee, O Nile, that issues from the earth and comes to keep Egypt alive! ...

He who makes barley and brings emmer into being, that he may make the temples festive. If he is sluggish, then nostrils are stopped up, and everybody is poor. If there be thus a cutting down in the food-offerings of the gods, then a million men perish among mortals, covetousness is practised ...

But generations of thy children jubilate for thee, and men give thee greeting as a king, stable of laws, coming forth at his season and filling Upper and Lower Egypt. Whenever water is drunk, every eye is in him, who gives an excess of his good ...

If thou art too heavy to rise, the people are few, and one begs for the water of the year. Then the rich man looks like him who is worried, and every man is seen to be carrying his weapons . . .

When the Nile floods, offering is made to thee, oxen are sacrificed to thee, great oblations are made to thee, birds are fattened for thee, lions are hunted for thee in the desert, fire is provided for thee. And offering is made to every other god, as is done for the Nile, with prime incense, oxen, cattle, birds and flame . . .

1 What is unusual about the Egyptian attitude concerning the source of the Nile? Does it indeed 'issue from the earth'? Is it possible the Egyptians didn't know its true source?
2 List the consequences to Egypt of a year in which the flow of water is below normal.
3 Explain the statement '. . . every man is seen to be carrying his weapons'.
4 Describe the celebrations that are carried out when the river has a good flow of water.

Document 5.3

The Narmer macehead shown in Fig. 5.7 is, like the palette, an important document in Egyptian history. When attempting to answer the questions below, refer to the Narmer Palette (Fig. 5.4 on page 93) for help.

1 Which figure is King Narmer? List three or four reasons to back up your choice. Be as specific as you can.
2 Who is the large figure on the bottom left-hand side? How did he serve the king?
3 Who are the three small figures carrying standards on the top right? Can you identify any of the figures on the standards?
4 The person under the sign is the vizier. What appears to be a difference between this person and the others on the macehead? What was the responsibility of a vizier?

Document 5.4

Born in Sicily, Diodorus Siculus was a Greek his-

Fig. 5.7 *The Narmer Macehead.*

torian who lived during the first century BC. *His famous work covering forty books was called Library of History. It covered much of the Mediterranean world. He travelled in Egypt between 60 and 57* BC, *and gathered much material from local sources. In this extract, he discusses the contribution of Menes (here called Menas) to Egyptian history.*

After the gods the first king of Egypt, according to the priests, was Menas, who taught the people to worship gods and offer sacrifices, and also to supply themselves with tables and couches and to use costly bedding, and, in a word, introduced luxury and an extravagant manner of life. For this reason when, many generations later, Tnephachthus, the father of Bocchoris the wise, was king and, while on a campaign in Arabia, ran short of supplies because the country was desert and rough, we are told that he was obliged to go without food for one day and then to live on quite simple fare at the home of some ordinary folk in private station, and that he, enjoying the experience exceedingly, denounced luxury and pronounced a curse on the king who had first taught the people their extravagant way of living; and so deeply did he take to heart the change which had taken place in the people's habits of eating, drinking, and sleeping, that he inscribed his curse in hieroglyphics on the temple of Zeus in Thebes; and this, in fact, appears to be the chief reason why the fame of Menas and his honours did not persist into later ages. And it is said that the descendants of this king, fifty-two in number all told, ruled in unbroken succession more than a thousand and forty years, but that in their reigns nothing occurred that was worthy of record.

Diodorus Siculus, *Library of History* I: 45 (translated by C. H. Oldfather), Heinemann, London, 1933, pp. 159, 161.

1 According to Diodorus, why is there virtually no record of the achievements of Menas (Menes)?

2 What is your opinion of Diodorus' account? Does it sound credible or incredible? Give reasons for your answer.

3 In the light of modern research, does Diodorus appear to have his facts right in the last sentence? Explain.

4 Diodorus is correct when he says there is little reference to Menes in Egyptian history. What is *your* explanation for this?

CHECK THE FACTS

Use information from this chapter to answer these questions.

1 Approximately when did the first people arrive in Egypt, and what kind of lifestyle did they lead?

2 What was the main difference in lifestyle between the people of the Paleolithic and Neolithic periods of history?

3 How did the people of the Tasian culture bury their dead?

4 In what ways was the Badarian culture superior to the Tasian?

5 What other name is often used to describe the Amratian culture?

6 In what ways were the burial customs of the Gerzean culture different from those of the Amratian?

7 When was Egypt united as one nation, and by whom?

8 Who was Manetho, and what was his contribution to the study of Egyptian history?

9 What are the main time periods into which Egyptian history has been placed?

10 What was a mastaba, and why was it so called?

GENERAL QUESTIONS

1 Study Fig. 5.8 carefully, then answer the questions below. The first four need only

Fig. 5.8 *This is a burial tomb dating from the late First Dynasty. The tomb was later covered by bench-shaped mastaba.*

one or two sentences each, but the last needs a paragraph.

a   How do you know that this burial chamber must be for a person of importance?

b   Why do you think the entrance to the burial chamber was sealed off with such a huge rock-door?

c   The burial chamber is obviously surrounded by other rooms. What would they have been used for?

d   What would have covered the tomb originally?

e   What was the Egyptians' view about life after death? What sort of goods were included with the corpse, and for what reason?

2   Imagine you are an Egyptian living in a small village along the Nile River in 4200. Give an account of a typical day's activities, and show how the Nile influences your life.

3   If you were a farmer living in the Gerzean period of Egypt's history, how would you compare the lifestyle you lead with that of a farmer living during the Amratian culture that preceded you?

4   You are the craftsman who has just been commissioned to fashion the now-famous Narmer Palette for the king. Explain the design you have worked out, and the significance of each of the details.

5   Write a paragraph about each of these topics from Egypt's history:

a   the seasons of the Egyptian year

b   the changing form of pottery from the Tasian to the Gerzean cultures

c   the union of Upper and Lower Egypt into one nation

d   sources for Egyptian history and their reliability

e   the Heb-Sed festival

6

THE OLD KINGDOM
(c. 2686–2180)

THE OLD KINGDOM

The Old Kingdom lasted for about five hundred years. It was a period of great stability and prosperity, and Egypt's essential greatness was forged in that time. Its kings were all-powerful, and they erected gigantic monuments to demonstrate their greatness. Many still stand today even after 4000 years, a lasting tribute to the skill of the architects and workers.

THE PHARAOH

At this stage it is appropriate to examine the position of the king. Henceforth he will frequently be referred to as *Pharaoh*. This term means 'great house' and signifies the royal palace. Although it was not specifically used to refer to the king himself until the New Kingdom period, it is generally employed by modern writers when referring to Egyptian kings of any era.

The Pharaoh held a unique position in Egyptian society, as he was both god and king. He was considered to be an embodiment of Horus, son of the god Osiris. Sometimes he was also referred to as the son of the gods Re or Amon, but this only meant that he had some of their attributes and powers.

The Pharaoh was responsible for all aspects of national life. He caused the Nile to flow and to flood, and if the overflow was too little or too great it was his fault. He was responsible for the fertility of the soil, the health of the nation's economy, the fortunes of the army and the maintenance of peace.

In theory, the Pharaoh owned all the land, but in fact rarely exercised that right. He was considered to be completely infallible, and his commands were obeyed in all matters. No one had the right to challenge his decrees, for who can dispute with a god? In works of art, he was always depicted as dwarfing his enemies, who could never expect to win against a deity.

In matters of law, the Pharaoh's judgment was final. He could make decisions without hearing the evidence because he was divine and knew where the truth lay. This same power lay with his officials who administered justice in his name. They were held to have the same powers of discernment because they were the Pharaoh's appointed officers. It was this dependence on the Pharaoh's divinity that explains the absence of any codified laws in Egypt.

THE VIZIER

Since the Pharaoh could not be in all places at once, he needed a civil administration of officials. Heading these was the vizier, who was second in importance only to the Pharaoh himself. The first viziers were royal princes, related to the Pharaoh. From the Fifth Dynasty on, viziers came from the ranks of nobles. The vizier headed a vast bureaucracy of officials and scribes who administered all aspects of the nation's affairs. These included the collection of taxes, the administration of law and order, the building of public works and supervision of the armed forces.

Several documents have survived which recount the duties expected of a vizier. One is called the *Instructions of Ptahhotpe*; a second, the *Installation of the Vizier*. Although the first is credited to Ptahhotpe, vizier to King Djedkare Isesi of the Fifth Dynasty, it is generally thought to have been written during the Twelfth Dynasty. The second appears on the wall of the tomb of Rekhmire, vizier to King Thutmose III of the Eighteenth Dynasty. Some of its instructions appear in Document 6.1 on page 118.

NOMES AND NOMARCHS

The country was divided into more than forty *nomes* (or provinces), each under the direction of a governor, or *nomarch*. The governor ruled his nome in the name of the Pharaoh and tried to make his administration effective. Some of the governors of outlying districts acted on their own in making decisions without consulting the central authority for direction. These governors tended to be quite independent in their outlook.

THE THIRD DYNASTY
(c. 2686–2620)

The first ruler of the Third Dynasty was Sanakht, but comparatively little is known about his reign. Far more important was his younger brother and successor Djoser (also known as Zoser). Unfortunately, there is no commonly agreed spelling of Egyptian

Fig. 6.1 *The famous Step Pyramid of King Djoser, designed and built by Djoser's vizier Imhotep. Situated at Saqqara, the Step Pyramid was the forerunner of many pyramids to come. What kind of tombs preceded this pyramid?*

names, and this is often confusing to students studying Egyptian history for the first time. Djoser was so successful in organising the resources and administration of the nation that he was the first Pharaoh to build a pyramid as a tomb. In so doing, he established a tradition which was eagerly followed for hundreds of years by his successors.

DJOSER'S PYRAMID

Located at Saqqara, Djoser's pyramid has become famous because of its shape. Today it is known as the Step Pyramid and appears as a series of six mastabas, one standing on the other. Credit for building and designing the pyramid is generally given to Imhotep, Djoser's vizier and architect. So great was Imhotep's fame that he was eventually made a god, one of the few non-royals to achieve this great honour.

The step pyramid was the most massive monument ever raised in Egypt up to that time. When finished, it stood just over sixty-two metres high. It was built of small stone blocks, then faced with a fine white limestone brought in from a quarry at Tura in the hills east of the Nile. Surrounding it were a number of buildings, of which the most important was the mortuary temple, where the priests conducted regular services for the dead king. Then there were some solid buildings with no rooms, doors or windows. These were make-believe chapels where Djoser's spirit could celebrate endless Heb-Sed festivals into the far eternities (see page 96). There was no need for proper rooms, as spirits could pass through solid brick unhindered. Finally, there were mastabas for his nobles, and the whole complex was surrounded by a high limestone wall.

Is there any significance in the pyramid design? We are uncertain on this point, but I.E.S. Edwards suggests that the stepped design may have been considered a means whereby the dead king could ascend to the sky to join the other gods there. He quotes pyramid texts which state: 'a ladder is set up for him that he may ascend on it' and 'a stairway to the sky is set up for you among the Imperishable Stars'.

OTHER PYRAMIDS

Djoser's successor Sekhemkhet also planned a step pyramid at Saqqara, but it was never completed. The workmanship was poor and it is apparent that it lacked the inspired supervision of an architect of Imhotep's abilities. It was only discovered in 1951, and to date has only partly been excavated.

Huni was the last ruler of the Third Dynasty. He tried to build a true pyramid (as opposed to a step pyramid) at Meidum, but failed. The construction of the first successful true pyramid had to wait for the accession of Sneferu, the first ruler of the Fourth Dynasty.

THE FOURTH DYNASTY (c. 2620–2480)

Sneferu came to the throne about 2620. Perhaps benefiting from the mistakes of Huni, he built two huge pyramids at Dahshur. In one, the angle of inclination had to be changed during the course of construction. It started as fifty-four degrees, but after a time was changed to forty-two degrees. As a result, this has become known as the 'Bent Pyramid'. The reason for the change of angle is not known for sure, but two suggestions have been made. One, by Kurt Mendelssohn, is that design faults and poor workmanship made the pyramid unsafe, and that a lower angle of inclination was therefore necessary. The second suggestion for the change is that the pyramid simply needed to be finished in a hurry.

Unlike other pyramids, the Bent Pyramid had two separate entrances. One was in the middle of the north face, about twelve metres above the ground. The other was on the west face. Each led to a separate chamber.

Sneferu's other pyramid lay a kilometre and a half to the north. This is the so-called 'Red Pyramid'. Its builders were now more concerned about safety, so it had a very shallow angle of inclination (forty-three degrees instead of the later norm of fifty-two degrees). When it was finished, the Red Pyramid became the first complete pyramid in history.

These first pyramids were truly massive structures, each being only slightly smaller than Khufu's Great Pyramid at Giza. The Tura stone which encased the Bent Pyramid is still largely in place, making this the best preserved of all the pyramids.

KHUFU AND THE GREAT PYRAMID AT GIZA

The son and successor of Sneferu was Khufu (known to the Greeks as Cheops). It was he

Fig. 6.2 *The pyramids of Giza.*

who built the mightiest pyramid of all — the Great Pyramid at Giza. The construction of this gigantic edifice shows how the resources of the whole nation were organised and channelled with a single-minded purpose and efficiency that defies description.

More than two million stone blocks, each weighing about three tonnes, were used in the construction. Most were limestone, but some were granite. Thousands of workers were conscripted to cut the blocks from the quarry, ferry them to the site, and manipulate them into position. Theirs was a huge task, given the fact that they worked with the simplest of implements, had no draught animals and did not use the wheel. Despite all difficulties, they accomplished most of their assignment within the Pharaoh's reign of twenty-three years.

When it was finished, the pyramid covered an area of over five hectares and rose to a height of 146 metres. Perfectly square, its sides conformed to the four points of the compass. It was later designated as one of the seven wonders of the ancient world and is the only one still standing.

The tomb

Twice during the building of the pyramid Khufu enlarged the tomb's plan. This meant abandoning two previous burial chambers before the construction of the final one. On each occasion the position of the chamber was raised higher within the pyramid. The inside of the pyramid was criss-crossed by various corridors, passageways and airshafts, and these also were the product of engineering genius. After the body of Khufu had been laid to rest in the burial chamber, together with his treasures, the entrances were sealed by huge blocks of stone to prevent thieves breaking in. Although this kept grave-robbers at bay for a few hundred years, the tomb was eventually broken into and the treasure stolen.

Khufu was the only king to have his burial chamber deep within the pyramid itself, and not in an underground chamber below it. We don't know why this is, but it may be that by being buried high above ground level, he was seeking to be free from the influence of Osiris, god of the underworld. Khufu was apparently a very autocratic ruler and as such was criticised by Herodotus (see Document 6. 2 on page 118).

During Khufu's reign, increasing attention and honour was given to Re, the sun god. After Khufu's death, nine of the next twelve Pharaohs incorporated the name of Re in their titles. The priests of Re also became more important, and held that position of power till the end of the Fifth Dynasty.

KHAFRE

Khufu was succeeded by his son Djedefre (Redjedef), but the new king only reigned for nine years before he died. He was succeeded in turn by his younger brother Khafre (or Chephren to the Greeks). Khafre married his sister Khamerernebti and his niece Meresankh for dynastic purposes, but also many other women as well, by whom he raised a large family.

Like Khufu, Khafre also had grand ideas about his own importance, and built an enormous pyramid that was only slightly smaller than his father's. It was not, however, as well built. He constructed a great valley temple built of huge granite blocks, and filled it with large dark-green diorite statues of himself. The temple was connected to the pyramid by a long causeway.

Fig. 6.3 *The Sphinx at Giza.*

THE GREAT SPHINX

Near the causeway an enormous sphinx was carved from limestone. With the body of a lion and the head of a human, it was seventy-three metres long and twenty metres high. It was supposed to represent Harmakhis, a manifestation of their sun god, but the face was carved in the likeness of Khafre himself.

Both Khufu and Khafre expected much from their people. It is likely they strained the resources of the nation in demanding the construction of such gigantic edifices to commemorate their greatness.

MENKAURE

Menkaure (Mycerinus to the Greeks) was the son and successor of Khafre, and he has come down in history as a pious and just king who wanted to reverse the harsh policies of Khufu. Like the kings before him, he too built a large pyramid, but it is the smallest of the three great pyramids at Giza. It was never finished in his lifetime, and had it been, it would have been considerably more expensive, as he planned to encase it with polished red granite. His successor Shepseskaf did indeed finish the pyramid, but did not proceed with the granite casing.

Menkaure also planned an elaborate mortuary temple on the same scale as his pyramid, to be built of limestone blocks and covered in granite. However, Shepseskaf refused to spend so much money on the dead king, and compromised with a dingy structure of mud-bricks which did not last long.

Fig. 6.4 *Menkaure is shown here standing between the goddess Hathor on the right, and the goddess of the Jackal nome. What sort of a reputation did Menkaure enjoy?*

SHEPSESKAF

Shepseskaf was the last king of the Fourth Dynasty. It is possible that he was Menkaure's son-in-law, but we are not certain. He did not reign long, and with his death the Fourth Dynasty came to an end. Unlike his predecessors, he did not build a pyramid, but reverted to the mastaba form of tomb.

WRITING

Egyptian writing started during the First Dynasty, but developed appreciably during the Fourth Dynasty when proud rulers were anxious to record their achievements for posterity.

Fig. 6.5 *This is a good example of hieroglyphic writing, giving praise to King Sesostris I, at Karnak. The king's name is in a frame, or cartouche. What would be the difficulty in learning to write like this?*

The Egyptians got the *idea* of writing from Mesopotamia, but devised their own form, which was quite different from the cuneiform writing of the Mesopotamians. Egyptian writing was essentially pictorial, and was known as *hieroglyphics*, from the Greek word meaning 'sacred carving'. It consisted of some 700 characters: stylised drawings of birds, animals, humans and a variety of everyday objects. Originally, each hieroglyph stood for a whole word or idea. Later, some were used for a rebus effect, for example the symbol for 'bee' followed by the symbol for 'leaf' could

mean 'belief'. Again, twenty-four hieroglyphs were selected to represent certain consonants, and this was the closest the Egyptians got to an alphabet. Theirs was not a true alphabet because they they never chose symbols to represent the vowels.

Once the Egyptians started using papyrus sheets as writing material, they developed a new form of script which was easier to write down. This was *hieratic* or 'priestly' writing, and it was almost as old as hieroglyphics. At first it was written vertically, but later was written horizontally from right to left. Very much later, after about 650, another script evolved. This was the *demotic* or 'popular' form. This replaced hieratic for everyday use, but hieratic continued to be used by priests for the writing of religious material for several more centuries.

THE FIFTH DYNASTY
(c. 2480–2340)

The change from Fourth to Fifth Dynasty occurred about 2480. It marked significant changes in the development of both religion and government. In relation to religion, the Fifth Dynasty kings continued to give special honour to the sun god Re. They included the term 'Son of Re' in their official titles, and built many temples to honour the god. By the time of Unas, the last ruler of the dynasty, the idea was also developing that all men and women, regardless of rank, would be judged after death by Osiris. This gave a new dimension to Egyptian religion, and gave all people hope for a more fruitful life after death.

The Fifth Dynasty rulers built pyramids, but on a relatively minor scale when compared with their predecessors. Although small, the pyramids were well constructed and contained many relief carvings to show the exploits of the kings in their expeditions to seek booty in neighbouring lands. Many of the early kings

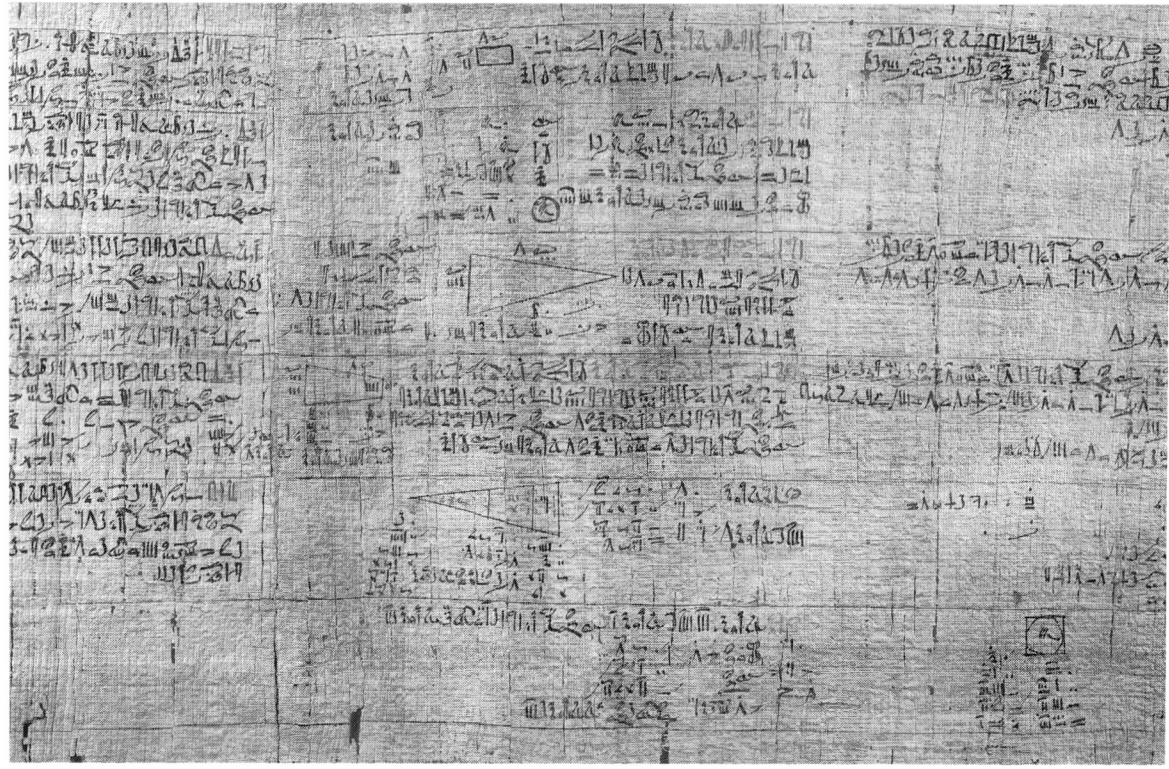

Fig. 6.6 *This is a section of the Rhind Mathematical Papyrus, dating from c. 1600 BC. Its subject matter deals with problems about triangles. Why did hieratic script replace hieroglyphics?*

built their pyramids at Abusir, so they would not be dwarfed by the huge pyramids at Giza. Indeed, Giza was never again used as a burial site. Six of the Fifth Dynasty monarchs also built special temples to Re in the Abusir region. These temples were generally very well built.

The style of government changed dramatically during the Fifth Dynasty. The Pharaohs began to lose their absolute predominance in government and were forced to concede much more freedom of action to the nobility and high officials. The royal house lost its right to fill the highest positions in the land, and central government became progressively weaker. This loss of power by the Pharaohs may have resulted from public disapproval of the burdens placed on them by the former

Pharaohs' demands for enormously expensive tombs.

PHARAOHS OF THE FIFTH DYNASTY

Userkaf (Weserkaf)

Userkaf was a descendant of Djedefre through his mother. Not a great deal is known about his reign, which is thought to have lasted for seven years. He was devoted to Re, and was the first Pharaoh to build a special temple to honour the sun. This was at Abu Gurab, some distance south of Giza. Most of his officials had previously served Shepseskaf, so the transition from the Fourth to the Fifth Dynasties was apparently peaceful.

Sahure

The son of Userkaf, Sahure reigned for twelve years. Reliefs from his pyramid and other buildings show that he sent a powerful expedition against the Libyans, and captured much booty from them. He also organised forays into Syria and Nubia. Information from the Palermo Stone shows that he traded widely with the land of Punt to the south. Today, no one knows for sure where Punt was, but it may have been part of the coastal region of modern Ethiopia and Somalia.

Neferirkare

Neferirkare is believed to have been Sahure's brother. Not a lot is known about him, including the length of his reign. We do know, however, that some of his high officials had magnificent tombs, so presumably his reign was a prosperous one.

Niuserre (Nyweserre)

Niuserre was another Pharaoh about whom not a great deal is known. He probably reigned for about eleven years; certainly long enough to build a pyramid at Abusir. Relief carvings here indicate that he had military victories over foreign enemies.

Niuserre apparently had some financial difficulties, for he took over the causeway and valley temple of his predecessor. This financial tightness is also indicated by the general lack of finish in the work that was done. Succeeding Pharoahs also apparently suffered from a similar shortage of funds.

Djedkare Isesi

We have already come upon Djedkare Isesi as the Pharaoh whose vizier Ptahhotpe was credited with the document *Installation of the Vizier*. He reigned for some twenty-eight years, and built a pyramid at Saqqara. He engaged in some battles with neighbouring peoples, and engaged in trading — apparently as far as central Africa.

Unas (Wenis)

The last Pharaoh of the Fifth Dynasty, Unas reigned for thirty years. He built a pyramid and funerary temple at Saqqara, and these have been preserved in a fairly good condition. They have been a valuable source of information for both historians and archaeologists.

THE SIXTH DYNASTY (c. 2340—2180)

The founder of the new dynasty was Teti, who came to the throne in about 2340. Surprisingly little is known about him, especially as he was the founder of a new dynasty. Manetho says he reigned for thirty years, but this lengthy period may be in doubt. Manetho also claimed that Teti was assassinated by one of his bodyguards. The decline in power of the Pharaoh, which commenced with the previous dynasty, continued in Teti's time. This is apparent when two of his viziers, Kagemni and Mereruka, built magnificent mastabas close to his own modest pyramid, demonstrating the increasing power and wealth of high officials.

Viziers were not the only officials to enlarge their power. Many governors became increasingly independent in the administration of their provinces. Although they acted in the Pharaoh's name, they were not backward in proclaiming their achievements and triumphs on the walls of their magnificent mastabas.

PHARAOHS OF THE SIXTH DYNASTY

Pepi I

The son of Teti, Pepi I reigned for at least twenty-five years. Much of the information we have about this Pharaoh comes from the biography of one of his high officials. According to this source, Pepi was involved in a number of military campaigns. Five were against a tribe of troublesome desert dwellers, and another against the people of Sheret (a place unknown today).

He built up an extensive trading link with Lebanon, and encouraged commerce with Punt. His agents went to all parts of Egypt to look for stone for his buildings, and much of this ended up at Saqqara, where he had his pyramid complex.

He had some problems with palace conspiracies against his rule, and towards the end of his life he may have shared the throne with his son Merenre in order to secure the lad's accession.

Merenre

Merenre came to the throne while still very young, and probably reigned no more than four years. During his short reign, he sent expeditions south into Africa to trade for ivory, ebony, incense and similar luxury items. He also sent officials abroad to locate fine granite to use in his pyramid and attendant buildings. When he died, he was succeeded by his half-brother Pepi II.

Pepi II

If we are to believe Manetho, Pepi II reigned for the incredible period of ninety-four years! He came to the throne at a very early age, and his mother acted as regent till he was old enough to exercise power in his own right. Throughout his long reign there were no challenges to his power, but he did have some problems pacifying several troublesome tribes from Nubia.

Because of the length of his reign, Pepi had at least two Heb-Sed festivals, and was able to build the largest of the pyramid complexes

erected by Sixth Dynasty kings. Soon after he died, the kingdom split and entered what is known as the First Intermediate Period.

THE FIRST INTERMEDIATE PERIOD (c. 2180–2040)

This was a period of great anarchy and turmoil for Egypt. Coinciding with the breakdown of the central authority was an apparent change in the weather. Rainfall patterns changed in many parts of Africa, with the result that the waters that fed the Nile were greatly depleted. The Nile diminished greatly, and both food and water became scarce. Famine and death stalked the land, and invaders, themselves driven by hunger, flocked to Egypt and added to the misery there. Against this disastrous background, provincial governors formed their own small independent states. They fought against their neighbours to extend their power, and the whole country was convulsed in a tragic civil war.

Historians have found it difficult to discover much about the Seventh Dynasty. Apparently some princely nobles attempted to exercise power from Memphis, but their area of effective control was small. The rulers of the Eighth Dynasty are also shadowy. They also were centred at Memphis, but they never controlled more than a small part of Upper Egypt.

NINTH AND TENTH DYNASTIES

Some move towards a reunification of Egypt eventually came from the governor of the Heracleopolitan nome, Akhtoy (or Achthoes). He was able to extend his power northwards to the Delta and southwards to Elephantine. His successors formed the Ninth Dynasty, but they were unable to build on Akhtoy's initial success.

The Tenth Dynasty was also centred on Heracleopolis. Its kings were well established in their own region, and they were strong enough to send expeditions to Syria. But their position was soon challenged by the rising power of Thebes to the south.

THEBES AND THE ELEVENTH DYNASTY

The final reunification of Egypt was the work of Mentuhotep II, ruler of Thebes. Coming to power in about 2080, he extended Theban power northwards and eventually defeated the rulers of Heracleopolis in about 2040. In thus reuniting Egypt, Mentuhotep II founded the Middle Kingdom.

SUMMARY OF MAIN EVENTS

c. 2686–2620	**Third Dynasty** Reign of Djoser; Step Pyramid built under the direction of Imhotep Reigns of Sekhemkhet and Huni
c. 2620–2480	**Fourth Dynasty** Sneferu builds the Bent Pyramid and the Red Pyramid Khufu builds the Great Pyramid at Giza Khafre also builds a mighty pyramid and the Sphinx Menkaure builds a lesser pyramid
c. 2480–2340	**Fifth Dynasty** Userkaf; Sahure; Neferirkare; Niuserre; Djedkare Isesi; Unas
c. 2340–2180	**Sixth Dynasty** Teti; Pepi I; Merenre; Pepi II
c. 2180–2040	**First Intermediate Period** Seventh to Tenth Dynasties Mentuhotep II unites Egypt; founds the Middle Kingdom

FEATURE

Egyptian embalming practices

Egyptians in the Old Kingdom period took great care to embalm their dead. They believed in a life after death, and maintained that the spirit of the departed would return to inhabit the body it had left at the time of death. The embalming was an elaborate and expensive process in the case of kings and nobles, but less complicated as the status of the deceased went down the social scale.

The best description of the embalming process is found in the writings of Hero-

dotus. He states that there were three separate processes, depending on the social status of the deceased. The most elaborate method is as follows.

The embalmers started by drawing out part of the brain with a crooked piece of iron inserted in the nostrils. The remainder was cleared by rinsing the brain cavity with drugs. The body was then cut open with a sharp knife and the internal organs such as the stomach, the liver, the lungs and the intestines taken out. The cavity

Fig. 6.7 *This picture shows the winged ba hovering over a mummy. The ba was a spirit, symbolising the physical survival of the dead. The mummy lies at rest on a lion-headed bier. Why did the Egyptians mummify their dead?*

was then filled with many kinds of spices and the wound sewn up. The body was then soaked in saltpetre or soda for forty days, then wrapped in fine linen bandages and smeared over with gum. It was then returned to the relatives who put it in a wooden case shaped in human form.

The organs were placed in separate jars called canopic jars which were either put in the four corners of the burial chamber, or placed together in a canopic chest. Each of these jars was guarded by a god. Dua-mutef the jackal-headed god guarded the stomach while the human-headed Imset protected the liver. Hapy the ape-headed god watched over the lungs and Qebekh-senuf the falcon-headed god took care of the intestines.

FEATURE

Pyramid complexes

A pyramid was never built as a single isolated building, but was always part of a complex of related buildings. Although each complex varied in some ways from another, it usually incorporated several common features. As an example, let us look at the complex built at Saqqara for King Djoser 's famous Step Pyramid (Fig. 6.8).

Note how the complex is surrounded by a high wall that runs for over 1. 6 kilometres and is ten metres high. It incorporates fourteen apparent gateways, but of these, only one is real. This is on the south corner of the east side.

On entering through the gate, the visitor passes along a corridor flanked by false columns till a large courtyard is reached. In this courtyard are two hoof-shaped markers. These mark the distance a king had to run during his coronation ceremony, and which he repeated during his Heb-Sed festival. At the southern end of this courtyard is a large tomb, with an adjacent chapel. The pyramid itself stands at the end of this courtyard, and behind that is the mortuary temple (see page 105).

On the east side of the complex are a number of buildings. They include chapels and store rooms and in their day contained many treasures kept for the use of the Pharaoh. A surprising thing about some of the buildings is that they have no interior. They are merely façades, for the insides are solid brickwork. Their purpose is described on page 105.

In most pyramid complexes there was

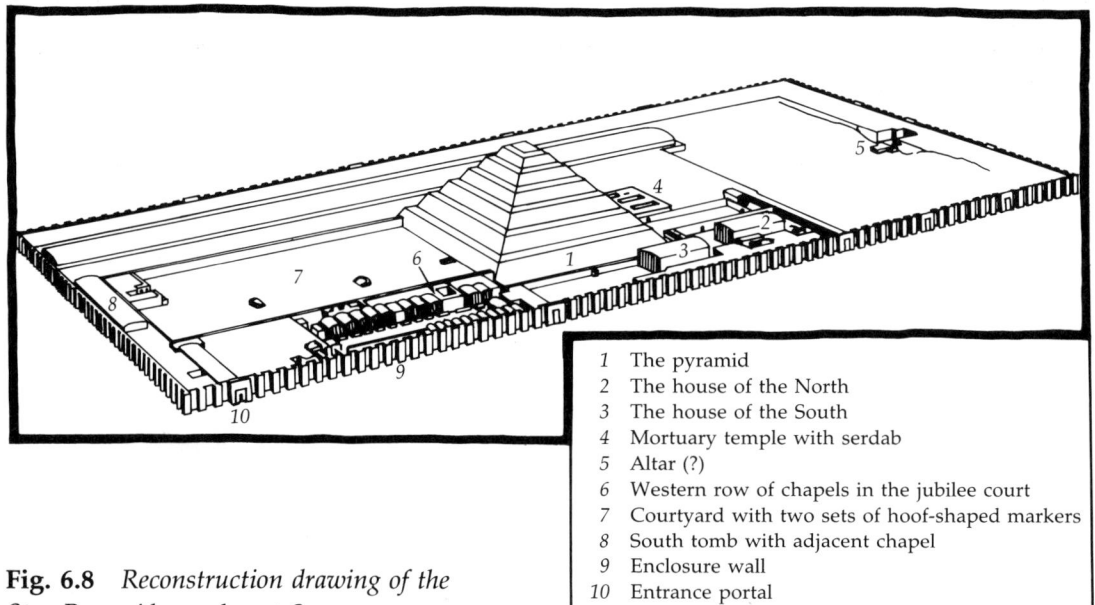

1 The pyramid
2 The house of the North
3 The house of the South
4 Mortuary temple with serdab
5 Altar (?)
6 Western row of chapels in the jubilee court
7 Courtyard with two sets of hoof-shaped markers
8 South tomb with adjacent chapel
9 Enclosure wall
10 Entrance portal

Fig. 6.8 *Reconstruction drawing of the Step Pyramid complex at Saqqara.*

provision for the high officials of the Pharaoh to have their mastabas. Here they were buried so they could serve their master in death as they did in life. These are particularly noticeable at the great pyramids at Giza.

In some pyramid complexes such as the Fifth Dynasty tombs at Abusir (see Fig. 6.9), there were long causeways linking the complexes with the Nile. At the river end of these causeways were elaborate valley temples.

Fig. 6.9   *Reconstruction drawing of the Fifth Dynasty pyramid field at Abusir.*

Document 6.1

The famous Installation of the Vizier *(see page 104) outlines some of the duties expected of a vizier. This extract advises how the vizier should take proper care in the administration of justice to the people.*

Do not make judgment improperly; God hates biased behaviour. This is an instruction, and you should act accordingly. See equally the man you know and the man you do not know, the man who is near you and the man who is far away. The magistrate who acts in accordance with this [instruction] will be successful here in this place. Do not dismiss a petitioner before you have considered his words. If there is a petitioner who makes petition to you, do not reject the things he has to say as being things already said. You should dismiss him only after you have let him hear the reasons why you dismiss him ... Do not lose your temper with a man improperly; lose your temper only in a matter worth losing your temper over. Establish fear of yourself that you may be feared; for a real magistrate is one who is feared ... He who will act justly before all people is the vizier. A man continues to exercise his office as long as he acts according to his commission. A man's reputation remains inasmuch as he does what he has been told to do. Do not act as you wish in matters about which the law is known. It is appropriate for arrogance that the Lord prefers fear to arrogance. You should therefore act according to what has been enjoined on you ...

T. G. H. James, *Pharaoh's People*, The Bodley Head, 1984, p. 61.

1   Indicate where the document says that a judge should be strictly impartial.

2   What are the vizier's obligations towards a petitioner? What code of conduct is he expected to abide by?

3   Under what circumstances is it permissible for a vizier to lose his temper?

4   What discretion does the vizier have in matters where the law is clear?

Document 6.2

In this extract, Herodotus passes judgment on Khufu (whom he calls Cheops) and gives some information about the building of the Great Pyramid. Herodotus actually visited the Great Pyramid, and saw its grandeur for himself.

Till the death of Rhampsinitus, the priests said, Egypt was excellently governed, and flourished greatly; but after him Cheops succeeded to the throne, and plunged into all manner of wickedness. He closed the temples, and forbade the Egyptians to offer sacrifice, compelling them instead to labour, one and all, in his service. Some were required to drag blocks of stone down to the Nile from the quarries in the Arabian range of hills; others received the blocks after they had been conveyed in boats across the river, and drew them to the range of hills called the Libyan. One hundred thousand men laboured constantly, and were relieved every three months by a fresh lot. It took ten years' oppression of the people to make the causeway for the conveyance of the stones, a work not much inferior, in my judgment, to the pyramid itself ... The pyramid itself was twenty years in building. It is a square, 244 metres each way, and the height the same, built entirely of polished stone, fitted together with the utmost care. The stones of which it is composed are none of them less than nine metres in length.

Herodotus, *The Persian Wars* II: 124, p. 179.

1 In what ways is Herodotus critical of Cheops?

2 Approximately how old was the Great Pyramid when Herodotus saw it? What changes would be evident today?

3 Why do you think the Egyptians were prepared to work so hard for Cheops for the twenty-year period?

4 What were the two sources of information that Herodotus used in compiling his report on Cheops and the Great Pyramid?

1 In what ways is the method of embalming using cedar-oil different from the method described on page 114?

2 Why were the Egyptians prepared to spend so much time and money on the embalming process?

3 What sort of health risks would an Egyptian embalmer be likely to undergo?

4 What other communities in the world have used mummification to preserve their dead?

Document 6.3

Here, Herodotus, after giving details about the most expensive method of embalming (see page 114), goes on to describe the two cheaper processes.

If persons wish to avoid expense, and choose the second process, the following is the method pursued: Syringes are filled with oil made from the cedar-tree, which is then, without any incision or disembowelling, injected into the bowel. The passage is stopped, and the body laid in natrum [saltpetre or soda] the prescribed number of days. At the end of the time the cedar-oil is allowed to make its escape; and such is its power that it brings with it the whole stomach and intestines in a liquid state. The natrum meanwhile has dissolved the flesh, and so nothing is left of the dead body but the skin and the bones. It is returned in this condition to the relatives, without any further trouble being bestowed upon it.

The third method of embalming, which is practised in the case of the poorer classes, is to clear out the intestines with a purge, and let the body lie in natrum the seventy days, after which it is at once given to those who come to fetch it away.

Herodotus, *The Persian Wars* II: 87, 88, p. 157.

Document 6.4

The end of the Old Kingdom meant troubled times for Egypt. The central power collapsed, and the various nomarchs fought among themselves for as much land as they could control. The conditions were so chaotic that they drew this lament from a man named Ipuwer.

Door keepers say: 'Let us go and plunder.' ... The laundryman refuses to carry his load ... Birdcatchers have marshaled the battle array ... Men of the Delta marshes carry shields ... A man regards his son as his enemy ... A man of character goes in mourning because of what has happened in the land ...

Why really, the face is pale. The bowman is ready. Robbery is everywhere. There is no man of yesterday ...

Why really, the Nile is in flood, but no one ploughs for himself, because every man says: 'We do not know what may happen throughout the land!'

Why really, women are dried up, and none can conceive. Khnum cannot fashion mortals because of the state of the land.

Why really, poor men have become the possessors of treasures. He who could not make himself a pair of sandals is now the possessor of riches ...

Why really, many dead are buried in

the river. The stream is a tomb, and the embalming place has really become the stream ...

Why really, the land spins round as a potter's wheel does. The robber is now the possessor of riches ...

Why really, the River is blood. If one drinks of it, one rejects it as human and thirsts for water.

Claudio Barocas, *Monuments of Civilization: Egypt*, Cassell, 1976, p. 50.

1 What is the overall picture of the conditions in Egypt at this time? How does Ipuwer make his point?

2 Quote passages to show that law and order have broken down.

3 How have the troubled times affected the lives of ordinary people? Explain how poor men have become possessors of treasures.

4 In what ways has the Nile become a river of blood? How was Egypt eventually rescued from this state of affairs?

CHECK THE FACTS

Choose the correct ending for each of these sentences from the words in brackets.

1 The term Pharaoh originally meant (son of Osiris, governor of a nome, great house, king's vizier).

2 The *Installations of the Vizier* was the work of (Ptahhotpe, Rekhmire, Djedkare Isesi, Djoser).

3 A provincial governor was called a (nomarch, vizier, Pharaoh, noble).

4 The architect and creator of the Step Pyramid was (Sanakht, Djoser, Sekhemkhet, Imhotep).

5 The first successful true pyramid was built at (Saqqara, Dashur, Meidum, Abusir).

6 This pyramid was built for (Huni, Djoser, Sneferu, Khufu).

7 The face of the Sphinx is supposed to be that of (Djedefre, Harmakhis, Khufu, Khafre).

8 The last form of Egyptian writing was called (demotic, hieratic, hieroglyphic, priestly).

9 The longest-reigning king in Egypt's history was (Pepi I, Pepi II, Menkaure, Unas).

10 The founder of the Middle Kingdom was (Manetho, Merenre, Niuserre, Mentuhotep II).

GENERAL QUESTIONS

1 Look at Fig. 6.1 on page 104 and Fig. 6.8 on page 116 and answer these questions. The first four can be answered in one or two sentences each, while the last needs a paragraph.

   a How were Egyptian kings buried before the Step Pyramid was built? How did the Step Pyramid's shape derive from these earlier tombs?

   b What was the Pyramid built of? In what way was this building material different from that which had been used previously for important buildings?

   c Why were some of the buildings in the complex completely solid, with only a façade of doors and windows?

   d What was the Heb-Sed festival, which was conducted in the southern courtyard?

   e Why did Djoser build such an imposing pyramid complex? What was the importance of the pyramid for future Egyptian kings?

2 Imagine you are a labourer who has been conscripted to work on the construction of Khufu's pyramid at Giza. Give an account of the difficulties you face every day in the

construction work. Express your ideas about the value of erecting such colossal edifices.

3 Write an account of Egyptian writing from the point of view of a scribe. Give some information about how the hieroglyphic script evolved, and detail the problems associated with learning to write it. Comment too on the introduction of hieratic and demotic script, and how they are currently being used.

4 You are an embalmer living in Egypt during the period of the Old Kingdom. Describe how you would embalm the body of a Pharaoh. What differences would there be if you were dealing with a poorer client? Explain why there is always such a steady demand for your services.

5 The following questions are all about the Pharaohs of the Fourth Dynasty. Answer each one with a paragraph.

a Who was the first king of this dynasty? What pyramids did he build, and in what ways were they different from the 'normal' pyramids that were built later? What models did he have to follow?

b What sort of king was Khufu? What evidences are there to suggest some clues about his personality? Say whether you agree with Herodotus' assessment of him, and why.

c In what ways was Khufu's pyramid different from all those which preceded or followed it?

d What were the building achievements of Khafre? What effects did his building programme and that of his father have on the nation?

e Why do you think Shepseskaf did not build himself a pyramid? List as many reasons as possible.

6 What factors led to the eventual collapse of the Old Kingdom and the introduction of the First Intermediate Period? What was life like during the latter period?

7
THE MIDDLE KINGDOM
(c. 2040–1786)

MENTUHOTEP II OF THEBES

Mentuhotep became King of Thebes in about 2061. His kingdom was in Upper Egypt, and extended from Aswan in the south to This in the north. An ancient city, This lay about 150 kilometres north of his capital of Thebes. At the time of his accession, Thebes had been engaged in a long warfare against the neighbouring kingdom to the north, based on Heracleopolis. In the fourteenth year of his reign, Mentuhotep launched an attack on his northern rivals, and after some twenty-five years finally defeated them.

In finally achieving control over a unified Egypt, Mentuhotep II established the Eleventh Dynasty. His new regime was generally welcomed by the people because a peaceful and settled life in a united country was obviously better than the horrors of unending civil war.

Achievements

Mentuhotep set about organising his new kingdom with great energy. He appointed many Thebans as new nomarchs, but in some cases allowed the previous nomarchs to retain their position provided they pledged their loyalty. Whatever their origin, he kept a tight rein on them all, and made them accountable to him personally. He made Thebes the new capital of Egypt, and appointed Thebans to the highest offices of the land.

Mentuhotep started a vigorous new building programme, and this provided a great bonus for quarry workers, builders and architects. He constructed temples and other public buildings all over Egypt, but naturally tended to concentrate on Upper Egypt. His largest building was his own temple and tomb complex at Deir el Bahri, near Thebes. Unfortunately, few of these buildings have survived to the present time.

Mentuhotep was very interested in trade, and sent an official named Akhtoy to look for metals such as copper, and precious stones such as turquoise and lapis lazuli. In order to protect his trade routes from unruly tribesmen, he was prepared to mount several campaigns. One was against the Bedouin in the Sinai. These tribesmen not only attacked trade caravans, but also raided the fertile lands of the Delta from time to time.

Nubia was of special interest to him. During the Intermediate Period, when Egypt had been weak and divided, Nubia had become powerful and threatening. To counteract this threat and to protect Egypt's southern borders, Mentuhotep occupied Nubia's northern regions.

Mentuhotep's reign titles

When Mentuhotep first became King of Thebes, he chose as his reign title the name Sankhibtawy (He Who Causes the Heart of the Two Lands to Live). Later, to celebrate his success in reuniting Egypt, he chose a new title: Smatowy (He Who Unites the Two Lands). He died after ruling for fifty-one years, and was given great honour as the king who saved Egypt from turmoil and division. During the New Kingdom period, his name was honourably linked with those of Menes (Narmer) and Ahmose — all being unifiers of a divided kingdom.

Some confusion exists in history books about kings bearing the name Mentuhotep. In this book he is called Mentuhotep II, because that was his title when he came to the throne of Thebes. Thus those who came after him were Mentuhotep III and IV etc. Some writers, however, prefer to label him Mentuhotep I, because he was the first king of that name to rule a united Egypt.

SANKHARE MENTUHOTEP III

The son of Mentuhotep II, Sankhkare Mentuhotep III came to the throne about 2010. Because his father had ruled for so long, he was middle-aged when he started his reign. The new king ruled for twelve years, and he showed a considerable interest in building, erecting many monuments in Upper Egypt. Because his reign was so short, his tomb did not get past the early stages of preparation before he died.

The highlight of his reign was the expedition of 3000 men that reopened the trans-desert route from Coptos to the Red Sea, from where trading missions were sent to Punt. Led by an official named Henenu, the expedition went by way of Wadi Hammamat, which was famous for its stone quarries.

Mentuhotep III was succeeded by Mentuhotep IV, whose rule was weak. It gave rise to a period of turmoil and confusion which only ended when Mentuhotep was challenged and overthrown by his vizier Amenemhet (or Amenemes) in 1991. In overthrowing the Pharaoh and taking his place, Amenemhet founded the Twelfth Dynasty.

TWELFTH DYNASTY: AMENEMHET I

The Pharaohs of the Twelfth Dynasty ushered in a period of great prosperity for Egypt. They re-established centralised authority, encouraged the spread of trade abroad, supported the arts and established the Theban god Amon as the national god of Egypt.

One of the early decisions of Amenemhet was to move the capital northwards from Thebes to a location some thirty kilometres south of Memphis. He did this because it was more central, and would make government of the country easier. The city was called Itj-towy (Seizer of the Two Lands) and is near the modern town of al-Lisht.

Since the rise of Amenemhet was due to the support of powerful governors, he had to reward them. He did so by re-establishing their former powers and privileges. However, in an effort to retain some control over their ambitions, he clearly defined their provincial boundaries and required them to raise troops on his behalf. Despite these precautions, some eventually became so powerful that they themselves became a threat to the royal house. This problem was later solved by the great Sesostris III (see page 128).

RELIGION

Because the Middle Kingdom Pharaohs originated in Thebes, they wanted to promote their local god Amon to a more exalted status. His worship thus became more important, and the priests of the god Re, who had been

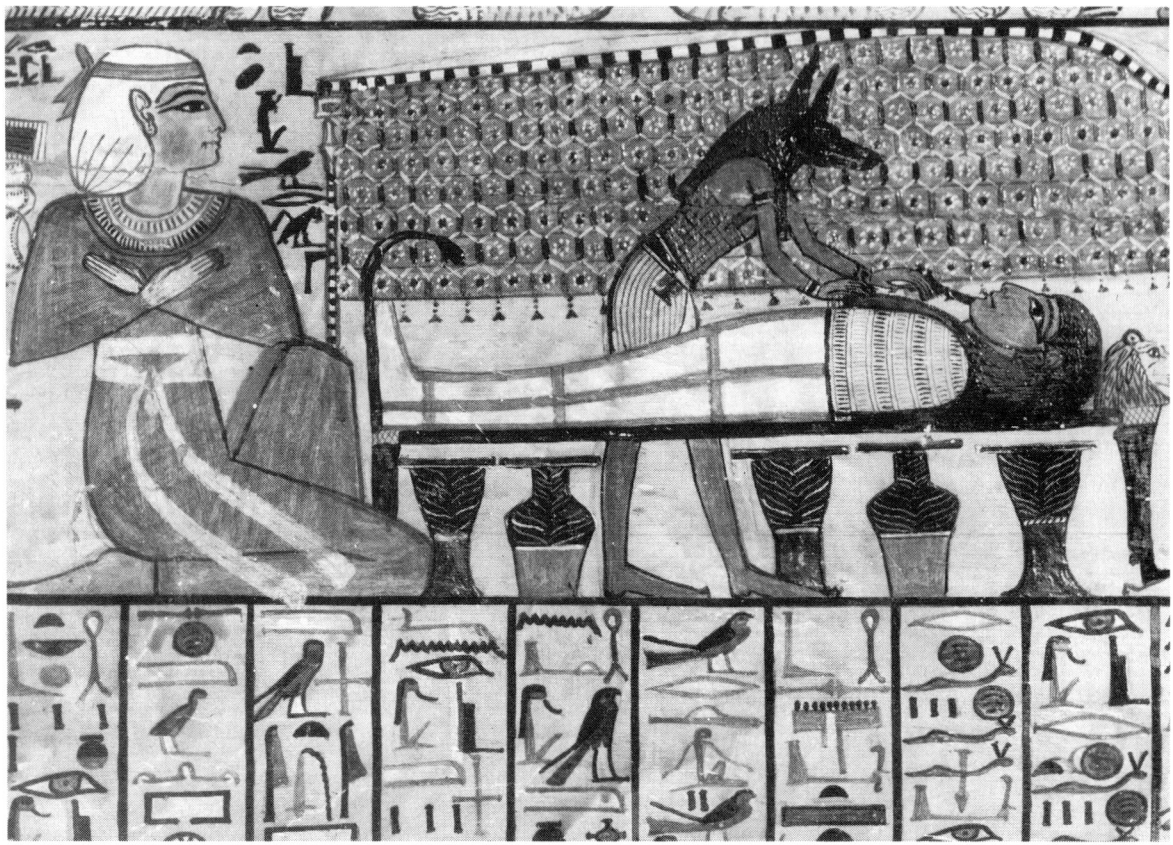

Fig. 7.1 *Here the jackal-headed god Anubis is shown performing a ceremony over a mummy. Anubis was the god of mummification, and assisted in the rites by which a dead man was admitted to the underworld. He wields the divine sceptre carried by kings and gods. What is the significance of Anubis' jackal head?*

dominant since the Fifth Dynasty, obliged the new rulers by merging the two gods as Amon-Re. This new emphasis on Amon was accepted without murmur by the people, as changes in religious ideas and practices had occurred since the earliest times.

The first Egyptians worshipped things in nature such as wind and water, trees and animals. They admired certain qualities found in animals, such as the ferocity of a lion, the strength of a crocodile, and the care of a cow for its calf. Because of this admiration, they first represented their gods in animal form. For example, Thoth, the god of learning and wisdom, was portrayed as an

ibis or a baboon, Anubis was represented by a jackal, and Horus took the form of a falcon.

Certain animals were associated with various gods, and so received honour. An ibis was kept at the temple of Thoth at Hermopolis, a cat representing the goddess of joy and love was kept at Bast, while a sacred bull, Apis, was lodged at Memphis. When they died, these animals were mummified just like the Pharaohs.

The Egyptians had an enormous respect for the sun, which they saw was necessary for life. They worshipped it as the god Re, and the main temple was situated at Heliopolis. Re was the first god to be worshipped throughout the whole land and he was always one of the most important gods of Egypt.

Gods in human form

As Egyptian civilisation progressed, the people began to worship gods in human form. Thoth, for example, was given a human body but he kept his ibis head. In the same way, Anubis was endowed with a human body while keeping a jackal head, and Horus got a man's body while retaining

Fig. 7.2 *Horus.*

his falcon's head. Still later, gods were given a complete human form. One of the first was Ptah, the god of craftsmen, whose main temple was at Memphis.

One of the most important gods was Osiris, lord of the after-life. He had an evil brother named Set, who was very jealous of Osiris. Set killed his brother, cut his body in bits and scattered them all over the world. Osiris' wife Isis searched for the parts, and brought Osiris back to life again. Later Horus, the son of Osiris and Isis, defeated Set and took away his powers. The Pharaohs were always identified with Horus. When he died, the Pharaoh became Osiris and ruled the underworld.

Amon was an invisible god who was present everywhere at once. Although he was sometimes represented as a ram, a goose or a snake, he was more often pictured as a crowned king. As we have seen, he was merged with the god Re during the Middle Kingdom.

THE ROLE OF THE PHARAOH

Although with the accession of Amenemhet the Pharaoh was once again the dominant political power in the land, this was because of each ruler's abilities and qualities rather than his divinity. The Pharaoh was still identified with the gods, and was known as the son of Amon-Re, but his continued dominance depended more on his personal capabilities than his supposed divine powers.

AMENEMHET'S FOREIGN POLICY

Amenemhet took a great interest in securing Egypt's defence and in increasing trade with foreign lands. To the south, he consolidated Egypt's hold on Nubia, and incorporated its northern region into Egypt as a province. The new territory was a valuable source of gold, and was much prized. As a means of securing it, Amenemhet placed several fortresses in the region of the Second Cataract.

Concern had been felt in the Delta too, because tribesmen from Palestine and Syria had infiltrated the region and caused trouble. Amenemhet responded by building a line of forts to keep out the intruders. Known as the 'Walls of the Ruler', the fortifications were a valuable asset for many years.

In the interests of promoting foreign trade, Amenemhet increased contact with the port of Byblos, and encouraged Egyptian ships to venture into the Aegean Sea. He also strengthened a trade route from Coptos on the Nile to the Red Sea from where trade missions went south to the land of Punt.

SESOSTRIS I (SENWOSRET)

After ruling for twenty years, Amenemhet made his son Sesostris co-ruler with himself in 1971, and this arrangement continued for the next ten years. Amenemhet's move was designed to ensure the smooth succession of his son and to remove the possibility of challenges from rival claimants. The worth of this move was well demonstrated when Amenemhet was assassinated while Sesostris was away fighting in Libya. On hearing of his father's death, Sesostris raced back to Egypt and using his authority as co-ruler, was able to assert his claim to the throne and foil the conspirators who had tried to usurp his position. The practice of having co-rulers persisted right through the duration of the Twelfth Dynasty and was very effective in maintaining political stability.

Sesostris as sole ruler

Early in his reign as sole ruler, Sesostris saw the need to consolidate his position against

any possible challenges. One way of doing this was by a propaganda exercise. He quickly gave widespread publicity to a document called *The Instructions of Amenemhet*. This was supposed to have been a letter from Amenemhet in which the right of Sesostris to succeed his father was stressed, together with a bitter condemnation of the conspirators. Modern research suggests that it may not have been written by Amenemhet, but perhaps by another writer acting on orders from Sesostris. Sesostris also distributed many copies of *The Story of Sinhue*. This was the story of a court official who had fled in fear after the assassination of Amenemhet. It was loud in its praises of Sesostris, and showed him in the best possible light.

Sesostris expands into Nubia

As sole ruler of his kingdom, Sesostris showed great drive and vigour and brought Egypt to the peak of its prosperity. Vitally concerned about Egypt's neighbours, he took a particular interest in Nubia. From a base at Elephantine (modern Aswan), he pushed deep into Nubia and built several forts at strategic points to keep a hold on the territory. He established the border at the Second Cataract, and built a strong fortress at Buhen. His interest in Nubia was twofold: to exploit the territory's minerals and safeguard the trade routes into southern Africa.

The nomarch of Elephantine was made responsible for administering the new conquests, and was ordered to send a steady supply of minerals to Egypt. These included gold, copper, amethysts and diorite. He also established a post at Kerma, from which trading expeditions were sent south into Africa.

Other areas of interest to Sesostris were Libya, Palestine and Syria. He sent at least one punitive expedition to Libya, with the result that Egypt was free from any threats from this region for the next 200 years. He also made important diplomatic contacts with Palestine and Syria, but to be quite secure, built a chain of forts across the Sinai.

Sesostris as a builder

On the home front, he initiated an extensive programme of public works which provided many opportunities for the building industry. Early in his reign he built a great new temple at Heliopolis, and continued to build all over Egypt. One of his last projects was to construct a large pyramid complex for himself at Lisht, a short distance from the capital. At Karnak in northern Thebes he built a temple to Amon, who by this time was beginning to gain prominence among the Egyptian gods.

Securing the succession

Two years before his death, Sesostris followed the example set by his father and made his son co-ruler. This was Amenemhet II, who succeeded to the throne peacefully on Sesostris' death c. 1929. Sesostris was very popular with his subjects, and he was worshipped as a god for centuries after his death.

AMENEMHET II

Amenemhet II had a peaceful reign of some thirty-four years, and did much to develop Egypt's trade abroad, especially with Syria and Punt. Many Egyptian works of art dating from Amenemhet's time (including several statues of the Pharaoh himself) have been found in Syria. Conversely, many Syrian and even Cretan items have been uncovered at a temple in Tawd (Upper Egypt). Towards the end of this reign he sent a large expedition to Punt, and this has been recorded on a black basalt stele erected at the port of departure. The expedition brought back many treasured articles including incense.

Amenemhet was keen to increase Egypt's supplies of gold and copper, and either led or sent expeditions to Nubia, Sinai and Kush to obtain them. In general he was very successful, and Egyptian artists had plenty of raw materials to fashion their works of art.

Amenemhet built his pyramid complex at Dashur. The pyramid had an outer casing of fine limestone, but had a core of rubble. It was surrounded by the tombs of his family. Elsewhere, in their respective nomes, many nomarchs built themselves fine tombs as well. This was a reflection of the importance of their role in keeping the kingdom peaceful and prosperous.

Three years before his death, Amenemhet made his son Sesostris II his co-ruler, thus following the pattern set by his predecessors.

SESOSTRIS II

Sesostris II ruled for about twenty years (c. 1897–1878), and was favoured with peaceful conditions. These allowed him to maintain Egypt's strong trading relations abroad and to start development of a great scheme to develop the Faiyum region.

As early as the first year of his reign, Sesostris sent a trading expedition to Punt, an event duly recorded on some rocks at the Red Sea port. He continued the development of goldmining in Nubia, and encouraged exploration for copper and amethysts. Palestine and Syria continued to be major trading partners, and the commercial deals were often strengthened by diplomatic marriages between the noble houses of the trading partners.

The Faiyum scheme

The Faiyum is a low-lying region just south of the apex of the Delta. At the time of Sesostris, much of it was covered by Lake Moeris, which received its water from a branch stream of the Nile. The marshy ground near the edges of the lake was far too wet to be of any use for growing food. Under Sesostris, a dam was built to regulate the flow of water into the lake. This flow was slowed down to such an extent that the formerly useless lakeside ground could now be used for crops. This reclamation project was very successful, and was later greatly enlarged by his grandson Amenemhet III.

Sesostris' pyramid complex

Sesostris built his pyramid complex at Lahun in the Faiyum region. The pyramid itself was built of solid rock and covered by a limestone casing which has long since been stripped away. An unusual feature of the pyramid was that the entrance to the tomb was on the southern rather than the northern side. It was surrounded by mud-brick mastabas covering the tombs of his immediate family. In one of these tombs, some beautiful jewellery was found belonging to one of the Pharaoh's daughters.

Not far from the pyramid complex was the town of Kahun which was specially built to house the servants of the mortuary temple. This town has been discovered in a fairly well-preserved condition, and has given archaeologists a valuable insight into the planning of Egyptian towns and what sort of lives the people led.

As the kingdom flourished under Sesostris, it attracted many visitors from other countries. Some came as traders, while others were artisans or even domestic servants. They all brought new ideas with them, and so Egypt was subject to foreign influences in a significant way.

SESOSTRIS III

Sesostris III, who ruled from 1878 to 1843, was the greatest ruler of the Twelfth Dynasty, and he started what was to be a golden age of Egyptian greatness. However, he had to deal

Fig. 7.3 *Sesostris III, greatest ruler of the Twelfth Dynasty. For what achievements is he famous?*

with two serious problems which not only challenged his own personal position, but that of the nation as a whole. The first problem concerned the position of the nomarchs; the second, the threat posed by an increasingly restless Nubia.

The nomarchs

During the reign of his predecessors, many of the nomarchs had become very powerful, especially those of Middle Egypt. They had received many privileges from the Pharaoh, and had built up important marriage alliances with the families of foreign rulers in Palestine and Syria. To show how exalted their positions were, they had built fine palaces and elaborate tombs, some even approaching the splendour of the Pharaoh himself.

About half way through his reign, it appears that Sesostris grew alarmed at this increase in provincial power, and saw it as a threat to his own position. Fearing a possible challenge, he moved decisively against his potential rivals. By means that are unclear, he suddenly stripped all the nomarchs of their power and abolished the provinces. In their place he divided the nation into three territorial departments. The first stretched from the Delta south to the capital, Itj-Towy. The second ran from the capital to Thebes, while the third included all the land south of Thebes. He created a hierarchy of officials for each region, and gave the vizier responsibility for overseeing the whole structure. By his actions, Sesostris made the nation's government highly centralised, and set the standard for future monarchs to keep a firm direct control over the nation's affairs.

Nubia

Soon after his accession, Sesostris was faced with a growing restlessness in Nubia. The tribes of western Nubia were interfering with Egyptian trade into southern Africa, and other Nubians were apparently planning an uprising against the Egyptian control of their northern territories. Sesostris personally led an expedition against them in the eighth year of his reign. To make the passage of his troops easier, he had a canal cut through the First Cataract at Elephantine. This allowed his warships and troop transports to progress much further south than usual, and appreciably helped his war effort. His campaign was a great success, and he repeated it with equal success on three other occasions over the next few years.

The Nubian forts

In an attempt to keep the Nubians in check, Sesostris strengthened three forts built by his predecessors, and constructed several new ones. These formed a network of defences which extended between the Second and the Third cataracts. Traders coming up from the south were allowed through the defended area until they came to Buhen. Here they sold their goods before returning to their homes.

Palestine

In addition to his concern about the threat from Nubia, Sesostris was also worried about the continuing infiltration of people from the Palestine region into Egypt. After his Nubian campaigns he led an army into Palestine, going as far as Shechem. He returned undefeated, but without any great victories or much booty. Still, the raid made the Palestinians think twice about any future infiltrations of Egyptian territory.

The tomb of Sesostris

Sesostris had a large pyramid built of mud-bricks at Dashur and encased it with a limestone cover. Surrounding it were the mastabas of his close family.

Herodotus wrote about Sesostris III, but confused his deeds with those of his predecessors of the same name and with Ramses II of the Nineteenth Dynasty. As a result, he made Sesostris a sort of super hero. These errors aside, Sesostris did achieve greatness in his own right.

AMENEMHET III

Amenemhet III succeeded his illustrious father Sesostris III in c. 1842, and ruled for forty-five years. His reign was a period of great prosperity, enhanced by peace both at home and abroad. One of his best-known contributions to the nation's prosperity was his devotion to the Faiyum reclamation project started by his grandfather Sesostris II.

The Faiyum reclamation scheme

Amenemhet devoted considerable time and energy into expanding the Faiyum project. He controlled the flow of water into Lake Moeris even more carefully than before, and as a result, brought an extra 62 000 hectares of fertile land into cultivation. This was watered by a series of new irrigation canals, and greatly increased the nation's food supply.

Amenemhet was so proud of his achievement in the Faiyum that he erected two huge statues of himself nearby. These were seen and written about by Herodotus when he visited Egypt. He also built his capital there. He called it Shedet, but it later became better known by its Greek name of Crocodilopolis (Crocodile City).

Trade and mining

Like his immediate predecessors, Amenemhet greatly encouraged trade with other countries. The main emphasis was with Palestine and Syria, and there is strong evidence that the trade extended to Crete as well. Numerous Egyptian artefacts have been found in all these places, confirming that a fairly vigorous trade existed.

Amenemhet was no less interested in mining than he was in trade. Most attention was given to the copper and turquoise mines of the Sinai, and the activity was so sustained that many miners and officials built permanent homes there.

Within Egypt itself there was great activity in limestone and granite quarrying, as there was such a demand for the products both for constructing buildings and making statues. Likewise, in Nubia, there was continuing interest in gold mining.

Amenhemet's pyramids

Amenemhet had two pyramids built. The first was at Dashur, and comprised a core of mud-bricks covered by a limestone casing. Although it was quite elaborate in construction, many scholars consider it was never used as a tomb, but rather as a cenotaph.

The second pyramid was at Harawa, and it was built along the same lines as the one at Dashur. It incorporated many ingenious

Fig. 7.4 *Head of Amenemhet III (?), c. 1850 BC. An example of Middle Kingdom portrait sculpture that is expressive of personality.*

features designed to prevent grave robbers from pillaging the tomb, but in time it was breached just as easily as its predecessors. Its mortuary temple was an enormous building measuring some 300 by 240 metres. It had so many rooms and corridors that it was a veritable maze. When he saw it, Herodotus was so astounded at its size and complexity that he called it 'the Labyrinth'. Unfortunately, only its foundations have survived to the present time.

The arts

During the time of Amenemhet, Egyptian art flourished in its many forms: sculpture, painting, handcrafts and literature. Many examples of sculpture have survived to the present. They show that the sculptors, in making statues both of Pharaohs and private individuals, were able to express their subjects' personalities effectively. Gone were the aloof and impersonal statues of the past.

Literature became more important than ever before, and many of the ancient Egyptian classics were written at this time. Great honour was given to literate men, and this inspired increasing numbers of people to learn the art of reading and writing.

At this period, the worship of Osiris was becoming more popular. Men and women of all social classes believed that through Osiris, they could look forward to a happy and fulfilling after-life.

THE SECOND INTERMEDIATE PERIOD (c. 1786–1567)

Soon after Amenemhet III died in about 1786, his successors began facing problems on two fronts. Firstly, the position of the vizier became ever more important, and this official tended to overshadow the Pharaohs who were supposed to be his master. A succession of weak kings then contributed substantially to a gradual breakdown of centralised government. The second problem involved the presence of a large number of foreigners in the eastern Delta. They had gradually infiltrated into the region from Syria and Palestine and had concentrated in tribal groups which tended to handle their own affairs and ignore any orders coming from the Egyptian government. They were eventually to be known to the Egyptians as Hyksos, meaning 'princes of foreign uplands' (from the Egyptian *hega-khase*).

THE HYKSOS DOMINATION

Although the kings of the Thirteenth Dynasty were able to maintain control of most of Egypt for about a hundred years, their power was obviously on the wane when the Hyksos occupied the fortress town of Avaris in the Delta in about 1720. From here they spread their area of influence and by about 1675 were in control of Memphis. Although retaining control of Memphis, the Hyksos made Avaris their capital and fortified it heavily. Memphis was the limit of their expansion southward, but it contributed to a general collapse of centralised power in Egypt. Once more Egypt fell into a state of chaos, with local rulers controlling their own regions as best they could.

The Hyksos kings found the Egyptian religion and culture very attractive, and tended to govern their new territories in the Egyptian manner. They took Egyptian names and according to some historians, founded the Fifteenth and Sixteenth Dynasties. But they also introduced into Egypt some ideas of their own. For example, they popularised the use of bronze instead of copper, and showed the value of the war chariot. Even weaving was improved when they demonstrated the advantages of a standing loom.

THE SEVENTEENTH DYNASTY

At the beginning of the sixteenth century before Christ, Egypt was effectively divided into three parts. To the north were the Hyksos, in control of all the land as far as Memphis. In the extreme south, the Nubians had pushed into Egypt and were intent on advancing further north along the Nile. Only in Middle Egypt was there an indigenous government, centred on Thebes. Its kings formed the Seventeenth Dynasty, and were probably descended from the monarchs of the Thirteenth Dynasty.

At first the Theban kings had to struggle hard merely to maintain their position against the hostile regimes to their north and south. Eventually, however, their strength improved, due in part to a growing national resentment of the Hyksos intruders and a desire to expel them from Egyptian lands. Fearful of the growing power of Thebes, the Hyksos king Apopi picked a quarrel with King Seqenere II and fighting broke out. No details are known about the outcome of the battle, but Seqenere was severely wounded, perhaps killed. Apparently neither side won a resounding victory, and an uneasy peace followed for several years.

When Seqenere's son Kamose became King of Thebes he determined to kick the Hyksos out of Egypt once and for all. He launched a surprise attack which caught Apopi off balance, and penetrated as far as Avaris. The Hyksos then recovered somewhat and salvaged their position, but they were seriously weakened. It was to be left to Kamose's younger brother and successor Ahmose to complete the final expulsion of the Hyksos. In so doing, Ahmose founded the Eighteenth Dynasty and ushered in the period of the New Kingdom.

SUMMARY OF MAIN EVENTS

c. 2040–1991	**ELEVENTH DYNASTY**
c. 2061	Mentuhotep II becomes King of Thebes
c. 2040	Mentuhotep II reunites Egypt; given great honour as the saviour of his country
c. 2010	Sankhare Mentuhotep III succeeds his father
c. 1998	Mentuhotep IV becomes king — a weak ruler

c. 1991–1786	**TWELFTH DYNASTY**
c. 1991–1962	**Rule of Amenemhet**
	Capital moved from Thebes to Itj-towy
	Nomarchs given considerable powers
	Amon made the national god of Egypt; Pharaoh known as the son of Amon-Re
	Expanded Egyptian territory, emphasised defence and encouraged foreign trade
c. 1971–1928	**Rule of Sesostris I**
	Conquered part of Nubia — exploited its minerals
	Freed Egypt from threats from Libya
	Made diplomatic and trade contacts with Palestine and Syria
c. 1929–1895	**Rule of Amenemhet II**
	Encouraged trade with Punt, Syria, Palestine
	Continued to exploit Nubian gold resources
c. 1897–1878	**Rule of Sesostris II**
	Continued emphasis on overseas trade
	Started land reclamation scheme in the Faiyum
c. 1878–1843	**Rule of Sesostris III**
	Introduced Egypt's golden age of greatness
	Curbed power of the nomarchs; centralised the government and strengthened the bureaucracy
	Crushed unrest in Nubia against Egyptian rule
	Raided Palestine to prevent infiltration of Egypt by Asiatic migrants
c. 1842–1797	**Rule of Amenemhet III**
	Greatly enlarged Faiyum reclamation project
	Encouraged trading and mining
	Sculpture, art, literature all flourished
	Built 'the Labyrinth' temple complex at Harawa
	Period of great prosperity for Egypt
c. 1786–1567	**Second Intermediate Period**
	Thirteenth Dynasty kings weak — challenged by foreign invaders in the Delta
	Hyksos kings govern Lower Egypt
	Seventeenth Dynasty kings expel the Hyksos

FEATURE

The Egyptian army

Throughout its long history, Egypt was in constant conflict with enemies of all kinds. Consequently, it had need for a large and well-trained army. In the earliest times, the army consisted entirely of infantry, but the Hyksos are believed to have introduced the horse and chariot into Egypt and thus widened the Egyptians' fighting capacity.

Soldiers from the standing army entered service at an early age and were subjected to a severe discipline during their basic training. Although at first required to live in barracks, they were later allowed to live with their families between campaigns. Most soldiers were native-born Egyptians, but there were usually many foreigners serving too. Of these, some were mercenaries, while others were prisoners of war who were conscripted into the Egyptian forces.

Life in the army was tough. One ancient scribe wrote about conditions in these terms: 'He [the soldier] is awakened while there is still an hour for sleeping. He is driven like a jackass and he works until the sun sets beneath its darkness of night. He hungers and his belly aches. He is dead while he lives.'

The main weapon used by the Egyptians was the bow and arrow. The archers used bows of wood and animal horn and carried quivers of twenty to thirty arrows each. Although most moved on foot, some were carried on war chariots which made them highly mobile and very effective in attack. In their battles with enemy forces, the Egyptian archers wreaked havoc with their arrows before their comrades engaged the enemy hand to hand with spears, scimitars, axes and daggers.

Upper class youths usually joined the elite chariot corps, which promised better conditions. Those with plenty of money often bought their own chariots rather than relying on government issue.

In times of war, all classes of society were expected to contribute men for battle. Even the Pharaoh himself went to the front.

FEATURE

Temples and priests

Temples were extremely important to the Egyptians. They were not like our churches, where worshippers gather for regular services, but were seen as the home of a god, and a place where ceremonies were conducted every day to honour that god. Gods and goddesses were believed to need food, clothing and shelter, and these had to be provided by the priests who served in the temple.

Fig. 7.5 shows a typical temple of the style built during the New Kingdom period. A worshipper would approach the temple through an avenue of assorted statues of animals, and then pass between two obelisks and huge statues of the Pharaoh who had built the temple. Entrance was through an enormous gateway called a pylon. One passed through the entrance into a large courtyard, which was often enclosed on several sides by columns. This was as far as an ordinary member of the public could go.

Only a privileged few could enter the hypostyle hall, noted for the massive columns which supported the roof and which took up much of the space of the hall. The sanctuary itself was reserved strictly for the Pharaoh and the chief priests.

The priests followed a set ritual every day. They arose at dawn and purified themselves by bathing in a sacred pool. Then after crossing the courtyard, they entered the temple. Once inside, the chief priest proceeded to the sanctuary where the god (in the form of a statue) was kept. The priest purified the air with incense, then removed the god's clothes and washed its body. Then he put on fresh garments and returned it to its place. After providing it with fresh food and drink, he closed the sanctuary door.

On special occasions the god was taken from his sanctuary and, accompanied by a whole throng of priests and followers, was

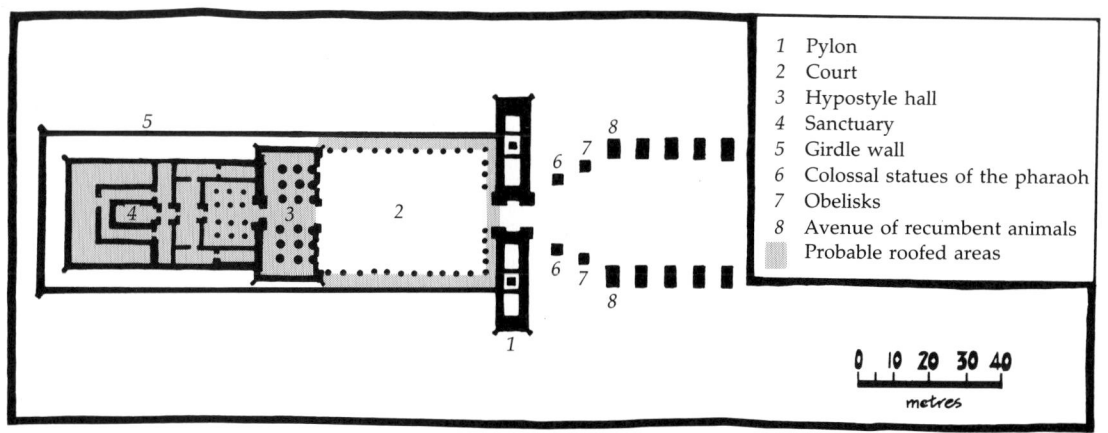

Fig. 7.5 *Plan of a typical pylon temple.*

paraded through the surrounding country-side. At such times the people were encouraged to watch the procession and to enjoy the colourful parade. The most spectacular festival was the one held at Karnak to honour Amon during the time of the flood. He was taken from his own temple to another not far away, and was away from home for about a month.

The priests held an honoured position in society. Many became priests because it was the family profession, but others joined from other occupations. Within the priesthood itself there was a strict hierarchy. The chief priests invariably came from the noblest families and their task was to attend to the personal needs of the god. Priests of lower rank were scholars, astrologers, scribes, musicians or even supervisors of temple building construction.

Document 7.1

This document is an extract from a report written by Henenu, an overseer of the expedition Sankhare Mentuhotep III sent to the Red Sea (see page 123).

My lord ... sent me to despatch a ship to Punt to bring him fresh myrrh from the chiefs over the desert ... Then I went forth from Coptos upon the road, which his majesty commanded me. There was with me an army of the South from [the name is blank] of the Oxyrrhyncus nome ... as far as Gebelen ... The army cleared the way before [us] , overthrowing those hostile toward the king, the hunters and the children of the highlands were posted as the protection of my limbs ...

I went forth with an army of 3000 men. I made the road a river and the desert a stretch of field, for I gave a leathern bottle, a carrying pole, two jars of water and twenty loaves to each one among them every day. The asses were laden with sandals ...

Now, I made twelve wells in the bush and two wells in Idehet, 20 cubits in one and 31 cubits in the other. I made another at Iheteb, 20 by 20 cubits on each side ...

Then I reached the Red Sea; then I made this ship, and I despatched it with everything, when I had made a sacrificial offering [to the gods] of cattle, bulls and ibexes.

Now, after my return from the Red Sea, I executed the command of his majesty, and I brought for him all the gifts, which I had found in the region of the God's Land. I returned through the valley of Hammamat, I brought for him majestic blocks [of stone] for statues belonging to the temple. Never was brought down the like thereof for the king's court; never was done the like of this by any king's companion sent out since the time of the god. I did this for the majesty of my lord because he so much loved me.

1 What evidences are there to show that Henenu was an important person?
2 Show what preparations were made to ensure that the expedition was a success.
3 Why do you think 3000 men were sent on such an expedition? What duties do you think may have been required of them?
4 What method do you think may have been used to transport the heavy blocks of stone back to the king?

Document 7.2

Fig. 7.6 shows a nobleman and his wife offering gifts to Osiris. This picture was found inside a tomb and was probably painted while the people were still alive.

1 What is the significance of the god being Osiris on this occasion? Would not another god have been just as significant?
2 If you had not have been told the identity of this god, could you have identified him? What is there about him that gives clues as to who he is?
3 Why were food and other gifts presented to the god? What items can you identify here?
4 What sort of writing is shown here? What sort of message is it likely to depict? In what way was this early Egyptian writing later changed?

Document 7.3

Early in his reign, Sesostris III mounted no less than four successful campaigns against the Nubians, who were becoming increasingly troublesome. On one of these campaigns, he left behind a

Fig. 7.6 *Homage to Osiris.*

stele at Semneh to commemorate his victory and to mark the new southern border. Here is its text:

Year 16, third month of the second season, occurred his majesty's making the southern boundary as far as Heh. I have made my boundary beyond that of my fathers; I have increased that which was bequeathed to me. I am a king who speaks and executes; that which my heart conceives is that which comes to pass by my hand; one who is eager to possess, and powerful, not allowing a matter to sleep in his heart, attacking him who attacks, silent in a matter, or answering a matter according to that which is in it; since, if one is silent after attack, it strengthens the heart of the enemy. Valiance is eagerness, cowardice is to slink back; he is truly a craven who is repelled upon his border;

since the Nubian hearkens to the mouth; it is answering him which drives him back; when one is eager against him, he turns his back; when one slinks back, he begins to be eager. But they are not a people of might, they are poor and broken in heart.

I captured their women, I carried off their subjects, went forth to their wells, smote their bulls; I reaped their grain, and set fire thereto. I swear as my father lives for me, I speak its truth, without a lie therein, coming out of my mouth.

J.H. Breasted, *Ancient Records of Egypt*, University of Chicago Press, 1906, pp. 295–6.

1 What *was* the boundary bequeathed to Sesostris III by his predecessors? Who had advanced into Nubia before him?

2 Judging by the words on this stele, what is your opinion of Sesostris' character?

3 Why was Nubia so important to Egypt? What policy has Sesostris adopted in relation to the Nubians?

4 What is the opinion of Sesostris about the Nubians? Does such an assessment heighten or diminish his victory over them?

Document 7.4

Herodotus visited the pyramid of Amenemhet III at Harawa and was astounded by the size of the mortuary temple there. In admiration he called it 'the Labyrinth', and described it as follows.

To bind themselves yet more closely together, it seemed good to them to have a common monument. In pursuance of this resolution they made the Labyrinth which lies a little above lake Moeris, in the neighbourhood of the place called the city of Crocodiles. I visited this place, and found it to surpass description; for if all the walls and other great works of the Greeks could be put together in one, they would not equal, either for labour or expense, this Labyrinth; and yet the temple of Ephasus is a building worthy of note, and so is the temple of Samos. The pyramids likewise surpass description, and are severally equal to a number of the greatest works of the Greeks, but the Labyrinth surpasses the pyramids. It has twelve courts, all of them roofed, with gates exactly opposite to one another, six looking to the north, and six to the south. A single wall surrounds the entire building. There are two different sorts of chambers throughout — half under ground, half above ground, the latter built upon the former; the whole number of these chambers is 3000, 1500 of each kind. The upper chambers I myself passed through and saw, and what I say concerning them is from my own observation; of the underground chambers I can only speak from report: for the keepers of the building could not be got to show them, since they contained (as they said) the sepulchres of the kings who built the Labyrinth, and also those of the sacred crocodiles . . . The upper chambers, however, I saw with my own eyes, and found them to excel all other human productions; for the passages through the houses, and the varied windings of the paths across the courts, excited me with infinite admiration, as I passed from the courts into chambers, and from the chambers into colonnades, and from the colonnades into fresh houses, and again from these into courts unseen before. The roof was throughout of stone, like the walls; and the walls were covered all over with figures; every court was surrounded with a colonnade, which was built of white stones exquisitely fitted together. At the corner of the Labyrinth stands a pyramid, 73 metres high, with large figures engraved on it; which is entered by a subterranean passage.

Herodotus, *The Persian Wars* II: 148, pp. 191, 192.

1 According to Herodotus, why was the Labyrinth built? How does his belief tie in with modern research?

2 What is Herodotus' opinion of the Labyrinth? With what other buildings does he compare it?

3 Why must we credit Herodotus with an accurate description of the Labyrinth? Why did he choose to call it by such a name?

4 What were the main features of the Labyrinth, and for what purposes would they have been used?

CHECK THE FACTS

Rearrange the following events so that they are in chronological order.

- The powers of the nomarchs abolished
- Sesostris I exploits the minerals of Nubia
- The Hyksos seize control of part of Egypt
- Amenemhet I makes Itj-towy the new capital of Egypt
- Mentuhotep II of Thebes reunites Egypt
- Kamose defeats the Hyksos and weakens their position
- Amenemhet III completes the Faiyum project
- Sankhare Mentuhotep III sends a large expedition to Punt
- The Walls of the Ruler are built to prevent foreign inflitration into Egypt
- The Faiyum reclamation project started

GENERAL QUESTIONS

1   Study Fig. 7.7 carefully, then answer the following questions. The first four can be done in one or two sentences each. Write a paragraph to answer the last.

   a   Which part of the temple would have been built first? What were the later additions? Explain your answer.

   b   Why did various Pharaohs build additions to the temple?

   c   Into what parts of the temple could the general public go? What parts were reserved for the priests?

   d   What was the purpose of having such a temple? What ceremonies were performed here?

   e   What various functions did priests perform in the temple? What part did they play in Egyptian society?

2   Imagine you are about to set out on the large expedition that Sankhare Mentuhotep III sent to Punt. Write an account of your exploits, mentioning such points as:

   a   who is coming on the expedition and what their functions are

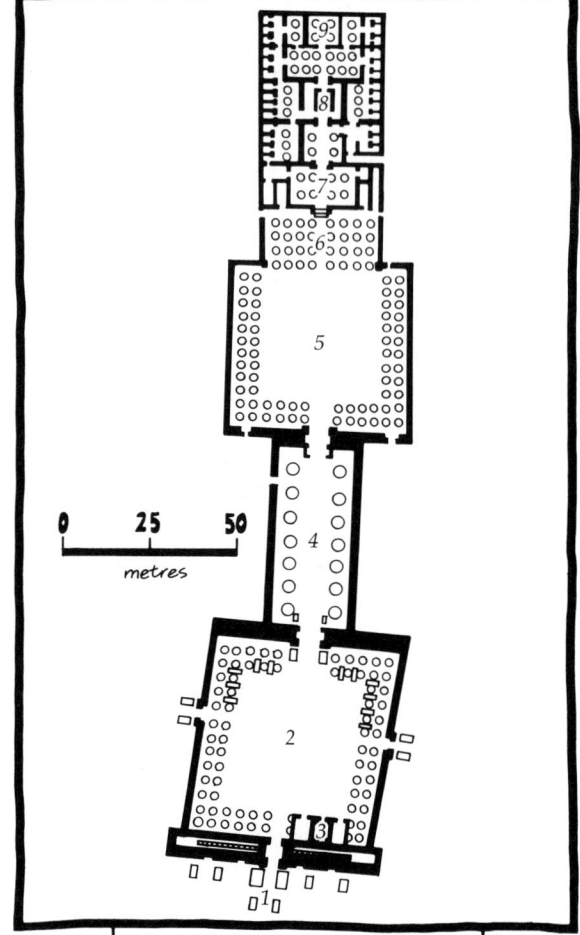

1   Entrance
2   Courtyard of Ramses II
3   Chapels of Thutmose III
4   Colonnade of Amenhotep III
5   Courtyard of Amenhotep III
6   Vestibule
7   Hypostyle hall
8   Sanctuary of the Sacred boat
9   Sanctuary

Fig. 7.7   *Plan of the Temple of Amon at Thebes, built during the New Kingdom.*

   b   the goods you expect to get
   c   the trading goods you will take with you
   d   the difficulties of travelling across deserts
   e   the dangers of sea travel

f the dangers of passing through hostile territory

3 Which kings showed an interest in Nubia, and what were their individual achievements in this region? Why was Nubia considered so important to Egypt? Give at least three reasons.

4 Both Mentuhotep II and Amenemhet I started new dynasties, and as such were very important in Egypt's history. Consider the achievements of each Pharaoh, and say which one, in your opinion, made the greater contribution to the nation. Give good reasons for your choice.

5 The following questions are based on the careers of Sesostris III and Amenemhet III. Answer each one with a paragraph.

a Why did Sesostris limit the powers of the nomarchs? How did he subsequently reorganise the government of the kingdom?

b What were the main aims of Sesostris' foreign policy? How did he achieve those aims?

c How did Amenemhet's land reclamation programme improve on that of his grandfather Sesostris II?

d What were Amenemhet's achievements in the fields of overseas trade, and mining?

e How did Amenemhet's reign affect the artistic culture of Egypt?

6 Do you agree or disagree with the statement 'The Twelfth Dynasty was generally a period of great prosperity for Egypt'? Write an essay to outline your reasons. Give an indication of how the dynasty finally went into decline.

8
THE NEW KINGDOM
PART 1 (c. 1570–1379)

THE EIGHTEENTH DYNASTY
AHMOSE

During the Eighteenth Dynasty, which lasted for 200 years, Egypt reached the peak of its power and glory. Basing their magnificent capital at Thebes, its Pharaohs launched into a series of audacious foreign adventures which created an extensive and prosperous empire.

The founder of the dynasty was Ahmose, who ruled from c. 1570 to 1546. Ahmose had as his first priority the expulsion of the Hyksos, whose position had already been weakened by his older brother Kamose. He started by defeating the Hyksos' allies in Middle Egypt, and capturing Memphis. Then he led a waterborne attack against the Hyksos capital of Avaris in the eastern Delta, and finally captured it after a siege. From there he pursued the fleeing Hyksos into Palestine, where they had another fortress, Sharuhen. He besieged this in turn, and the city finally fell after three years. Most of the survivors were given to his officers and soldiers as slaves, and the Hyksos were never again a threat to Egypt.

Nubia

Ahmose had also to contend with the Nubians, who had taken advantage of Egypt's weakness to seize their independence. With a powerful force he pushed them back to the Second Cataract, where he built a new temple at the old fortress of Buhen (modern Wadi Halfa). This campaign regained the lost Egyptian territories. To administer these territories, he created a new office: Overseer of Southern Foreign Lands. The overseer was second only to the vizier in importance, and was directly responsible to the king for the defence of the region and the collecting of tribute.

Administration

Ahmose's military successes influenced most formerly independent nobles to throw in their lot with him and give him their support. Those who did were well rewarded. So too was the army. Its victorious officers and men received much booty, and their morale grew immensely. A career in the new and well-equipped army soon became an attractive proposition to members of both the nobility and the middle class. The army thus became a professional and highly trained organis-ation, with a great deal of prestige. Ironically, much of its success came about because of the weapons and tactics copied from the Hyksos.

Anxious to restore the prosperity of Egypt, Ahmose reopened the copper mines at Sinai

Fig. 8.1 *This picture shows workmen clearing the Middle Kingdom fortress at Buhen. It was near here that Ahmose defeated the Nubians, and built a new temple. What was the importance of Nubia to Egypt?*

and resumed trade with the cities on the Syrian coast. He restored neglected temples, built chapels for his family and planned ever more ambitious projects for the glory of the nation.

Sister-marriage

Ahmose followed a tradition started during the Seventeenth Dynasty by marrying his sister Ahmose-Nofretari. This was to ensure the purity of the royal line and to emphasise the idea of divine kingship. She received the title of God's Wife of Amon, and was given great honour. The practice of brother-sister marriages only lasted for the first two reigns of the dynasty.

THE BUREAUCRACY

The bureaucracy of the early New Kingdom Pharaohs followed that of the Middle Kingdom, with the vizier still being the chief official of the kingdom. After a time, governmental affairs became so complex that the Pharaohs had to appoint two viziers – one for Lower and one for Upper Egypt.

To administer the affairs of government, many scribes were needed, and there was a keen demand by families to have their sons educated and go into government service. It is interesting to note that people trained as priests were often given government appointments and vice versa. Although many government posts were hereditary early in the reign, the Pharaoh gradually moved away from this practice, making appointments on merit rather than through family background. Many of the new appointees were army officers who had come to the Pharaoh's notice by distinguished service during military campaigns. Their promotion meant the decline of families which had formerly monopolised government appointments.

AMENHOTEP I

Also known as Amenophis, Amenhotep I succeeded his father Ahmose, ruling from c. 1546 to 1526. Eager to widen Egypt's boundaries, he began a programme of expansion which led to the start of the Egyptian empire. His first campaign was against the Nubians. He defeated them conclusively, and made the whole of Nubia an Egyptian province. To consolidate the Egyptian position, he brought in Egyptian colonists and appointed a viceroy with the title of 'King's Son of Kush'. Encouraged by his success in Nubia, he launched a new attack into Palestine and Syria and pushed as far east as the Euphrates. He won victory after victory and came home laden with the spoils of war.

The incoming booty gave a great boost to the national economy. Huge sums were spent in building temples and monuments to thank Amon-Re for his help in securing the national victories. This helped many thousands of workers and led to a general state of prosperity in the land. Unfortunately, there is little remaining of Amenhotep's grand building programme today. This is because later rulers plundered his buildings for materials for their own constructions.

We are not sure where Amenhotep was buried. It may have been in the Valley of the Tombs of the Kings, but there is no clear evidence of this.

THUTMOSE I

Sometimes also known as Thothmes, Thutmose succeeded Amenhotep as Pharaoh about 1525. Thutmose was not of royal blood, but had been a successful general and was Amenhotep's son-in-law. Like his predecessor, the new Pharaoh was keen to expand Egypt's borders. In the second year of his reign he pushed deep into Nubia and went past the Fourth Cataract, setting up a new boundary at Kanisa Kurgus. To secure his gains, he built several new forts in the conquered territories. He made a repeat attack in the next year, and on this occasion cleared the canal that Sesostris III had built at Elephantine. This had become clogged with rocks over the years and was no longer navigable.

Following his success in Nubia, Thutmose turned north and stormed through Syria. He crossed the Euphrates and won a great victory over the Mitanni at Carchemish, where he erected a victory stele. Although his reign was short, ending in 1512, he added appreciably to the Egyptian domains.

Thutmose as a builder

Thutmose was a great builder. He completely renovated the Middle Kingdom temple of Amon at Thebes and added important extensions as well. The end result was a style that became the standard for New Kingdom temples.

Thutmose refused to build a pyramid, and introduced the rock-cut tomb as a more secure form of burial for Pharaohs. Thereafter, with the exception of Akhenaton (see page 161), all New Kingdom rulers were buried in hidden tombs in the Valley of the Tombs of

Fig. 8.2 *An early photograph of the Valley of the Kings. Note the extremely desolate nature of the terrain in which the tombs were located. Why did the Pharaohs choose such a dismal location?*

the Kings near Thebes. Separated from the tombs but not far distant were the mortuary temples, devoted to the service of the dead Pharaoh. In these temples, priests performed daily funerary rites, and made offerings to the dead king's *ka* (protective spirit). The services and offerings were supposed to go on forever. Mortuary temples were a feature of Old and Middle Kingdoms also, and were located close to the pyramid (see page 155).

THUTMOSE II

The son of Thutmose I by a lesser wife, Thutmose II married his half-sister Hatshepsut to strengthen his claim to the throne. In 1512, the first year of his reign, there was a serious uprising against Egypt in Nubia. Thutmose sent a strong force to put down the rebels,

and it acted with great ferocity in putting down the rebellion. Most of the Nubian men were killed, although one prince was brought back to Egypt, presumably to educate him in Egyptian ways and later send him back as a friendly and pliable ruler of the region.

Thutmose also had problems in southern Palestine, where some Bedouin were in revolt. He sent another force there, and defeated his enemies. A considerable number of slaves were brought back as a result of this campaign.

Apart from the Nubian and Palestinian campaigns, little else is known about the reign of Thutmose. There is even some doubt as to the length of his reign. Although 1504 is traditionally given as his final year, there is some evidence to suggest that the real date may have been 1490.

QUEEN HATSHEPSUT

When he died, Thutmose had a daughter by Hatshepsut and a ten-year-old son (later to become Thutmose III) by a lesser wife. The boy was too young to rule, so his stepmother Hatshepsut at first acted as regent in his place. After about a year, however, she had herself crowned as Pharaoh (c. 1503), and thereafter exercised the full powers of a monarch in her own right until her death some twenty years later. She always maintained that she had every right to do this, as she was the daughter of a king. She was aided in her seizure of power by a group of loyal and influential officials, chief of whom was Senenmut. The young Thutmose was made a priest of Amon, and kept in the background. He had to bide his time before he could finally assert his own authority.

Hatshepsut was a remarkable woman. She was determined to rule despite her sex, and many statues show her dressed as a man. Sometimes she was even depicted wearing the traditional false beard of the Pharaoh.

Hatshepsut at war

Although Hatshepsut is generally portrayed as being devoted to peace, there is evidence to suggest that she was involved in several campaigns. Inscriptions on the walls of her famous temple at Deir el-Bahri tell of one campaign against the Nubians and another against the Asiatics of Palestine. Other sources reveal that Hatshepsut may well have personally led two separate campaigns into Nubia, each one being highly successful.

Trade

Although apparently forced into some military campaigns, Hatshepsut was more interested in the affairs of peace, particularly trade. She sent a large trading expedition to Punt which returned with a fabulous cargo of gold, ebony, animal skins, baboons, pro-cessed myrrh and living myrrh trees. These items, together with large quantities of tribute from Asia, Nubia and Libya, brought a dazzling splendour to her reign.

Hatshepsut as builder

Hatshepsut completed an extensive building programme, largely dedicated to honour Amon-Re. Among her achievements were the restoration of the damages done to public buildings by the Hyksos kings, and the renovation of her father's hall at Karnak, where she installed four huge obelisks (each thirty metres tall) and added a chapel. At Beni-Hassan in Middle Egypt she built a rock-cut temple known by its Greek name of Speos Artemidos (the Shrine of Artemis).

By far the best known of all her works was the magnificent mortuary temple at Deir el-Bahri, designed and built by Senenmut. Built in three colonnaded terraces connected by ramps, the temple is a masterpiece of Egyptian architecture. It was decorated with some 200 statues, and its walls covered with reliefs telling about her birth, coronation and great deeds. Splendid gardens of exotic plants adorned the terraces, and the whole complex was a delight to behold.

There is an interesting story connected with this temple about the later downfall of Senenmut from Hatshepsut's favour. According to this tale, he had several small images of himself carved in unobtrusive places on some of the walls, presumably so he could share the queen's eternal blessedness. When Hatshepsut discovered his impudence, she dismissed him, and wrecked the tomb he had prepared for himself. This story lacks verification, and Senenmut may well have fallen for other reasons.

Hatshepsut in decline

Towards the end of her reign, Hatshepsut's position started to weaken in relation to Thutmose. As her supporters grew older and

Fig. 8.3 *The beautiful mortuary temple of Queen Hatshepsut at Deir el-Bahari.*

weaker, his became stronger and more demanding as they sensed that the queen could not cling to power for ever. By the twentieth year of her reign she was forced to recognise Thutmose's claims to the succession, and made him co-ruler. Two years later she died.

There has been considerable speculation about the cause of her death. Some say she died of natural causes while others have maintained there was a conspiracy against her. Nothing definite is known either way. What *is* certain, however, is that Thutmose later tried to remove her name from all monuments, and to substitute those of Thutmose I and II. It was a deliberate attempt to obliterate her achievements from human memory, and clearly demonstrates the ill-will he bore her for keeping him so long from his birthright.

THUTMOSE III

Thutmose III occupied the throne as sole ruler from c. 1482 to c. 1450. However, he preferred to date his rule from the time he should have been king (c. 1504). During the long period that Hatshepsut ruled in his place, he was well cared for, and given a royal education. He was well trained in military activities, and was an outstanding archer and horseman. Towards the end of Hatshepsut's reign, he was probably given command of the army on one of the Nubian campaigns.

The challenge from Kadesh

Since Hatshepsut had generally concentrated on peaceful pursuits, some of Egypt's neighbours interpreted her position as one of weakness. The Syrian kings who had formerly sent tribute to Thutmose I stopped sending it to his successors, and were no longer respectful of Egypt's might. About the time of Hatshepsut's death, a large force of troops from Palestine and Syria gathered at the fortress town of Megiddo ready to invade Egypt. It was commanded by the king of Kadesh, heading a large coalition of other princes, and probably backed by the king of Mitanni.

As the new Pharaoh, Thutmose took to the field against this threat. By taking an unexpected route that was considered too dangerous, he was able to surprise his enemies and defeat them convincingly. He then besieged Megiddo, whence they had fled, and finally captured it after eight months. He later had his exploits here recorded on the walls of the temple he built at Karnak.

Mitanni

In about 1471, Thutmose led an invasion of the kingdom of Mitanni. This kingdom had long since ceased to pay tribute to Egypt, and had actively supported its enemies in Syria and Palestine. Thutmose planned his cam-

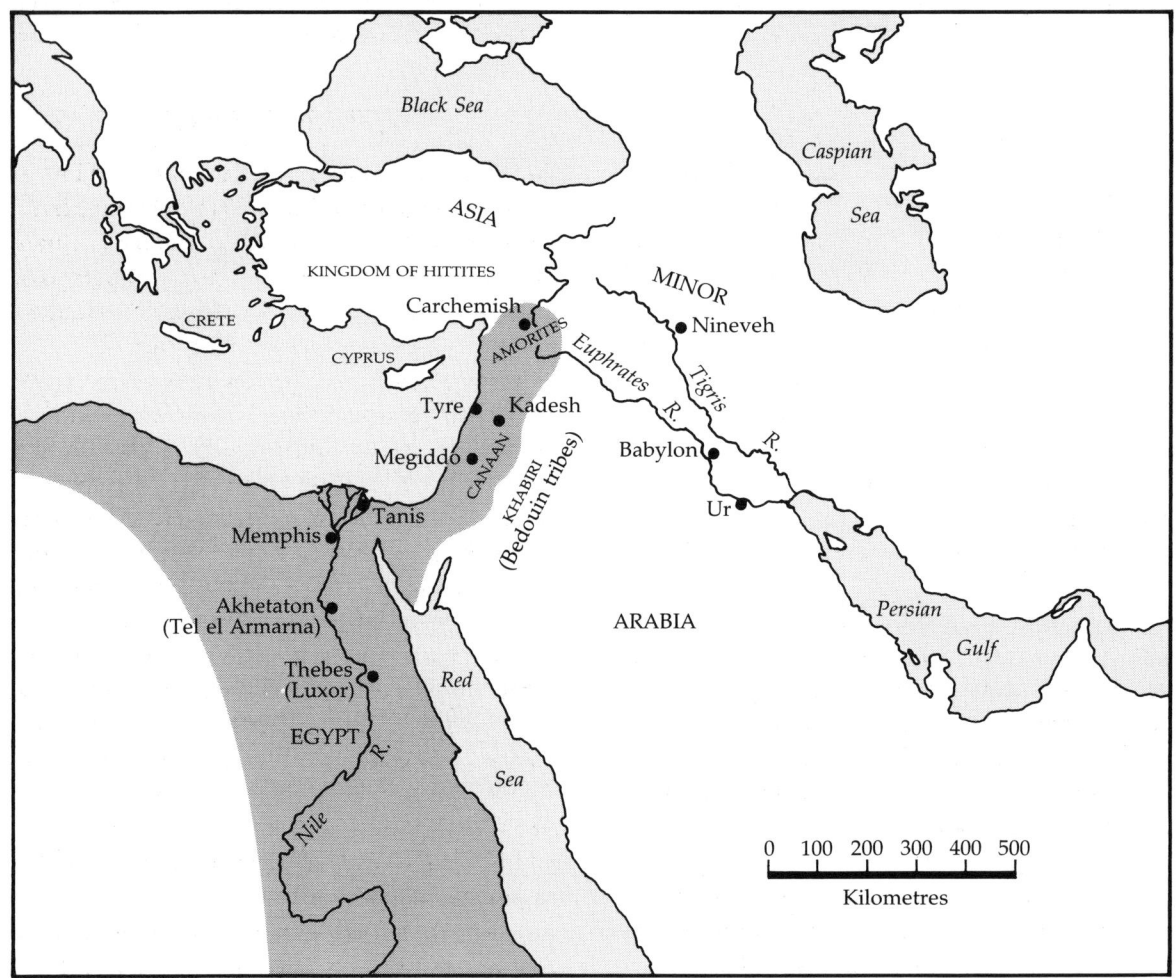

Fig. 8.4 *Egyptian Empire under Thutmose III, c. 1450 BC.*

paign well, transporting boats from Syria to ferry his troops across the Euphrates. The crossing was not contested, and the two armies subsequently met in a ferocious battle. The Egyptians defeated the Mitannians with great loss, and captured much booty. To mark his victory, Thutmose erected a victory stele next to the one originally set up by his grandfather Thutmose I. On his way home he hunted elephants in the Orontes Valley, and on returning to Thebes held a great victory celebration.

The later campaigns

In all, Thutmose conducted seventeen campaigns. These were necessary to retain control over the empire he had won for Egypt. In establishing the new empire, Thutmose generally appointed local rulers to act as Egyptian vassals. They swore to remain loyal to Egypt, to keep the peace and to pay tribute regularly. As a sign of good faith, they had to send their sons to the Egyptian court as hostages. Egyptian garrisons were scattered throughout the region in strategically situated forts, from which Egyptian officials kept a close watch on local political developments. But despite all their efforts, the Egyptians were never able to inspire loyalty from the conquered lands. The subject peoples were forever plotting to cast off the Egyptian yoke, and paid their tribute grudgingly.

Prosperity

Under Thutmose, who has come to be known as 'the Alexander the Great of Egypt', Egypt reached the peak of its power and prosperity. Tribute flooded into Thebes from Palestine, Syria and Nubia: cattle, horses, grain, timber, metals and precious stones. This new and never-ending flow of wealth enabled Thutmose to embark on a magnificent building-programme that reflected the grandeur of the empire. He paid particular attention to the great Temple of Amon at Karnak,

enriching it with many new buildings and obelisks. An obelisk which he built at Heliopolis now stands in London, and is known as Cleopatra's Needle. As a result of his efforts, Thebes became a capital of great magnificence.

The last years

In the last few years of his life, Thutmose appointed his son Amenhotep II as co-ruler. When he died c. 1450, he was buried in the Valley of the Tombs of the Kings. As with other Pharaohs, his tomb was later discovered and looted, and his mummy was discovered by archaeologists in 1899 in a hiding place apparently prepared by the kings of the Twenty-first Dynasty.

AMENHOTEP II

Amenhotep came to the throne c. 1450 at about the age of eighteen. Very strong physically, he was proud of his ability as an athlete and warrior and often gave public displays of his skills (see page 158). When he died in 1425, his bow was buried with him.

Early in his reign Amenhotep was forced to campaign in Syria, where there was a rebellion against Egyptian authority. He crushed the uprising with great severity, and executed seven princes of the region. He sent their bodies back to Thebes and to Napata in Nubia to be displayed in the streets as an example of the fate of rebels.

Several years later, Amenhotep had to return to the region to deal with a rebellion of the coastal city of Ugarit. This was an important operation, for the Egyptians relied on the Syrian ports for getting supplies to their garrisons in the region. The rebellion was crushed, and so Egyptian influence in the region remained firm.

The last seventeen years of Amenhotep's reign were peaceful, and he was able to turn his attention to building. He built many

Fig. 8.5 *This is the burial chamber of Thutmose III. Note the two large pillars supporting the ceiling. It had been looted by grave robbers long before its discovery in 1898. By what name is Thutmose often called by historians?*

THUTMOSE IV

Although the son of Amenhotep II and his chief wife, Queen Tiaa, Thutmose was apparently not the heir apparent. A stele found between the paws of the Sphinx at Giza tells an interesting story about his situation. This was that the Sphinx spoke to him one day and promised to make him king if he would clear away the sand which had banked up against it over the centuries. It is apparent from this that Thutmose was not the first choice to be the next Pharaoh after his father. The story is obviously an attempt

by Thutmose to give his eventual accession to the throne c. 1425 an appeal of legitimacy and divine favour.

The alliance with Mitanni

Early in his reign, Thutmose had to squash several minor rebellions in Syria and Palestine. While in the region, he sensed that the growing power of Mitanni could spell danger for Egypt if it was not contained. He therefore decided to defuse the danger by diplomatic rather than military means. He opened negotiations with King Artatama of Mitanni, and as a result, was able to conclude a treaty of friendship between the two powers. As a means of cementing the new relationship, he married Artatama's daughter Mutemwa. The peace thus created lasted for many years, and saved both sides much bloodshed.

Nubia

In the eighth year of his reign, Thutmose was faced with a rebellion in Lower Nubia. He moved rapidly against the rebels and defeated them soundly. A swift response to any threats from Nubia was always required from a Pharaoh, as that country's gold resources meant so much to the Egyptian economy.

Thutmose's empire extended from Karoy in Nubia to the south to Naharin, on the border of Mitanni to the east. It remained peaceful after his foray into Nubia, and allowed him to concentrate on the affairs of peace.

Thutmose's building programme

Since Thutmose only reigned for about nine years, his building programme was not extensive. At Thebes he erected a large obelisk which now stands in front of the Church of St John Lateran in Rome. Elsewhere at Thebes he built a small mortuary temple, and a wayside chapel for the barque of Amon. In Nubia he completed a temple which had been started by Thutmose III, and left behind a few memorials in the city of Memphis, where he had spent much of his youth.

A feature of Thutmose's reign was his strong devotion to the sun god Aton (or Aten). This god was always depicted as the solar disc which emitted rays terminating in human hands. The Pharaoh kept his personal enthusiasm in bounds, however, and so did not offend the all-powerful priests of Amon. The more forceful enthusiasm for the Aton later shown by Thutmose's grandson Akhenaton was to have serious consequences.

When Thutmose died in 1417 he was still a relatively young man. He was succeeded by his son Amenhotep III, whose mother was the Mitannian princess Mutemwa.

AMENHOTEP III

Amenhotep, who is sometimes known as Amenhotep the Magnificent, came to the throne about the age of twelve c. 1417. After about ten years he married a commoner named Tiy, who became his principal wife. By so doing, he departed from the former practice of the Pharaoh marrying a royal princess of his own family. He obviously adored his wife, who was both beautiful and talented. He had a special lake constructed so she could go boating in private, and built a temple for her worship in Nubia. Tiy was devoted to the Aton, and Amenhotep encouraged her interest in the god.

Foreign policy

In the fifth year of his reign, Amenhotep faced a serious revolt in Nubia. He sent an expedition which crushed the rebellion, and thereafter he had peace in the southern regions. Some time later, there were some troubles in the Nile Delta, but these were rectified by an important official named Amenhotep, son of Hapu (see page 156).

Amenhotep was keen to use diplomacy rather than military means in maintaining good relations with other mighty powers. We know quite a lot about this period because the king's correspondence with foreign powers has been uncovered at Tell el-Amarna. These so-called 'Amarna Letters' have been extremely valuable in giving the thoughts and ideas of Amenhotep and those kings with whom he corresponded.

Among the records we find that Amenhotep made political marriages with princesses from both Mitanni and Babylon, and these cemented peaceful relations between the powers concerned. King Tushratta of Mitanni was particularly concerned about Amenhotep's health as the Pharaoh grew old, and sent a special image which was supposed to have curative powers. On the level of trade relations, we know that the Egyptians sent gold to Asia in return for copper, horses and lapis-lazuli.

Amenhotep's emphasis on peace and his failure to display Egyptian military might in Syria apparently led some of the princes there to suspect that Egypt was getting soft. Towards the end of his reign several of them became extremely restless and rebellious.

Building projects

The Egyptian empire reached its peak of prosperity under Amenhotep, and the vast amounts of tribute that poured into the royal treasury were largely spent on public buildings of various kinds. He ordered the construction of a huge pylon (an elaborate gateway to a temple) at Karnak and a magnificent temple to Amon at Luxor. He followed these up with his own gigantic mortuary temple at

Thebes. Most of this is now in ruins, the only remains being the famous Colossi of Memnon. These are two huge statues of Amenhotep, some twenty metres high and each hewn from a single block of stone. He also constructed an elaborate palace at Malkata, one of the few examples of Egyptian palaces still remaining.

The last days

Towards the end of his reign of thirty-eight years, Amenhotep suffered from ill-health, and his grip on the affairs of state weakened. He seemed more interested in his own personal pleasure than in attending to his political duties, and this adversely affected his position. This decline in the prestige of the Pharaoh was soon to be accentuated by his son and successor Amenhotep IV.

Fig. 8.6 *These two statues of Amenhotep III are all that remain of his mortuary temple at Thebes. Twenty metres high, they are each carved from a single block of stone. Why are they sometimes known as the Colossi of Memnon?*

SUMMARY OF MAIN EVENTS

c. 1570–1546 BC **Rule of Ahmose**
Defeated the Hyksos and the Nubians
Made army an attractive career: many officers became government
   officials; promotion on merit
Viziers for Lower and Upper Egypt

c. 1546–1526 **Rule of Amenhotep I**
Victories in Nubia, Palestine and Syria
Spent freely on public works

c. 1525–1512 **Rule of Thutmose I**
Successful campaigns in Nubia and Mitanni
Introduced standard style for temples
Started practice of kings being buried in rock tombs
   (Valley of the Kings)

c. 1512–1504 **Rule of Thutmose II**
Crushed rebellions in Nubia and Palestine

c. 1503–1482 **Rule of Queen Hatshepsut**
Started great programme of public buildings
Sent major expedition to Punt
Kept the future Thutmose III from becoming Pharaoh for over
   20 years

c. 1482–1450 **Rule of Thutmose III**
Led numerous campaigns and extended Egypt's boundaries to
   their widest points
Massive tribute spent on enormous public buildings at Thebes

c. 1450–1425 **Rule of Amenhotep II**
Crushed two rebellions in Syria

c. 1425–1417 **Rule of Thutmose IV**
Made alliance with Mitanni

c. 1417–1379 **Rule of Amenhotep III**
Crushed rebellion in Nubia
Preferred diplomacy to war
Spent heavily on public works

FEATURE

Thebes and the Valley of the Tombs of the Kings

Thebes was the capital of Egypt during its heyday. It was located on the Nile, about 670 kilometres south of Cairo. Today, the modern city of Luxor occupies part of the site. Ancient Thebes straddled the Nile, and was in fact in two parts. The main area, where most of the people lived, was on the east bank. Here the rulers of the Eighteenth Dynasty built huge temples and palaces, and the busy streets were filled with officials, traders, craftsmen and soldiers. At the northern end of the eastern city was the place known as Karnak. This was the site of many fabulous temples, the largest of which was the famous temple dedicated to Amon-Re.

The western part of the city was known as 'the city of the dead'. Here were the mortuary temples of the kings, together with the houses of all those who served in those temples: priests, craftsmen and labourers. Beyond these temples lay the Valley of the Tombs of the Kings, where the New Kingdom Pharaohs were buried. There were some sixty tombs located here, each carefully sited so as to be free from the depredations of grave robbers. Unfortunately, all except one were robbed sooner or later. The only tomb to escape unscathed over the centuries was Tutankhamen's.

FEATURE

Mortuary temples

A brief reference was made to mortuary temples on page 145. In the Old and Middle Kingdoms, such temples were usually built close to the pyramid which formed the tomb of the dead monarch. They usually had an open court with pillars, several shrines and a chapel where priests performed their daily rites. Fig. 8.7 shows a plan of Khafre's mortuary temple.

In the New Kingdom, pyramids were replaced by tombs cut in solid rock, but they still had adjacent mortuary temples. Endowments of land were set aside to pay for the ministrations of the priests, presumably for ever.

Without doubt the most impressive mortuary temple ever built was the one constructed for Queen Hatshepsut at Dier el-Bahri around 1500. It rises from the valley floor in three colonnaded terraces connected by ramps, and blends well with the rocky cliffs behind it. The pillars forming the colonnades are either rectangular or chamfered into sixteen sides, and are beautifully proportioned and spaced. Fitting tastefully into the scheme of things were some 200 statues.

Most of the walls were covered with brightly painted low reliefs which portrayed various important times in the queen's life. The whole temple was set off with fragrant gardens full of exotic plants imported from faraway lands. Fig. 8.3 on page 147 shows how well the temple has been preserved to the present day.

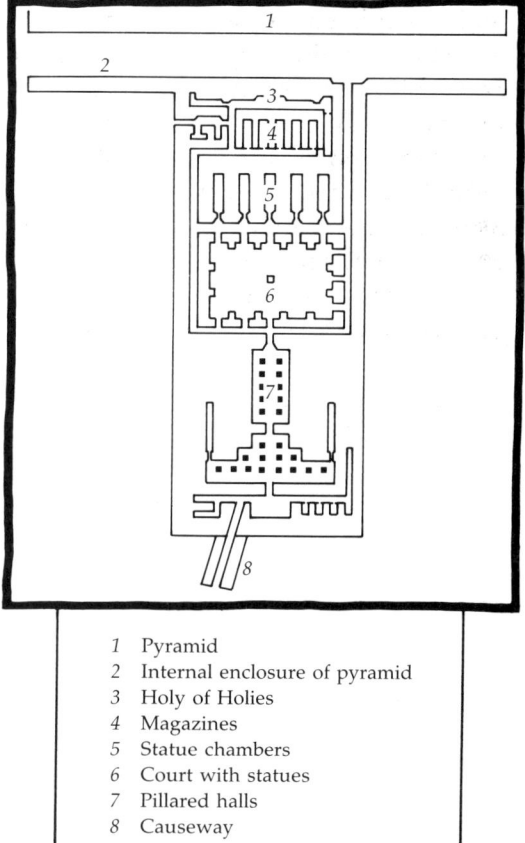

1	Pyramid
2	Internal enclosure of pyramid
3	Holy of Holies
4	Magazines
5	Statue chambers
6	Court with statues
7	Pillared halls
8	Causeway

Fig. 8.7 *Plan of Khafre's mortuary temple at Giza.*

FEATURE

Amenhotep, son of Hapu

Fig. 8.8 *Amenhotep, son of Hapu had a great reputation as a wise man, and in this statue he is shown writing his wise sayings on a papyrus scroll. In what ways did Amenhotep serve his royal master best?*

Amenhotep, son of Hapu was the most important official of Amenhotep III. He was born into a noble family about 1460 at Athribis in Lower Egypt and like most of his class, entered government service. Under Amenhotep III he became Scribe of the Recruits, a military position something like that of a general. Posted to the Delta, he was made responsible for safeguarding the region from infiltration by foreigners. To keep out seaborne intruders he stationed troops at strategic points along the Nile. Against the Bedouin, he built forts on Egypt's eastern borders.

Later in his career, Amenhotep, son of Hapu was made supervisor of the king's building programme and was responsible for overseeing the construction of the buildings mentioned on page 152. So pleased was the Pharaoh with his efforts that he ordered the building of a small funerary chapel for his loyal servant next to his own. This was the highest honour a Pharaoh could give to one of his subjects.

Amenhotep, son of Hapu was always considered a sage, and many wise sayings were credited to him. He was associated with healing, hence many statues were made to honour him as a means of curing people from illnesses. Many years after his death he was deified, and associated with the god Thoth.

Document 8.1

This is a hymn to the god Amon composed by the painter Merisekhmet who lived in New Kingdom times.

Praise to thee, Amon-Re-Atum-Harakhti, who spoke with his mouth and there came into being men, gods, cattle, and all goats in their totality, yea and all that flieth and alighteth.

Thou didst create the regions and the Habenu, they being settled in their towns; also the fertile meads made pregnant by the Nun and later giving birth; yea, also good things without limit of their number to be sustenance for the living.

Valiant art thou as a herdsman tending them for ever and ever. Thus are bodies filled with thy beauty, and eyes behold through thee, and thy fear is upon everyone. Their faces are turned unto thee. Good art thou at all times. All mankind live by the sight of thee ...

Do not the widows say, 'Our husband art thou', and the babes 'Our father and mother'. The rich boast concerning thy beauty, and the poor adore thy face. The prisoner turneth towards thee, and he that hath a malady calleth upon thee.

Thy name will be protection for every lonely one; safety and health for him that sails upon the waters, rescuing from the crocodile; a memory good at the moment of turmoil, rescuing from the mouth of fever. Everyone hath resort to thy presence that they may make supplication to thee.

Alan H. Gardner (ed.), *Hieratic Papyri in the British Museum* 3rd Series, British Museum, London, 1935, p. 31.

1 Why does the author address Amon by four connected names? What does this practice reveal about the way gods were worshipped in Egypt?

2 According to the author, why should Amon be given so much praise and honour?

3 In what ways is Amon of benefit to human beings? Give some specific examples.

4 What circumstances led to Amon becoming the dominant god of Egypt for such a long period?

Document 8.2

As mentioned on page 148, King Thutmose III attacked and defeated a collection of princes from Palestine and Syria at Megiddo. The following extract is part of a record of this important event which was carved on the walls of the Great Temple of Amon at Karnak.

Behold, the command was given to the entire army to move ... His Majesty set out in a chariot of fine gold, arrayed with his weapons of war, like Horus the Smiter, lord of power, like Montu of Thebes, while his father, Amon, strengthened his arms. The southern wing of the army of his majesty was on a hill south of the brook of Kina, the northern wing was at the northwest of Megiddo, while His Majesty was in the centre, with Amon as the protector of his person in the crush of battle, and the strength of Seth was pervading his limbs. Then His Majesty prevailed against the enemy at the head of his army. When they saw that His Majesty was prevailing against them they fled headlong to Megiddo in fear, abandoning their horses and their chariots of gold and silver. The people hauled them up, pulling them up into the city by their clothing, for they had closed the gates of the city, and lowered clothing to pull them up into the city. Now, if only the army of His Majesty had not given their hearts to plundering the possessions of the enemy, they would have captured Megiddo at this moment, while the wretched enemy of Kadesh and the wretched enemy of this city were hastily hauled up to get them within the city. The fear of His Majesty had entered their hearts, their arms were powerless, and his serpent diadem had overpowered them.

Then their horses and their chariots of gold and silver were captured easily; they lay stretched out like fish on the ground. The victorious army of His Majesty went around counting their shares of the plunder. Behold, the tent of that wretched foe was captured. The whole army rejoiced, giving praise to Amon for the victory which he had granted to his son on this day. They praised His Majesty, exalting his victories. They presented the plunder which they had taken, consisting of hands, living prisoners, horses, chariots of gold and silver ...

Then His Majesty commanded his army, saying: 'If you had captured this city, I would have given ... Re this day; because every prince of every country that has revolted is within it: the capture of Megiddo is the capture of a thousand cities. Capture it ...'

C. Forbes and G. Garner, *Documents of the Egyptian Empire (1580–1380)* Australian Institute of Archeology, Macquarie University, Sydney, 1982, p. 27.

1 Indicate in the extract where the king's name is linked with various gods. Why do you think this practice was adopted?
2 What evidence is there to show that the battle was a decisive victory for the Egyptians? What did the enemy do in their panic?
3 Why was the Egyptian army's desire for plunder against the king's wishes? Comment on the nature of that plunder, especially the reference to 'hands'.

4 Explain the king's words: 'The capture of Megiddo is the capture of a thousand cities.'

Document 8.3

Amenhotep II was very proud of his physical skills. He had the following inscription carved on a stele near the Sphinx:

Now then His Majesty appeared as a king, as a beautiful youth who was well developed and had completed eighteen years upon his thighs in strength. He was one who knew all the works of Mont [the god of war]; he had no equal on the field of battle. He was one who knew horses: there was not his like in this numerous army. Not one among them could draw his bow; he could not be approached in running.

Strong of arms, untiring when he took the oar, he rowed at the stern of his falcon boat as the stroke oar for two hundred men. Pausing after they had rowed half a mile, they were weak, limp in body, and breathless. His Majesty was strong under his oar of twenty cubits in length. He stopped and landed his falcon boat only after he had done three miles of rowing without interrupting his stroke. Faces shone as they saw him do this.

He drew three hundred strong bows, comparing the workmanship of the men who crafted them, so as to tell the unskilled from the skilled. He also came to do the following, which is brought to your attention. Entering his northern garden, he found erected for him four targets of Asiatic copper, of one palm in thickness, with a distance of twenty cubits between one post and the next. Then His Majesty appeared on the chariot like Mont in his might. He drew his bow while holding four arrows together in his fist. Thus he rode northward shooting at them, like Mont in his panoply, each arrow coming out at the back of its target while he attacked the next post. It was a deed never yet done, never yet heard reported: shooting an arrow at a target of copper so that it came out of it and dropped to the ground …

[For the Egyptians, a cubit was the distance from the elbow to the extended finger tips–about 52 centimetres in the metric system]

M. Lichtheim, Ancient Egyptian Literature Volume II: The New Kingdom, University of California Press, 1976, p. 41.

1 What is your opinion of the claims made for Amenhotep? Do you think he was as talented as the stele makes out? Give reasons for your answer.

2 Why do you think such an inscription was made? What purpose was served by such an announcement of skill?

3 What is your assessment of the character of Amenhotep, judging by this extract?

4 Do modern leaders make announcements of their greatness? What techniques of communication are used today to publicise national leaders?

Document 8.4

Amenhotep III built a temple at Thebes, and on it erected a stele with this inscription.

Behold, the heart of His Majesty was satisfied with making a very great monument; never has happened the like since the beginning. He made it as his monument for his father, Amon, lord of Thebes, making for him an august temple on the west of Thebes, an eternal, everlasting fortress of fine white sandstone, wrought with gold throughout; its floor is adorned with silver, all its portals with electrum; it is made very wide and large, and established forever; and adorned with this very great monument (i.e. the stele on which the inscription appears). It contains numerous royal statues, of Elephantine granite, of costly gritstone, of every splendid costly stone, established as everlasting works. Their stature shines more than the heavens, their rays are in the faces of men like the sun, when he shines early in the morning. It is supplied with a 'Station of the King', wrought with gold and many costly stones. Flagstaffs are set up before it, wrought with electrum; it resembles the horizon in heaven when Re rises therein. Its lake is filled with the great Nile, lord of fish and fowl.

Lionel Casson, Ancient Egypt, Time-Life Books, 1966, p. 120.

1 What are the similarities between this extract and the previous one?

2 Find the meanings of these terms: electrum, gritstone, Station of the King.

3 What does the king say of his relationship with the god Amon? How is this relationship also reflected in the king's name? With what other gods were the Pharaohs associated?

4 What is the essential message of this inscription?

CHECK THE FACTS

Fill in the blank spaces in the sentences below.

1 The Hyksos capital was located at _____ .

2 The founder of the Eighteenth Dynasty was _____ who ruled between the years _____ .

3 The king who introduced the rock-cut tomb as a burial form was _____ .

4 Queen Hatshepsut's expedition to Punt resulted in the import of such items as ————— , ————— , ————— and ————— .

5 King Thutmose III is sometimes given the title of ————— by historians.

6 ————— was the Pharaoh who was so proud of his athletic prowess.

7 Thutmose IV made up a story about his imaginary conversation with the Sphinx because ————— .

8 The two kings who preferred diplomacy by negotiation and marriage rather than war were ————— and ————— .

9 The 'Amarna Letters' are so called because ————— , and they are important because ————— .

10 The Aton was ————— , and was always depicted as ————— .

GENERAL QUESTIONS

1 Look at Fig. 8.3 on page 147, and answer these questions. The first four can in answered in one or two sentences. The fifth requires a paragraph.

   a What buildings, apart from this one, did Hatshepsut construct during her reign?

   b Why is this building especially important to archaeologists?

   c Who supervised the construction of this building, and what allegedly happened to him?

   d What sort of ceremonies would have been performed in a temple such as this?

   e What were the circumstances of Hatshepsut becoming Pharaoh? What were her main achievements while in power? What was her eventual fate?

2 If you were a young man during the period of King Ahmose, what advantages would you see in pursuing a career in the army? Would there be any corresponding disadvantages?

3 Imagine you are Thutmose I, and explain your decision to have a rock-cut tomb instead of building another pyramid.

4 If you were an Egyptian, would you have preferred to live during the reign of Thutmose I or Amenhotep III? Give reasons for your choice.

5 The following questions are based on the life of Thutmose III. Answer each one with a paragraph.

   a How was Queen Hatshepsut able to keep the young Thutmose III away from his rightful position for so long? In what ways did she try to compensate him?

   b What was Hatshepsut's justification for assuming the powers of the Pharaoh? Did she have a right to exercise so much power?

   c How did Thutmose deal with the challenge of Kadesh early in his reign? Why was his campaign so successful?

   d How did Thutmose attempt to keep his empire under control? How successful was he in this matter?

   e In what ways did Egypt prosper under Thutmose's rule? How did Thutmose demonstrate the grandeur of his successes?

6 Write an essay to show how important Nubia was to Egypt, and outline the campaigns that various Pharaohs mounted to make sure that Nubia stayed under Egyptian control.

9
THE NEW KINGDOM
PART 2 (c. 1379–1085)

AMENHOTEP IV
(AKHENATON)

The reign of Amenhotep IV lasted from c. 1379 to 1365. He is best remembered for his unsuccessful attempts to substitute Aton for Amon as Egypt's chief god and thus install monotheism (the worship of a single god) in Egypt. In being almost totally preoccupied with religion, Amenhotep gave little attention to the preservation of the empire, which was coming under increasing attack from the Hittites and other enemies.

Amenhotep appeared a conventional monarch till the fifth year of his reign, when as a demonstration of his devotion to the god Aton, he changed his name from Amenhotep ('Amon is satisfied') to Akhenaton ('He who serves the Aton'). Aton was not a new god, and had long been associated with Re, the sun god, but under Akhenaton he was given prime importance. Under orders from Akhenaton, artists and sculptors depicted Aton as the sun disc, a single, universal god who was the source of all life and who brought light and warmth to all the world. Akhenaton called himself the son of Aton, and demanded that his subjects worship the god by worshipping him. All other gods were to be abandoned.

As a further move to honour Aton, and as a means of distancing himself from the priests of Amon at Thebes, Akhenaton built an entirely new capital city. This was 300 kilometres north of Thebes, near the present site of Tell el-Amarna. He called his new city Akhetaton, 'the Horizon of Aton'. It contained temples, palaces, public buildings, splendid houses for high officials and lesser quarters for labourers. Elaborate tombs were cut into the high desert cliffs surrounding the city, and their walls were decorated with carved murals which have given modern archaeologists a clear picture of what life was like in those days. Many scenes show Akhenaton and his beautiful wife Nefertiti in pleasant domestic situations such as playing with their children.

Akhenaton tried to encourage the worship of Aton by lavishly rewarding officials who supported his actions and demoting those who remained faithful to the old gods. He also launched a savage attack on Amon, ordering his workers to erase Amon's name from temples and monuments and cutting funds off from the priests who maintained temples dedicated to that god. Despite all his efforts, it is apparent that most people were unaffected by this new attention to Aton.

Fig. 9.1 *Akhenaton and his wife Nefertiti worshipping the Aton. The rays from the sun envelope the worshippers and give them strength. Akhenaton is shown much larger than his wife and family because he is considered a god. What comment can you make on Akhenaton's physical appearance?*

They preferred to remain true to the old, trusted gods.

The empire

Akhenaton's preoccupation with religion led to problems with the adequate defence of the empire. In what is now Turkey, a people called the Hittites rose in strength and put

considerable pressure on Egypt's ally Mitanni. As a result, the region of Syria and Palestine was destabilised, and most of Egypt's vassal kings were threatened by enemies who wished to take advantage of Egypt's apparent weakness. Many of these kings sent letters to Egypt begging for help. Some of these have survived and are part of the Amarna Letters. Although some aid was undoubtedly sent, it was generally ineffective, and Egyptian prestige in the region slumped severely. Egypt also suffered badly from a consequent loss of tribute, and its economy felt the pinch.

Smenkhkare

Towards the end of Akhenaton's reign, he had to contend with moves within the palace to overthrow him. His position was weakened considerably when his chief supporter, Queen Nefertiti, died. He was then forced to accept his half-brother Smenkhkare as co-ruler. When Akhenaton died, Smenkhkare made peace with the priests of Amon and tried to appease their god.

Smenkhkare did not long survive his half-brother. He reigned for only three years, dying c. 1361.

TUTANKHAMEN

Tutankhamen is probably the best known of all the Pharaohs. This is not because of the importance of his reign, which lasted only nine years, but because of the discovery of his virtually untouched tomb by the archaeologist Howard Carter in 1922.

Tutankhamen was probably Smenkhkare's brother. Known at first by the name Tutankhaten, he became Pharaoh in 1361 at about the age of nine. In order to strengthen his claim to the throne he married one of Akhenaton's daughters. Because he was so young, he depended on his vizier Ay and the general of his armies Horemheb (or Harmhab) for guidance in state affairs.

Under their direction he soon moved the capital from Akhetaton (Amarna) to Memphis and in the fourth year of his reign changed his name to Tutankhamen (also written Tutankhamon, Tutankhamun). Although at first remaining loyal to the god Aton, he later changed course, restoring all the temples, images, personnel and privileges of the old gods. He also declared publicly that Akhenaton had erred in trying to introduce the worship of Aton.

In 1352, the last year of his nine-year reign,

Fig. 9.2 *The entrance to Tutankhamen's tomb a year after its discovery by Howard Carter. Why was the tomb hidden from the world for so long?*

he sent an army under General Horemheb to Syria to help his Mitannian ally against the Hittites. While this war was taking place, Tutankhamen suddenly died at about the age of eighteen. As he had no surviving children, he was succeeded by Ay, who married his widow. Ay's position was extremely precarious, and he only lasted as Pharaoh for four years. In c. 1348 he was deposed in a coup mounted by the army and backed by the priests of Amon. The new Pharaoh was Horemheb, who soon proved to be a strong and vigorous ruler.

Tutankhamen's tomb

Tutankhamen's original tomb was appropriated by Ay for himself, and the boy-king was given another. Within a few years it was twice entered by would-be plunderers, who were, however, caught after doing only minor damage. During the reign of Horemheb, the so-called 'Amarna kings'—Akhenaton, Smenkhkare, Tutankhamen and Ay—were all publicly condemned and their names taken from the royal lists. The location of Tutankhamen's tomb was forgotten. Later, during the Twentieth Dynasty, workmen constructing the tomb of Ramses VI unknowingly dumped tonnes of rubble on the site of Tutankhamen's tomb, thus keeping it safe from would-be robbers. It remained hidden from the world till Howard Carter eventually unearthed it in 1922.

HOREMHEB

Horemheb was the last Pharaoh of the Eighteenth Dynasty. He was totally devoted to Amon, and was crowned in that god's temple at Luxor. He pulled down the temples and monuments dedicated to Aton that had been erected by his predecessors and used the materials for buildings honouring Amon.

One such was the famous hypostyle hall at Karnak, the largest room ever built in Egypt. Furthermore, he removed the names of Akhenaton and his successors (the Amarna kings) from the list of Pharaohs because of their heresy against Amon.

Horemheb concentrated heavily on domestic affairs, trying to clear up the confusion that had started with the religious experiment of Akhenaton. He punished corrupt officials and reorganised the legal system so that the average citizen had a better chance of getting justice. Since he was himself a former soldier, Horemheb appointed military commanders as his high officials, by-passing the established families which had tended to dominate the civil service.

Abroad, Horemheb resumed the trading expeditions which had ceased during the time of his predecessors. These brought much-needed goods to Egypt, and reminded foreigners that Egypt was still a power to be reckoned with.

As he had no son, Horemheb's death c. 1320 brought an end to the Eighteenth Dynasty. He appointed his general and vizier, Ramses, as his successor.

RAMSES I

The founder of the Nineteenth Dynasty, Ramses I came from the eastern Delta region. Since he was already an old man when he ascended the throne, he quickly made his son Seti co-regent. This was both to help him cope with the rigours of office and to ensure Seti's subsequent accession as Pharaoh.

Ramses only ruled for about sixteen months, so his achievements were necessarily limited. He concentrated on building, adding to temples that were already under construction. In foreign affairs, he ordered Seti to plan a campaign that would regain the lost possessions in Syria.

Fig. 9.3 *The enormous burial chamber of Seti I.*

SETI I

Seti, who ruled from c. 1318 to 1304, is best known as a competent military leader who restored Egypt's prestige in Palestine and Syria by regaining the territories lost during Akhenaton's reign. His first campaign was in Palestine, where he defeated his enemies with comparative ease and took control of the country. He later moved against the Hittites in Syria and although he was able to capture Kadesh, his hold on the city was shaky and it was subsequently lost. On another occasion, Seti was able to defeat a Libyan invasion of the western Delta region, thus securing Egypt against external attack.

Seti was proud of his military achievements and had his artists carve many relief pictures on temple walls to show battle scenes in which he was victorious.

RAMSES II

Son of Seti I, Ramses II had the second-longest reign in Egyptian history, from c. 1304 to 1237. His exploits were so widely known that he was later called Ramses the Great by early Egyptologists.

While still very young, Ramses was made co-ruler with his father, who appeared very anxious that he should eventually succeed to the throne. The young Ramses also accompanied Seti in his campaigns in order to gain military experience which would be valuable when he eventually became Pharaoh.

Early in his career, Ramses built a new residence city for himself which he called Per-Ramesse (House of Ramses). It was located in the eastern Delta region and was a convenient base for his later military campaigns into Palestine and Syria.

Military campaigns

Ramses' reputation as a strong and capable Pharaoh depends both on his military prowess and on his energy as a builder. His first campaign started in the fourth year of his reign when he led an army into southern Syria where he defeated several local rulers who had declared their independence from Egyptian control.

The next year Ramses undertook a more important task — to capture the fortress city of Kadesh from the Hittites. He reached the city with only part of his army, and was struck by the full force of the Hittites who were lying in wait from him. Many of his troops fled in disorder, but Ramses held on desperately till the rest of his force arrived and saved the day. The battle had a twofold result for the Egyptians. They won a tactical victory because they were the victors for the day. However, they sustained a strategic defeat because they were unable to capture Kadesh. Since neither side was able to resume fighting, an armistice was concluded and the Egyptians returned home.

Ramses was very proud of his courageous stand against great odds at Kadesh, and made sure his praises were recorded by scribes, poets and artists.

The aftermath of Kadesh

Ramses' failure to capture Kadesh had disastrous results for Egypt. Many local rulers in Palestine and southern Syria concluded that Egypt was a spent force, and so rebelled against their Egyptian overlords. The Pharaoh was thus forced to reassert his authority, and this entailed a whole series of campaigns. Although these restored Egyptian control in the region, the problem of the Hittite threat remained.

The Hittites

Ramses fought an intermittent and inconclusive war of sixteen years with his Hittite enemies, but at last realised that the situation was a stalemate. In about 1283 he signed a peace treaty with the Hittite ruler, Hattusilis III. Both monarchs pledged peace in the future, and mutual help against outside attack. They promised to help each other against internal rebellion and even to extradite fugitives. In signing the treaty, Hattusilis was probably concerned about the rising power of nearby Assyria. Likewise, Ramses may have been worried about an invasion from Libya.

As it turned out, this treaty was beneficial to both sides, as thereafter they maintained friendly relations. This friendship was later cemented further when Ramses married the eldest daughter of Hattusilis.

Ramses' only other campaign of importance was against the Libyans, who invaded the western Delta region. The Libyans were halted, and Ramses gained more fame for his victory.

Ramses' building programme

Ramses has emerged as the greatest Egyptian builder of all time and this activity, coupled with his military fame, gave him so much honour and prestige in his own time that all

nine kings of the Twentieth Dynasty took his name as the ultimate honour.

Following his construction of Per-Ramesse, Ramses embarked on a major building programme. He began by completing two projects started by his father. One was a great hypostyle hall at Karnak devoted to Amon, and the other a temple at Abydos. He continued by constructing Seti's funerary temple at Luxor, and later built another for himself (called the Ramesseum). Added to this was another large temple at Abydos, and four others at Per-Ramesse.

Some of his most famous edifices were in Nubia, where he built no less than six temples. The best known are the two at Abu Simbel, above the First Cataract. These were carved out of a cliffside, and featured four colossal statues. These represented Ramses himself, and three other gods: Amon of Thebes, Ptah of Memphis and Re-Herakhty of Heliopolis. In a major engineering feat of

Fig. 9.4 *The entrance to Queen Nefretari's temple at Abu Simbel. Four of the statues represent Ramses II and two his wife Nefretari.*

the 1960s, these temples were raised to a higher level when the construction of the Aswan High Dam threatened to leave them under many metres of water.

With many of his buildings, Ramses used stone from the buildings of his predecessors. This material was readily available and was much cheaper than bringing in fresh stone from the quarries.

Personal life

Not much is known of Ramses' personal life. His first and favourite wife was Nefretari, but she appears to have died early in the reign. Ramses had several other wives and a large harem, and had more than a hundred children. Isinofre was the queen who bore Ramses' successor, Merneptah.

The reign of Ramses marked the last peak of Egyptian power. He was a competent and popular king, and was looked on as a classical model of what a Pharaoh should be like. Ramses' many achievements cannot be denied, but he undoubtedly helped posterity to remember him by indulging in the ancient Egyptian version of a widespread publicity campaign.

MERNEPTAH

Egypt's power began to decline after the death of Ramses. His son Merneptah was already old when he ascended the throne c. 1236, and he lacked the vigour to mount new campaigns of conquest. Indeed, much of his time was spent in repelling attacks on his own land. In the fifth year of his reign he was faced with a serious incursion into the western Delta region by an army of Libyans and Sea Peoples. The latter had originated in Anatolia (modern Turkey) and had come to Libya by sea to find new homes. They now joined with the Libyans to gain a foothold in Egypt, and were threatening Memphis and Heliopolis.

Merneptah marched out to meet them at a spot somewhere to the west of the apex of the Delta. The invaders anticipated a hand-to-hand battle, but Merneptah held his men in check, and instead, showered his enemies with arrows for about six hours. At last the invaders turned and fled, and it was then that the infantry and the chariots finished off the fleeing enemy. Many captives were placed in military camps and later served as mercenaries for the Egyptians.

To celebrate his victory, Merneptah ordered the carving of four great stelae. One of these has come to be known as the 'Israel Stele' because it refers to the crushing of a revolt of one of the nomadic Israelite tribes somewhere in Palestine. Merneptah also squashed a rebellion in Lower Nubia, as another stele attests.

CONFUSION

There was a period of confusion in Egyptian politics following the death of Merneptah c. 1223, with a number of court factions competing for the vacant throne. This situation probably resulted from Ramses II having such a large family. In a period of twenty-two years there were no less than four monarchs, each ruling only for a short time. The last was Queen Tausert. When she was overthrown in c. 1200, the Nineteenth Dynasty was at an end.

THE TWENTIETH DYNASTY: RAMSES III

The confusion that swamped the last kings of the Nineteenth Dynasty was ended by Setnakht, who founded the Twentieth Dynasty. Of obscure origin, he only ruled for three years, and was then succeeded by his son Ramses III. Ramses, who ruled from c. 1198 to 1166, was the last of Egypt's great Pharaohs. After his reign, the power and prestige of both Egypt and its rulers steadily deteriorated.

Much of the first half of Ramses' reign was given over to a series of great defensive wars against formidable enemies. Firstly, in the fifth year of his reign, there was an invasion of Libyans in the western Delta region. This invasion was halted with great slaughter, if scenes from the walls of Ramses' funerary temple are to be believed.

The Sea Peoples

Three years later, Egypt faced an even greater threat. This was from a powerful force of Sea Peoples who advanced on Egypt by land and sea. They were so strong that they had over-run the Hittites, and had secured a firm base at Amor in Syria as a base for their invasion of Egypt. Ramses faced them in two very important confrontations. One was a land battle in Palestine, and the other was a naval engagement in one of the Delta channels.

Ramses' victories in both conflicts were crucial for Egypt's survival as a nation.

Thwarted from settling in Egypt, some of the Sea Peoples sailed further west. It is believed that the Sicilians, the Sardinians and the Etruscans probably descended from them. A land-based group, the Philistines, settled in southern Palestine and controlled the land till they were eventually conquered by the Hebrew king David (see page 68).

The Meshwash invasion

Egypt was still not entirely secure, because after three years there was another threat to the nation — an invasion by the Meshwash tribes from Libya. Ramses defeated these invaders as he had the others, and branded the prisoners of war with his name. They were then settled in military camps in Egypt, where they served in the Egyptian army. After the Meshwash invasion, Egypt was safe for the rest of Ramses' reign.

Fig. 9.5 *This line drawing shows an Egyptian warship fighting against a contingent of Sea Peoples, in this case Philistines. Who won the struggle between the Egyptians and the Sea Peoples?*

Domestic decline

Ramses' defensive wars were costly, and brought little of the profit that the offensive wars of some of his predecessors had gained. As a result, the amount of funds available for the building and running of temples declined dramatically. The scope of buildings lessened, and the workmanship in them suffered badly. Things got so bad that there is on record the report of a sit-down strike by temple builders who were protesting because they had not received payment of grain for work done.

Despite the troubled times, Ramses tried to encourage trade and industry. He sent a large seaborne trading mission to Punt, and exploited the copper mines at Sinai and the gold mines in Nubia.

Toward the end of his reign, Ramses was threatened by a plot hatched by one of his minor wives who wanted her son to succeed him. Although the conspiracy had widespread support, it was discovered in time and the conspirators executed. Although there is no evidence that Ramses was injured as a result of the plot, he died soon afterwards. He was succeeded by the middle-aged crown prince Ramses IV.

RAMSES IV

Soon after he ascended the throne c. 1166, Ramses prepared a long document in which he listed his father's gifts to the gods and made a general résumé of his reign. This was apparently an act of devotion to his father's memory. Now known as the Harris Papyrus, this document has proved valuable to today's Egyptologists.

Although the country's prosperity was declining, Ramses at once launched into an extensive building programme. He opened up new quarries, and set his workmen to build several temples at Deir-el-Bahri and Karnak. But these works were never com-pleted by Ramses as his reign was a mere six years. They were disappointing years, especially as his powers were constantly challenged by Ramsesnakht, the grasping chief priest of Amon.

RAMSES V TO RAMSES XI

The era when Egypt was ruled by kings named Ramses is called the Ramesside period. At this point it is not necessary to examine each of the remaining seven Ramesside kings' activities in detail. Of them, only two reigned longer than eight years. Their reigns were largely unremarkable, and plagued by common problems. They had to contend with challenges to their position by an increasingly powerful priesthood, and cope with dynastic disputes. As well, they faced periods of economic hardship when rising prices caused strikes among their workforce. To top it all, they had to endure the depredations of Libyan tribesmen who entered the land in ever greater numbers as the strength of the Egyptian army withered.

The last Pharaoh of the Twentieth Dynasty was Ramses XI. When he died in c. 1085 he was succeeded by Smendes, who founded the Twenty-first Dynasty.

SOME ASPECTS OF NEW KINGDOM SOCIETY

The civil service

During the New Kingdom period, the occupation of scribe became popular because it was seen as a means of achieving an influential and lucrative position in the civil service. Although some families tended to dominate the higher positions of the civil service, there were definite opportunities for advancement by talented men with humble backgrounds. In this way, social mobility was a fact in New Kingdom Egypt.

The army

As an imperial power, Egypt needed a strong and efficient army. This led to the growth of a professional military class whose skills were needed to keep the troops disciplined and in a constant state of readiness. In the days when the army was continuously victorious, officers were rewarded with land, slaves and other booty. This was an incentive for many families to enlist their sons in the army as a means of advancing the family fortunes.

Army officers were usually appointed as tutors to royal princes. This gave them influence with the prince when he eventually became Pharaoh, and increased their power and that of the army. Military officers were thus frequently among the closest of the Pharaoh's advisers.

The common people

The great bulk of the Egyptian people were uneducated labourers working in a predominantly agricultural economy. They tilled the soil and were allowed to keep part of the harvest, the rest going to the landlord. At certain times of the year they were required to perform compulsory labour on state projects such as irrigation.

Slavery

Slavery was a widespread institution, with most slaves entering bondage as prisoners of war. They could be bought and sold like any other kind of portable property. Although most households had few slaves, there were many serving in the temples and others engaged in state mining and quarrying projects.

Women

Although women were generally debarred from the high offices of state (with the exception of queens), they were given considerable prestige in the home. There was no religious ceremony for marriage, which was a civil matter involving the families of both bride and groom. Brother and sister marriages were reserved only for the royal family. Monogamy was the main form of marriage, although wealthy men might have a minor wife or concubine who lacked the first wife's status.

Women had equal legal rights with men, and could start legal proceedings in courts of law. Women also served in the temples, although they were subservient to the male priests.

SUMMARY OF MAIN EVENTS

c. 1379–1365   **Rule of Akhenaton**
Encouraged the worship of Aton, as the only god
Built new capital at Akhetaton (Amarna)
Decline in Egypt's position abroad
Succeeded by Smenkhkare

c. 1361–1352   **Rule of Tutankhamen**
Moved capital from Amarna to Memphis
Returned to the worship of Amon
Sent Horemheb to Syria to aid Mitannian allies

c. 1348–1320   **Rule of Horemheb**
Appointed soldiers as high officials
Constructed many buildings to honour Amon
Resumed profitable foreign trading expeditions
Last Pharaoh of the Eighteenth Dynasty

c. 1318–1304   **Rule of Seti I**
Recaptured lost Egyptian territories
Encouraged building, with scenes showing his victories

c. 1304–1237   **Rule of Ramses II**
Built the city of Per-Ramesse
Fought against the Hittites at Kadesh
Defeated the Libyans
Initiated an enormous building programme
Known as Ramses the Great

c. 1236–1223   **Rule of Merneptah**
Defended Egypt against Sea Peoples and Libyans

c. 1200   Death of Queen Tausert ends Nineteenth Dynasty

c. 1200–1085   **Twentieth Dynasty**

FEATURE

The Treasure of Tutankhamen

Since immense treasures were always buried with the Pharaohs, their tombs were constantly at risk from hordes of grave robbers. Over the centuries, every Pharaoh's tomb except one was despoiled, and that belonged to Tutankhamen. In fact, thieves did break into the ante-chamber of his tomb just ten years after he was buried, but the tomb was resealed, and remained hidden for the next 3000 years.

The man who discovered the lost tomb was Howard Carter, a British archae-ologist. In 1922 he finally unearthed the door of the tomb after six years of previously unfruitful digging in the Valley of the Kings. His discovery delighted admirers of Egypt's history because he revealed to the world the majesty of an Egyptian royal burial. Tutankhamen's tomb was the only one to withstand the onslaught of would-be robbers, and so modern people were able to see at first hand the splendour of the Egyptian past. After his discovery, Carter spent eight

Fig. 9.6 *Howard Carter working on the third coffin in the tomb. Getting through the series of coffins to the mummy inside was a difficult task requiring great skills and knowledge.*

years in removing, cataloguing and restoring the 2000 objects he found in the tomb.

And what objects they were! They ranged from ivory game boards, vases and ornaments to weapons, statues of animals, gods and humans, items of furniture, a dismantled chariot, boxes of precious jewels, and many exquisite works of art. Since Tutankhamen was only a very young and relatively unimportant king, one wonders what the tombs of more important Pharaohs like Thutmose III and Ramses II might have revealed had they remained intact!

Perhaps the greatest treasure of all was the mummy itself, not only because of the gold and precious stones contained in the coffins, but because no archaeologist had ever discovered a royal mummy still encased in its original covering. The mummy was contained in a series of cases, which fitted snugly one inside the other. Firstly, there were four outer cases, made of wood and shaped like the dead king. Each one was richly gilded and decorated. Then came a sculptured stone sarcophagus, and inside that, three more coffins. The last, which weighed over a tonne, was made of solid gold. The face of the mummy was covered by a spectacular mask in beaten gold, and the effect was one of serene beauty.

Document 9.1

Excerpt from Akhenaton's 'Hymn to the Aton'. This is an excellent example of Egyptian lyrical poetry.

All beasts are content with their pasturage;
Trees and plants are flourishing.
The birds which fly from their nests,
Their wings are stretched out in praise to
   thee.
All beasts spring upon their feet.
Whatever flies and alights,
They live when thou hast risen for them.

The ships are sailing north and south as
   well,
For every way is open at thy appearance.
The fish in the river dart before thy face;
Thy rays are in the midst of the great green
   sea.

How manifold it is, what thou hast made!
They are hidden from the face of man.
O sole god, like whom there is no other!
Thou didst create the world according to
   thy desire,
Whilst thou wert alone:
All men, cattle and wild beasts,
Whatever is on earth, going upon its feet,
And what is on high, flying with its wings.

Lionel Casson, *Ancient Egypt*, p. 145.

1 In what ways does animal life honour the Aton?
2 How did Akhenaton's views of god differ from those of most other Egyptians?
3 What effects did Akhenaton's views about religion have on the Egyptian way of life?
4 This prayer has often been compared with Psalm 104 in spirit. Read this psalm for yourself, and show why you agree or disagree with this statement.

Document 9.2

A French archaeologist named Gaston Maspero made many important discoveries of Egyptian tombs in the late nineteenth century. Here is his account of the body of Ramses II after the bandages had been removed.

The chest is broad; the shoulders square; the arms are crossed upon the breast; the hands are small and dyed with henna; the feet are long, slender somewhat flat soled and dyed, like the hands with henna ... the head is long, and small in proportion to the body. The top of the skull is quite bare. On the temples there are a few sparse hairs, but at the poll the hair is quite thick, forming smooth, straight locks about five centimetres in length. White at the time of death, they have been dyed a light yellow by the spices used in the embalmment. The forehead is low and narrow; the brow ridge prominent; the eyebrows are thick and white, the eyes are small and close together; the nose is long, thin, hooked like the noses of the Bourbons, and slightly crushed at the tip by the pressure of the bandages; the temples are sunken; the cheek bones very prominent; the ears round, standing far out from the head, and pierced like those of a woman for the wearing of earrings; the jawbone is massive and strong; the chin very prominent, the mouth small but thick lipped, and full of some kind of black paste. This paste being partly cut away with the scissors, disclosed some much worn and brittle teeth, which, however, are white and well preserved ... Finally, it may be said the face of the mummy gives a fair idea of the face of the living king.

John Romer, *Valley of the Kings*, Michael Joseph and Rainbird, 1981, p. 147.

1 How successful do you feel the Egyptians were in preserving Ramses' body? Justify your answer.

2 What feelings might you have experienced had you been present with Maspero at the unravelling of the bandages?

3 No mention is made of Ramses' body organs. Explain why this is so, and what would have happened to them.

4 Research the life of Maspero, and see what contributions he made to the field of Egyptology.

Document 9.3

Fig. 9.7 is a painted limestone relief of King Smenkhkare and his wife Meritaten. It was created around 1360 BC at Tell-el-Amarna and is considered to be an excellent example of the art of the so-called Amarna period.

Fig. 9.7 *Smenkhkare and Meritaten.*

1 In what way is Smenkhkare different in appearance from Pharaohs previously depicted in Egyptian art? In answering, comment on his stance, dress, and presence of flowing lines in the drawing.

2 Illustrate your answer more fully by referring to a specific picture shown elsewhere in the book.

3 Why do you think the two figures are shown the same size? What was the previous convention about the size of the Pharaoh in relation to other figures?

4 What appears to be the theme of the picture? Find some appropriate adjectives to describe the style.

Document 9.4

The following is a prayer to Amon supposed to have been addressed to Amon by Ramses II during his war against the Hittites.

And His Majesty said: 'What is it then, my father Amon? Hath a father indeed forgotten his son? Have I done ought without thee? Have I not gone or stood still because of thine utterance? And I never swerved from the counsels of thy mouth. How great is the great lord of Thebes, too great to suffer the foreign peoples to come nigh him! What are these Asiatics to thee, Amon? Wretches that know not God! Have I not fashioned for thee very many monuments, and filled thy temple with my captives? I have built for thee my temple of millions of years, and have given thee my goods for a possession. I present unto thee all countries together, in order to furnish thine offering with victuals. I cause to be offered unto thee tens of thousands of oxen, together with all sweet-smelling plants . . .

'I call to thee, my father Amon. I am in the midst of foes whom I know not. All lands have joined themselves together against me, and I am all alone and none other is with me. My soldiers have forsaken me, and not one among my chariotry hath looked round for me. If I cry to them, not one of them hearkeneth. But I call, and I find that Amon is worth more to me than millions of foot-soldiers, and hundreds of thousands of chariots, than ten thousand men in brethren and children, who with one mind hold together. The work of many men is nothing; Amon is worth more than they. I have come hither by reason of the counsels of thy mouth, O Amon, and from thy counsels have I not swerved.'

Adolf Erman, *The Ancient Egyptians: A Sourcebook of Their Writings,* Harper Torchbooks, 1966, pp. 263–4.

1 What is the significance of Ramses calling Amon his father?
2 List as many reasons as you can as to why Ramses feels justified in getting assistance from Amon.
3 How important does Ramses assess the help from Amon?
4 At what stage of Ramses' fight against the Hittites might this prayer have been written? What was the eventual result of his war with them?

CHECK THE FACTS

Write a sentence to answer each of these questions.
1 Why did Amenhotep IV change his name to Akhenaton?
2 What is 'the Amarna period', and how did it get its name?
3 Explain how Tutankhamen's tomb came to be lost for so long.
4 What was Horemheb's attitude towards the worship of the Aton?

5 Who was the founder of the Nineteenth Dynasty, and how long did he reign?
6 In what regions did Seti I conduct campaigns, and with what result?
7 How did Ramses II cement his relationship with King Hattusilis of the Hittites?
8 Who erected the Israel Stele, and what does it commemorate?
9 What was the Ramesside period? Why was it so called?
10 What is the Harris Papyrus, and why is it important?

GENERAL QUESTIONS

1 Look at Fig. 9.5 on page 169 and answer the following questions. Use one or two sentences for the first four, and a paragraph for the last.
   a What sort of warships did the Egyptians use? How were they powered?
   b What methods of fighting at sea did the Egyptians employ?
   c In what ways were the Sea Peoples' uniforms different from the Egyptians'?
   d If this battle was fought somewhere in the Nile Delta, what advantages would the Egyptians have over the Sea Peoples?
   e Where did the Sea Peoples come from, and in what places did they end up? What was the fate of the group called the Peleset?
2 Do you think Akhenaton was a profound religious reformer or a headstrong fanatic whose actions plunged Egypt into disaster? Justify your choice with as many arguments as possible.
3 What were the problems facing Tutankhamen when he came to the throne? Why was he so poorly equipped to deal with them?
4 Imagine you are a scribe in the service of Merneptah. Write an account of his efforts

to free Egypt from invasions and rebellions. Try to use the style as demonstrated in Document 8.2.

5 These questions are based on the life of Ramses II. Answer each one with a paragraph.

a What training was given to Ramses when he was still young to ensure his later success as Pharaoh?

b Where did Ramses' military campaigns take him, and with what result?

c What were the main achievements of Ramses' building programme?

d Why is Ramses known as 'the Great'? How did he help to cultivate the image of a great and successful Pharaoh?

e Which of Ramses' successors had, in your opinion, the most success? Give reasons for your choice.

6 In your opinion, which of the three great periods of Egyptian history (Old, Middle and New Kingdoms) has been the most interesting? Write an essay to discuss the main aspects of the period you have chosen.

ACKNOWLEDGEMENTS

For permission to reproduce photographs we would like to thank the following: Archeological Museum, Palermo, Fig. 5.5; The Australian Institute of Archeology, Fig. 6.2; The Australian Jewish News, Fig. 4.4; Bildarchiv Preussischer Kulturbesitz, Figs. 2.7, 9.7; Trustees of the British Museum, Figs. 1.6, 1.7, 2.2, 2.5, 2.9, 4.1, 4.5, 4.6, 5.2, 6.6, 6.7, 7.3; Calouste Gulbenkian Foundation Museum, Lisbon, Fig. 7.4; Egyptian Museum, Cairo, Figs. 5.4 (both), 6.4, 7.1, 7.2, 6.4, 9.1; Griffith Institute, Ashmolean Museum, Oxford, Fig. 8.2; Hirmer Verlag Munchen, Figs. 6.5, 8.3, 8.8; Iraqi Museum, Baghdad, Fig. 1.2; Louvre Museum, Paris, Figs. 1.4, 1.5; Mansell Collection, London, Figs. 2.1, 4.7; Trustees of the National Museums of Scotland, Edinburgh, Fig. 5.3; Oriental Institute, University of Chicago, Fig. 2.4, 3.4, 3.5, 4.2; Photographie Giraudon, Paris, Fig. 6.3; Roger-Viollet, Paris, Figs. 3.1, 3.2, 3.6, 3.7, 3.9.

While every effort has been made to trace and acknowledge copyright, in some cases copyright proved untraceable. Should any infringement have occurred, the publishers tender their apologies.

INDEX

Abraham 71
Achaemenes 45, 46
Adad-nirari I 23
Adad-nirari II 23
Ahab 75
Ahmose 142, 143
Ahura Mazda 52, 53, 56
Akhenaton 141, 151, 161–4
Akkad 1, 6–8, 14
Alexander the Great 56, 57, 60
Amarna Letters 151, 162
Amenemhet I 123–6
Amenemhet II 127
Amenemhet III 129–31
Amenhotep I 144
Amenhotep II 149, 150
Amenhotep III 151, 152
Amenhotep, son of Hapu 151, 156
Amon 123, 124, 127, 136, 146, 150, 161, 164, 167
Amorites 9, 14, 15, 22
Amratian Culture (Naqada I) 91
Anu 9, 16
Ark of the Covenant 71–3, 81
Artaxerxes I 54
Artaxerxes II 54–6
Artaxerxes III 56
Assur 22, 23, 31
Assurbanipal 29, 30, 44, 45, 78
Assurnasipal II 23, 24
Assur-uballit 22
Assyria 1, 15, 22–34, 43, 45, 74
Aton 151, 161, 163

Baal 75
Babylonia 1, 6–8, 14–17,

22–34, 44–6, 53, 74, 78
Badarian Culture 91
Bardiya 47, 48
Bent Pyramid 105
Black Obelisk 76
Byblos 67, 68, 126

Cambyses 47, 48, 50
Carter, Howard 162, 173, 174
Croesus 45, 46, 59
cuneiform writing 2, 3, 15, 18, 68
Cyaxares 45
cylinder seals 18, 93
Cyrus the Great 34, 45–50

Darius I 48, 50, 51, 53, 60
Darius II 54
Darius III 56, 57
David 72–4
Deioces 44, 45
Djedkare Isesi III
Djoser 96, 104, 116

Ea (Enki) 10
Elamites 43–5
Enlil 5–9, 11, 16
Esarhaddon 29, 78

Faiyum scheme 127–30

Gilgamesh 11, 30
Gerzean Culture (Naqada II) 91, 92
Great Pyramid 105, 106
Gutians 8

Hammurabi's Code 10, 14–17, 22, 43, 44
Hatshepsut 145–7
Hebrews 69–79

Heb-Sed 96, 105, 112, 116
Hezekiah 27, 28, 77
Hittites 17, 23, 44, 45, 162, 166, 169
Horemheb 164
Huni 105
Hyksos 131, 132, 134, 142

Imhotep 104
Indo-Europeans 44
Ishtar 9, 10
Israel 72–5

Jehu 24, 75, 76
Jeroboam 75
Jezebel 75, 81
Judah 32, 72, 75, 77, 78

Kalakh 23, 24
Karnak 127, 136, 146, 148, 150, 152, 154, 164, 167
Kassites 17, 23, 44
Khafre 107, 108
Khufu 105–8

Lydia 45, 46

Magi 52, 53
Manasseh 78
Manetho 94, 111, 112
Mardonius 50, 53, 54
mastaba 95, 96, 104, 105, 117
Marduk 10, 16, 33, 34, 46, 53
Medes 44, 46
Menes 94
Menkaure 108
Mentuhotep II 113, 122, 123
Merenre 112
Merneptah 168
Middle Kingdom 122–32

Mitanni *22, 23, 44, 148–51, 162*
Moses *71, 81*

Nabonidus *34, 45, 46*
Nabopolassar *31, 32*
Naram-Sin *7, 8*
Narmer *93–5*
Nebuchadrezzar *31, 32–4, 44, 46, 78, 81, 83*
Nefertiti *161, 162*
New Kingdom *142–71*
Nineveh *28–32, 45*
Niuserre *111*
Noah *1*

Old Kingdom *103–13*
Osiris *109, 125, 131*

Palermo Stone *94, 111*
papyrus *98*
Pepi I *111, 112*
Pepi II *112*
Persepolis *51, 54, 60, 61*
Persia *43–57*
Philistines *68–73, 81*
Phoenicia *1, 45, 56, 67, 68, 71, 72, 74, 81*

Ramses II *166–8*
Ramses III *168–70*
Ramses IV *170*
Re *107, 109, 123*
Red Pyramid *105*
Rehoboam *75*

Sahure *111*
Sankhare Mentuhotep III *123*
Sargon II *26, 37, 38, 77*
Sargon of Akkad *6, 8*
Saul *72*
Sealanders *17*
Sea Peoples *169*
Senenmut *146*
Sennacherib *26–9, 77*
Sesostris I *126, 127*
Sesostris II *127, 128*
Sesostris III *128, 129, 144*
Seti I *166*
Shalmaneser I *23, 24*
Shalmaneser III *24*
Shamash *10, 15*
Sneferu *105*
Solomon *74, 75*
Solomon's Temple *82, 83*
Sphinx *107, 108*
Standard of Ur *8*
Sumer *1–15*

Tasian Culture *90, 91*
Thebes *122, 123, 131, 142, 144, 149, 151, 154*
Third Dynasty of Ur *9, 43*
Thutmose I *144, 145*
Thutmose II *145*
Thutmose III *146–9, 151*
Thutmose IV *150, 151*
Tiglath-Pileser III *25, 26, 77*
Tutankhamen *22, 154, 162–4, 173, 174*

Ubaids *1*
Unas *III*
Ur-Nammur *9, 12*
Userkaf *110*
Utnapishtim *11*

vizier *103, 104, 111, 129, 131, 142–4*

Xenophon *55*
Xerxes *53, 54, 60, 61*

Yahweh *71, 72, 75, 78, 79, 81, 83*

ziggurat *12, 13, 33*
Zoroaster *52, 53*